PRAISE FOR KEEPING LIFE IN FOCUS

Jeremiah 3:15 says, "I will give you shepherds after my own heart who will lead you with knowledge and understanding." Todd Wright is a Jeremiah 3:15 leader. He is a leader with a heart after God and he has the knowledge and the understanding to lead people. Todd is a proven leader and his new book *Keeping Life in Focus* is a great resource for every leader's library. In this new book, you will find real life wisdom from a tried and tested leader.
Ken Adams, Pastor of Crossroads Church,
Newnan, GA

Todd Wright is a natural encourager. The kind of person who people love to be around. His newest book, *Keeping Life in Focus*, will encourage and bless you, not just for a day or two but for 365 days. It's practical, common sense, inspirational and biblical devotions for you and your family.
Tim Lee, Evangelist, Author of Born on the Fourth of July
Garland, TX

In *Keeping Life in Focus*, Todd Wright gives practical, biblical wisdom for every day of the year. This book is a wealth of wisdom and a great source of truth to be lived out daily by the man or woman of God. What a great tool for kingdom living for the body of Christ!
Ebo Elder, Author of The Great Comeback,
Pastor and Bible Teacher, Former World Ranked Boxer
Hogansville, GA

My friend Todd Wright has given us the help we need in a clear, hope-filled book of short devotional insights that will encourage your heart. Each writing is born out of his own journey of faith and demonstrates how a relationship with Jesus Christ will bless and encourage each day of your life.

Tim Dowdy, Lead Strategist for Pastor Wellness, Georgia Baptist Mission Board
McDonough, GA

Start your day off right with a dose of pithy, practical wisdom. Todd's clear, challenging style will draw you close, encourage your heart and help you experience the right focus that will change you from the inside out, one day at a time.

Roger Patterson, Pastor, Author of A Minute of Vision for Men,
Houston, TX

Todd Wright's leadership and guidance has greatly impacted my family and me. Each page of *Keeping Life in Focus* is filled with wisdom, insight, and perspective that penetrates through the surface and addresses the deep and personal challenges of everyday life.

Paula Waters, Real Estate Agent
Carrollton, GA

Todd Wright is not afraid to be "real." In his new book, he shares his own story, his struggles with humility and humor, and gives a firsthand account of how God works in his life daily. I am looking forward to sharing a little bit of that perspective on a daily basis!

Edith (Edie) Haney, Probate Court Judge
Carrollton, GA

Keeping Life in Focus is well written, poignant, timely, inspirational, wise, and motivational! It's designed to be a daily reading, but block off some time when you begin reading this book because you won't put it down! Read it...be blessed...pass it on and gift copies to those in whom you want to invest!

Dr. Larry D. Reesor, Founder, Global Ambassador, Global Focus International
Acworth, GA

Todd provides a simple yet powerfully challenging daily devotion to keep us connected to our true source of hope. The message is clear, and the application concise! This devotional will help you focus on growing your relationship with Jesus every day.

David Daniels, Owner/Operator
Chick-fil-A Carrollton
Chick-fil-A Bankhead
Carrollton, GA

KEEPING
LIFE *in* FOCUS

365
MOTIVATIONAL
MINUTES

by

TODD WRIGHT

Foreword by Johnny Hunt

MISSIONAL PRESS
—NASHVILLE, TN—

ISBN: 978-0-578-68163-4

Cover design by Katie Shull.

Published by:

Missional Press, a subsidiary of 610Media.
Nashville, TN
missionalpressbooks.com

Printed in the United States of America.

KEEPING
LIFE *in* FOCUS

by

TODD WRIGHT

Author's Note

It was the autumn of 2011, but that was not the only season impacting the life of my wife Lisa and myself. Both of our daughters, Hannah and Olivia, had gotten married that year and we became empty nesters. We had celebrated both weddings at our farm with the best of friends, family, my parents, and my favorite horse, Cutter, craving attention and watching from over the pasture fence. The next season of life would encompass extreme relational losses that would shake my very core. Parents, best friends, horse, and my last living uncle—gone! Grief, sadness, loneliness, and confusion would become daily obstacles through which to navigate my private and public life.

Just before entering that difficult and dark season, I felt what I believed to be a divine tug in my soul to become more intentional and accountable with my writing and in my devotional life. I carried out that tug by writing a short devotional talk I would record to be played on local radio stations each week in West Georgia. The talks would be practical, authentic, instructional, introspective, Bible-based, and to the point.

They would be written to add good perspective to both Christian and secular audiences. Leaders needing wisdom. Parents needing help. Single parents needing encouragement. Desperate people needing hope. Broken people needing healing. Vulnerable people needing a warning. Betrayed people who need to forgive. Confused people needing guidance and clarity. Each talk ended with the tag-line: "I'm Todd Wright, from Midway Church, helping you keep life in focus!" I began the first week of January 2012.

After over seven years on the radio, I'm excited to offer to you 365 weeks of these devotional talks in this book, Keeping Life in Focus: 365 Motivational Minutes. In each talk, I committed to become better; day after day and week after week, just better. The most important part of each page is a scripture focus. Get a Bible. Find the scripture and read it. God's Word for your soul is so much more impacting than anything I could say. After each talk, ask yourself the questions that can actually help you improve. Join me in becoming better!

I want to thank my wife Lisa, our kids Nick and Hannah Neely, and Brian and Olivia Long for seeing me at my worst during that difficult and dark season, yet they continued to love me the most! I want to thank the people of Midway Church who continued to love me and show up each week to listen and follow a hurting, flawed, and broken pastor. Midway Church also paid for the radio airtime for these talks to invest daily in the people of West Georgia. I want to thank all of my Midway Staff for their diligence through the years, but I must specifically thank my Executive Pastor Chad Clifton who has helped carry my personal and professional load for over 20 years. I want to thank Michael Vincent for recording and editing every radio broadcast for the last seven years. I want to thank Marty Duren and Missional Press for helping me put these talks into book form and getting it published.

I want to dedicate this book to my five grandchildren: Boaz, Clark, Hank, Ada, and Walt. Their births brought new sunshine into my cloudy season. I pray they will learn and live by the principles in this book.

I love you all!

"I'm Todd Wright, Helping You Keep Life in Focus!"

Foreword

I personally believe each day of my life is different because of the way I choose to begin each day.

Each morning after I arise, I put the coffee on and grab my Bible. I want to read God's perspective on my life and on life in general as well as specifically. After reading my Bible I turn to a couple of different personal devotionals that speak into my life. I am of the deep conviction that this book that Todd Wright has written, *Keeping Life In Focus,* will help you to begin your day in such a way that you will have a chance to get God's perspective before you hear everyone else's perspective on life.

As you open this book each morning you will first find the precious Word of God. You will have a chance to read and reflect on scripture. Then Pastor Todd will help you as he gives a brief application of your morning reading. After the application, Todd provides questions for personal application. These are referred to as one-minute motivations or devotionals. They are simple, practical and yet they give a great perspective to everyone, not just to the believer but even to those that are struggling with whether that life of following Christ is for you or not.

I can recommend this book with deep conviction because of its author's personal life. He's been a pastor for over three decades and is a leader of thousands of people. From a corporate perspective God has allowed Todd to lead a large portion in his region of the body of Christ; even on a broader perspective he is a missionary pastor. God has used him in numerous countries around the world to transport the same truth that you and I can possess in our own personal lives.

I trust that you will not only read *Keeping Life In Focus* but you will pass it on to family, friends, and neighbors who can be encouraged with the same wonderful Biblical truth.

Pastor Todd Wright thank you for your encouragement to the body of Christ.

Blessings,

Johnny Hunt
Senior VP of Evangelism and Leadership, North American Mission Board (SBC)
Pastor Emeritus, First Baptist Church Woodstock, GA
Former President of the Southern Baptist Convention

April 18, 2020

January 1
Time/Seasons

Scripture for Today: Ecclesiastes 3:1-8

"What time is it?" That's a question we have to answer every day to assure we are not late for the many events that define our lives.

But what time is it for you personally? What season of life are you currently going through? Is it a time of birth or death? A time of stability or change? A time of laughter or grieving?

In the Book of Ecclesiastes, King Solomon wisely wrote: "For everything, there is a season; a time for every purpose under heaven." I certainly enjoy some seasons more than others, but I have learned that each exists for God's intended purpose. I have also learned that each season will soon end, and another will begin.

It's important to know what to do in the different seasons of life. If a farmer plants in the wrong season, failure and disappointment are sure to follow. For now, winter has arrived, but so has the beginning of a New Year.

What actions do you need to take during this season to guarantee you have the most successful life possible?

How does knowing God is in control of the seasons encourage you in the different seasons of life?

January 2
Worth of Your Soul

Scripture for Today: Mark 8:34-37

What is your greatest possession? Your financial portfolio or home? Maybe the car you drive? In recent years we have experienced the declining value of possessions. It's been painful to see many things we worked hard for become virtually worthless.

Some place the highest value on their physical appearance, but they too face the deep pain of loss as the years pass and their external beauty fades.

Jesus warned us not to place such a high value on possessions and physical beauty. Things that thieves can steal, rust can destroy, and death can take away.

He placed the highest value on a person's soul. He asked, "What profit is it to a man if he gains the whole world and loses his own soul?"

It is from our soul that we think, feel, make decisions, and find the courage to live each day. It is our soul that will live forever long after our bodies have returned to dust. In what condition is your soul? It might help to read your Bible or go to church this week. Perhaps there, you can get some good soul food!

Why do we tend to focus on the physical things of life rather than eternal things?

What steps will help you shift from a physical focus to a soul focus?

January 3
Tolerance

Scripture for Today: Matthew 7:1-5

Just how perfect are you? Have you ever noticed how quickly we judge and condemn others because of their failures? We sometimes live in constant critique of those around us, just hoping to find some flaw that we can criticize behind their backs! We hold them to a very high standard. Yet, we don't want that same standard applied to us. We want others to overlook our own failures and we are frustrated when they don't. The fact is we have enough faults of our own to work on without critiquing the shortcomings of others.

Jesus asked, "Why do you see the speck in your brother's eye, but do not even notice the log in your own eye? First, take the log out of your own eye. Then you can see clearly to take the speck out of your brother's eye."

You know that high standard you hold everyone else to? Well use that one for yourself and lighten up on the people around you. There has only been one man who is perfect, and HE died for the rest of us!

Who have you been wrongfully criticizing lately? Do you have any apologies to make?

What logs are in your own eye that you need God to remove?

January 4
Thanks

Scripture for Today: Psalm 95:2, 1 Thessalonians 5:18

How hard is your life right now? Failing health. Fleeting dreams. Constant disappointment. These are realities we all face, but we cannot allow them to be our main focus.

Several years ago, I found myself in the back of a truck late at night, riding a jungle road in West Africa. A 15-year-old African boy named Junior was with me. In between our conversations he constantly smiled, laughed, and sang. I asked him, "Junior. What's your favorite song?" He began to sing a hymn I'd heard in church throughout my childhood: "Count your many blessings. Name them one by one. Count your many blessings. See what God has done!

Junior had lost his parents to disease several years earlier and some neighbors took him in. He lived in a mud and stick hut with a straw roof and dirt floor. No running water and no electricity. But Junior knew the key to a joyful life in spite of the hardships we face! Count your many blessings, not your disappointments! Pause to see what God has done and say thanks!

Pause right now and make a list of at least five ways God has blessed you. Use the margin or a page in the back if needed.

In prayer, thank God for these and any other blessings that come to mind today.

January 5
Good Noise

Scripture for Today: Ephesians 5:19, 1 Thessalonians 5:11

Do you ever get tired of the noise? The TV playing. Engines running. Cell phones ringing. Dogs barking. People complaining. My goodness! The list goes on and on!

For me, I have learned that some noises are actually good, peaceful, and soothing to my soul: A leather saddle, slightly squeaking as I ride my horse. My feet hitting the pavement as I go for a casual afternoon jog. My parents or grandparents talking about the past as the whippoorwill sings at the end of a warm summer day, and the porch swing gently squeaks in the background. These are all noises I love to hear.

Have you ever wondered what noises God loves to hear? Well, God loves the sound of your voice! He'd love to hear your voice tell Him how good He is today. He'd love to hear your voice say a kind word to someone who's disappointed or down. He'd love to hear your voice giving thanks for the good things in life.

Be a noise that God loves to hear. You'll find that others like it too!

What do you need to say to God today? Say it now.

Who can you encourage with your voice today? Try to encourage someone this morning, this afternoon, and this evening.

January 6
Quitting

Scripture for Today: Hebrews 12:1–2

Do you ever want to quit? Just walk away and never come back to your job? Marriage? School? Even life?

Quitting is a habit that's easily developed. As a kid, I started playing the piano and quit. Then the saxophone and quit. I even joined the football team and quit.

You see, I enjoyed the excitement of starting something new: the shine of a new instrument, the feel of a new uniform, the thrill of a new start. But when things got tough…well, it was time to quit!

The fact is, it feels good to quit—at least for a little while. But soon the reality of another dead dream begins to sink-in and a feeling of failure and defeat overwhelms us. Quitting seems like the easy way out, but instead it's a detour from the best life possible. The Bible teaches us to "run the race of life with endurance." In other words, finish what you start and don't quit. It's the only way you will enjoy the thrill of victory instead of feeling the agony of defeat!

What in your life right now are you about to quit but you need to keep going?

Pause and ask God for strength not to quit, but to completely do His will.

January 7
Memories

Scripture for Today: John 14:26

Have you thanked God today for your memory? I know. There are lots of things you'd love to forget! But life's not all bad and if you'll reflect for a moment, your memory will prove it.

I remember swimming at Talley Valley Pool in Tallapoosa with my mom and brothers in the summertime. I remember the unique sound of Three Dog Night singing, "Jeremiah was a bullfrog" on the jukebox. I remember the fresh taste of BBQ potato chips, the laughter of all the kids having fun, and the breeze blowing through the trees. It was 1972 and I was just eight years old, but I remember it clearly and it was awesome!

I also remember that was the year I invited Jesus into my life to be my Lord and Savior. I was baptized at Ward's lake a couple of weeks later. It was a simple, child-like faith but it provided a new dimension of life that I continue to enjoy today.

Take a stroll down memory lane and enjoy the journey! There's a great memory somewhere just waiting to be found.

Can you remember a specific memory that brings you a lot of joy?

Can you remember something specific God has done in your life recently? If so, thank Him right now for what He did for you.

If you have a specific and hurtful memory, ask God to bring healing to it in the name of Jesus.

January 8
Regrets

Scripture for Today: Proverbs 3:21–26

If you could start your life all over again, what would you do differently? As one song says, "Some people say they wouldn't change a thing. Oh, but I would. I'd do a lot of things different." As we look back in life, sometimes we regret things we did or didn't do. Either way, regrets are a challenge for all of us, and they often even keep us awake at night.

In the Bible, King Solomon gives us some great advice.

He said, "Keep sound wisdom and discretion. They will be life to your soul and grace to your neck. Then you will walk safely in your way, and your foot will not stumble. When you lie down, you will not be afraid; yes, when you lie down, your sleep will be sweet."

Every current regret we have came from some dumb decision in the past, and every dumb decision today will lead to a new regret tomorrow. That thought reminds me of something else I heard from a song. "Don't be stupid!" Life will be much better in the days ahead.

Are there any regrets you have been carrying that you need to drop? Ask God for strength to drop them now.

Ask God to help you, starting today, make decisions that won't cause future regrets.

January 9
Rumors and Gossip

Scripture for Today: James 3:3–12

When was the last time you heard a good rumor? Have you heard that Sally's pregnant? Johnny is losing his house? Fred's on drugs? Sue is having an affair with Joe?

You see, bad news travels fast even if it isn't true. Rumors are destructive, unfair, and unnecessary, even if they are true. God did not create and appoint you to publicize the difficulties and failures of other people. I'm sure you have had a few failures and difficulties of your own that you'd prefer the whole world not know.

Gossip can be a hard habit to break, but it is worth the effort to do so. In the book of James, the Bible warns us that though our tongue is small, it is powerful and destructive. It reminds us that our tongue is much like a small fire that can burn an entire forest.

If you just have to say something about someone, make sure you say something good. If you have nothing good to say, well, it's best to say nothing at all.

Have you hurt anyone recently with your words that you need to reconcile with?

Why not commit to God right now that you will not damage others by spreading rumors and gossip?

January 10
The Second Law of Thermodynamics

Scripture for Today: Proverbs 16:9

Have you noticed how hard it is to get your life in order, and how easy it is for it to get out of order again? This tendency applies to all areas of life. Everything in the Universe wears out, runs down, decays, or dies. Every new car will someday be in a junkyard, but no car in the junkyard will ever be new again. Scientists call this the Second Law of Thermodynamics. It states that everything in the universe has a tendency to get out of order.

A great life requires hard work and discipline because chaos and disorder are always on the prowl. So, in addition to your car, you need a good maintenance plan for your health, your marriage, your finances and, most importantly, your spiritual life. Left unattended, these areas will not get better, they will get worse.

What's your maintenance plan for a great life? If you don't have one or don't know where to begin; ask God. He created you and He will help you to succeed.

Is there an area of your life that has fallen into disarray?

Where is the best place to start your life maintenance plan? Reading your Bible? Prayer? Regular church attendance? Reconciling your marriage? Ask God for wisdom to begin today.

January 11
Engaged

Scripture for Today: James 4:8

"Are you engaged?" I'm not talking about a commitment for marriage, but about your spiritual life. When two gears are linked and begin to move together, they are engaged to produce energy and purpose. They are no longer in neutral, but have become engaged, and as a result have become productive.

Think of God as one gear and think of yourself as the other. With that in mind, once again I ask, "Are you engaged?"

We are told in the Biblical book of James, "Draw near to God and He will draw near to you." The image is simple, yet powerful. Each step you take toward God, He moves closer to you. Soon, the two of you connect and become engaged to produce energy and purpose. That's life at its best.

God has already moved in your direction and is waiting for you to move toward Him. What's your next move? Wipe the dust off your Bible? Go to church this Sunday? Get on your knees and pray? Whatever it is, get out of neutral and get engaged with God. It's what you were made for!

Are you engaged with God right now? If not, how long has it been?

What's the next step to getting your gears engaged with God's?

January 12
Invest and Mentor

Scripture for Today: 2 Timothy 2:2

Do you have a good investment strategy? We all want to know what to invest in for the greatest return. It might be that the best place to invest is not a "what," but a "who"!

I'm thankful for my parents who have been the greatest investors in my life. However, there are some others for which I am also grateful: men like Ernest, Arthur, Donald, and Donnie who invested in me as a kid, and Malone who gave me a great opportunity. Now, Bob, Stephen, John, and Larry who continue to be great mentors.

All of these men were much older than I when our paths first crossed. Some of them have since passed away, but their investment continues to impact me greatly.

As time passes, the roles shift, and we soon become the "old people" whose words and time are greatly treasured. If you are young, find an old person to hang out with. If you are old, invest in a young person. It's likely that both of your lives will increase in value and produce dividends long after you are gone.

Who are the people who have invested in your life? Thank God for them right now!

Who could you be mentoring right now? Who could be mentoring you? Why not set things in motion soon?

January 13th
Complaining

Scripture for Today: Philippians 4:1-7

Are you a consistent complainer?

I heard about a monk who joined a monastery and took a vow of silence. He was allowed only two words every ten years. After his first ten years, his superior asked what he had to say. His response was, "Food bad!" After his next ten years, his superior asked what he had to say. His response was, "Bed hard!" After his next ten years, his superior asked what he had to say. His response was, "I quit!" To which his superior responded, "Well that doesn't surprise me. You've done nothing but complain since you got here!"

If you're a consistent complainer, it's a habit you really need to break. Complaining is not good. It is not helpful. And it is not normal. We all have bad days. And yes, we have a right to speak up about things that could and should be better. But if complaining has become a habit, learn to practice gratitude, prayer, and graciousness, and the peace of God which surpasses all understanding will invade and heal your complaining soul!

What are the things you are most likely to complain about? Which ones of them can you change?

Pause and ask God to give you the kind of outlook that will help you avoid complaining.

January 14
Tomorrow

Scripture for Today: Job 7:7, Matthew 6:34

What are your plans tomorrow? It's a question we often ask, but it's built on the assumption that we will be alive tomorrow.

In 1982, I was making my daily trip from my hometown of Tallapoosa, Georgia to Floyd College in Rome, where I was a freshman in College. I had the 45-minute drive down to a science, but everything changed when a large truck drifted into my lane of traffic. The couple of seconds before we collided shifted to slow motion as I reviewed my life, certain those were my last moments to live. Obviously, I survived to see another day.

In 1993, my brother Richie was also in a serious accident, but he did not survive.

Life is fragile and uncertain; thus, each day should be lived with purpose. The Bible warns, "Don't boast about tomorrow, for you don't know what a day may bring." It also says, "Life is like a vapor. It appears for a little while and then vanishes away.

Don't put off until tomorrow what should be done today, because tomorrow may never come. Someday, it won't.

What have you been delaying that you need to do now?

Ask God to help you live each day for the purpose He has for you.

January 15
Giving and Happiness

Scripture for Today: 2 Corinthians 8:1–6

What will it take to make me happy? I know you've thought about it. Sooner or later the answer comes around to more money to spend. Money itself is not the problem and it's certainly needed to function in today's society. But the Bible gives us a warning that the love of money is the root of all kinds of evil! Money is a wonderful thing to have, but too often it simply feeds our own selfish desires to purchase and accumulate things we don't need to impress people we don't like. Then the payment comes due and more misery follows!

The Bible teaches a different way! It states, "It's happier to give than to receive."
II Corinthians 8 tells the story of some very poor people who gave a generous gift to others who were also poor. When they gave, it says they experienced "an abundance of joy" and happiness. If you want to be happy, don't purchase something. Instead, give something away to help someone in great need. That's where real happiness is found.

Who in your life do you consider a generous person?

How can you cultivate more generosity in your own life?

January 16
Directions

Scripture for Today: Proverbs 16:25

Do you have a GPS navigation device or app? If not, there are times when you wish you did. I have one on my mobile phone and recently, when traveling out of country in Rio de Janeiro, Brazil, it led me straight to a restaurant I couldn't find. Now that was nice!

Several years ago, while on an evening elk-hunting trip, I got lost in the Colorado Mountains. A friend of mine and I wandered aimlessly in the dark night and frigid weather until 2 or 3 in the morning when we were found. We had started the evening confident we knew where to go, but we were wrong. Our instincts had failed us.

Too often in life, we trust our instincts to guide us. But just because something feels right, doesn't mean it is. We are warned in Proverbs 16 verse 25: "There is a way that seems right to a man, but instead it's the way of destruction and death."

When you're not sure, ask God for directions. He can be trusted every time.

Write down below any ways in which you feel you've lost your orientation.

If you have lost all sense of direction about a particular challenge, ask God for guidance about it now.

January 17th
Why Do We Suffer?

Scripture for Today: Philippians 1:21-26

Is there any purpose to the sufferings we sometimes face? It's a question asked from every human heart. What is this pain and heartache all about?

I don't have a concise and complete answer but reading through the small book of Philippians in the Bible will help you gain a good perspective. Paul is the author and he wrote it from a prison cell. He would ultimately receive a death sentence. The church at Philippi were the recipients. They were extremely poor and were also being persecuted for their faith in Jesus. So, the book of Philippians is a message from a suffering man writing to a suffering people. Paul wrote about how to have joy and confidence in the midst of suffering.

He emphasized that suffering can enlarge our capacity to love God and people, to learn and discern, and increase our capacity to do good works that honor God. In reality, suffering can take us to a depth and intimacy with God that blessing never can!

Are you undergoing heavy suffering at this time of your life?

In humility, ask God to bring people into your life to help bear your burdens.

January 18
Self-Talk

Scripture for Today: Proverbs 23:7, Matthew 15:10–11

Do you ever talk to yourself? It's not a sign of getting old or going crazy. Actually, we all do it every day, and it's likely that the most impacting voice we hear is our own. On any given day, we tell ourselves that life is good or bad, our spouse is good or bad, that God is trustworthy or not, or that we're going to succeed or fail at a particular task. We've usually said all of that before breakfast each day.

It really matters what you say to yourself, because you are always listening and you usually believe what you've heard, even if it isn't true. The Bible wisely reminds us that, "as a man thinks in his heart, so is he." Given enough time, we begin to live out our thoughts and self-talk. Your self-talk today has a big influence on the person you'll become tomorrow. So be nice and speak with respect, especially when you're talking to yourself. What you say is paving the way to your future.

Do you more often say to yourself "Good job!" or "Why are you so dumb?"

Ask God to help you see yourself as He does and talk to yourself the same way.

January 19
Dependability

Scripture for Today: 1 Peter 5:12

Just how dependable are you? Can you be counted on when it counts? Dependability is a quality we don't always recognize when present, but we certainly know when it isn't. When we have it, we're an asset, but when we don't, we're a big liability.

I've never been very athletic, but regardless of the sport, I love to watch someone play that consistently makes the shot, hits the home run, or makes the field-goal when it's their responsibility to do so. No complaining and no excuses, they simply deliver time after time. We call them winners!

It's a quality that's also required in our military. Even knowing it might cost their own life, they deliver. We call them heroes!

That's also the example Jesus gave us, and for that we call Him Savior.

What responsibilities do you carry? Mom, dad, son, or daughter? Employee or leader? Whoever you are and whatever you do, just make sure you deliver. Somebody is counting on it!

Why do some people struggle to come-through in a tough spot?

When called on for help, are you more likely to come-through or be found wanting?

Ask God for the diligence and faithfulness to always be counted on when it counts.

January 20
Meekness

Scripture for Today: Galatians 5:22–23

How high is meekness on your list of values? Meekness is all about being teachable. We don't know all the answers, and we're ready to learn.

In the year 2000, a beautiful palomino colt was born in my arms as his mother struggled to give birth. I named him Cutter, after his famous grandfather Cutter Bill. Over the next two years I watched him evolve into an unruly and arrogant stallion that was a danger to be around. I was so frustrated I almost sold him. Then I read an article from a master trainer that explained everything I needed to know. He said a horse has to have pressure applied to him until he becomes meek. Once he is meek, his spirit becomes teachable.

Well, it took lots of pressure, but Cutter did become teachable. Throughout the rest of his life even a child could ride him with great joy and ease. A spirit of meekness gave him and everyone around him a better life.

Could it be that the pressures of life are a gift from God to make us teachable? Just how much pressure is it going to take for you to embrace meekness?

Do you generally think meekness is the same thing as weakness?

A desire to learn is not weak; it's a strength. Ask God to instill in you a spirit of meekness as you follow Him.

January 21st
Die Climbing

Scripture for Today: Philippians 3:12-16

As life passes, are you moving upward?

Moving upward is something we aspire to in many areas of life, but are you moving upward in your spiritual life? The Bible speaks about "letting go of those things which are behind and reaching forward to those things which are ahead." It then says we are to reach for the "upward" call of God. As God calls us upward, we can't go "up there" carrying all of "that down there"! So, we must learn to let go of some things each day to continue to move upward—bitterness, resentment, jealousy, anger, and such. Let go of that stuff. Hold on tightly to your faith!

The Swiss Alps are breathtakingly beautiful! But in the midst of the beauty, it's a challenge to those who climb. At the base of one mountain is a sign commemorating a man's life. It reads simply, "He died climbing!" Make sure you hold on to the right stuff and let go of the bad stuff. Keep moving to the upward call of God!

Are you trying to climb a mountain with a weight you can't carry?

Take a personal inventory of bad motives, bad attitudes, and other things that hold you down. Confess them to God, ask Him to remove them and their weight so you can climb ever upward.

January 22
Big Goals

Scripture for Today: Genesis 6:11-22

Where are you going? We have to answer that question for every journey we take. Are you going from good to great? Or from bad to worse? You'd better know the difference! Jim Collins wrote a book called "Good to Great." It's a great book about business, but it also applies to life. In it, he writes about the difference between good and great companies and what keeps a company great. He says that every great company has BHAGs that keep them striving for excellence. I believe the same is true about life.

BHAG is an acronym for a Big, Hairy, Audacious Goal. What are your BHAGS?

Throughout the Bible, God challenged many with tasks that fit in the BHAG category. For Noah, it was to build the ark to save mankind and the different species of the earth. For David, it was to kill the giant, Goliath. For Paul, it was to preach the gospel where no one had ever preached before.

Make sure you're moving from good to great. What are your BHAGs?

What is a goal you are pursuing that is so big it will never be reached without God's help?

What is the next step you can take toward its fulfillment?

January 23
Climb Mountains

Scripture for Today: Psalm 18:30–33

Have you climbed any mountains lately? The journey can be a challenge, even deadly. But going to the top is rewarding. Each year several people, young and old, die attempting to climb Mt. Everest. Every year many make the attempt for the first time, while others try again. Those who make it to the summit celebrate the accomplishment of a lifetime.

Life is full of challenging mountains that are worth the climb, and they should be celebrated. Birthdays. Wedding anniversaries. Work anniversaries. Each journey has at times been difficult, but the climb is worth it and rewarding.

Jesus took the most difficult climb in history. He climbed while carrying the cross He would be nailed to once reaching the summit. He also carried my sin and yours on His shoulders all the way to the top, and for that we should celebrate every day.

Write down two or three mountains you have climbed and take a moment to celebrate the victories again.

What mountains are you facing at this point in your life? Pause and ask for God's help in climbing them.

January 24
Grace

Scripture for Today: Philippians 4:4–7

How gracious are you? Grace is a beautiful word, and even more beautiful as an action! I was on a safari with some friends in South Africa when I saw a massive giraffe moving through the trees. Its awkward and disproportionate body moved in perfect and beautiful harmony that can only be described as graceful.

Our South African hosts showed us great kindness and love. They cared for us with such attention and beauty, it could only be described as gracious.

Upon returning home, the expenses we had charged had a ten-day grace period. Now that was beautiful!

The Bible teaches that God showed His love toward us while we were still sinners. For that thought John Newton wrote, "Amazing Grace how sweet the sound that saved a wretch like me. I once was lost but now am found. Was blind but now I see!"

Philippians 4:5 says, "Let your graciousness be known to everyone because the Lord is near." Show someone grace today and thank God for His towards you. Grace is always a beautiful thing.

How has God shown you grace recently?

How can you show grace to someone today?

January 25th
History Makers

Scripture for Today: Hebrews 11

What is your mission in life, and are you living it?

Throughout history God has raised up people from humble beginnings to positively impact the world, to make it a better place, to right wrongs, and to guide others to have peace with God. They are history makers! They change the course of history for individuals, families, and nations. In the Bible, ordinary people like Noah, Abraham, Joseph, David, Mary, Peter, Paul, and many others. Then there's the pioneer leaders, researchers, explorers, teachers, missionaries, and preachers of recent history: the Abraham Lincolns, Billy Grahams, Martin Luther Kings, and Mother Teresas. They were all history makers and people's lives are better because of theirs.

I was in Ethiopia working with a group of church leaders from Somalia, where it's dangerous and deadly to be a Christian. One man said, "For most of my life I have been a history speaker. Speaking about things that happened in the past. But from this day forward, I want to be a history maker!" All of us need to make that decision. Have you?

Have you ever held a dream to be a history maker? What was it about?

Take some time to dream again, then ask God to lead you in the way that will see it fulfilled.

January 26
Unfair Life

Scripture for Today: Psalm 73:1–3

What do you do when you think life is unfair? Actually, life often seems unfair, but seldom in our direction. It seems like it's always the other guy who gets the job or the other lady who gets the new furniture!

Perhaps we worked harder and longer, but someone else got the promotion. We respond with harshness and say, "I do not deserve to be treated this way!" Such thoughts often lead to anger, resentment, and lifelong bitterness.

But keep in mind that each of us has been blessed with many good things that we don't necessarily deserve: our family, food, and friends or maybe a place to call home. What about the freedom we enjoy in this awesome country of ours?

Have you ever been to a city park and noticed all the pigeons sitting on the various statues? To the statue, I'm sure life doesn't seem fair and perhaps the pigeon has the advantage. Well, some days I'm the pigeon and some days I'm the statue, but I'm just thankful to be in the park!

Have you experienced unfairness in life whether in your education, business, or home? Did you respond well?

No one in history has been more unfairly treated than Jesus who was crucified as a common criminal, even though He was pure, perfect, and without sin. He is our guide when we are treated unfairly, so rely on Him for endurance.

January 27
Honesty and Trust

Scripture for Today: Proverbs 20:6

Are you tired of dealing with people you can't trust? It's frustrating to be lied to, or to be betrayed with broken promises without a real explanation or apology. When you hear certain people speak based upon your previous experience with them, you now simply assume they aren't telling you the truth. I once had an old coonhound like that. The way he was barking up that tree, I was convinced there was something up there, but he consistently lied. That's where we get the phrase, "You're lying like a dog!"

It's said of others, "They're as honest as the day is long!" or "Their word is their bond." These people have proven to be trustworthy and they are a pleasure to do business with or interact with.

When people think about you, which category do they put you in? When they hear your name, do they think *trust* or *distrust*?

Trust is the foundation of every successful friendship, marriage, business, or leadership journey. It's impossible to be a success without it, so be honest and trustworthy.

What separates the trustworthy people you know from the people you can't trust? Which would you rather deal with?

Do people you interact with consider you trustworthy or not trustworthy? If you aren't sure, ask God to reveal any inconsistencies in your life.

January 28
Legacy

Scripture for Today: Psalm 78:1–4

What will they say about you when you die? Besides the common visitation phrase, "Don't they look good?" It's an important question to address now because you're still around to help write the answer. Whatever is said will define your entire life in a single sentence or two, so it's important to get it right. No, I'm not talking about the sentence, but life itself!

No one lives without mistakes, tragedies, and failure, but it's how you deal with your failure that matters. As a leader and a friend, I've had to change course, correct my actions, or apologize for my failures many times. And it's humiliating and painful. My apologies aren't always accepted, but that's okay. There is still something special that happens in my own soul every time I go through the process; I become a better me. To do the right thing is always a step in the right direction. Your legacy is in your hands.

We live. We lead. We die. Start today and make plans to do all three extremely well.

What kind of legacy are you leaving? Does it reflect an emphasis on the things God emphasizes?

What kind of legacy would you like to leave? If you need a course correction, ask God to help you build a legacy that honors Him.

January 29
Conflict

Scripture for Today: Matthew 18:15–16, Philippians 4:2–4

How do you deal with conflict? Conflict is simply a fact of life, unless you're the only person left on the planet. Even then, it's likely you'd have an argument with yourself at some point.

All conflict results from violated expectations. We all experience it in the relationships of life, but it doesn't always have to be a bad thing. It can possibly serve as a tool to deepen our understanding of others and ourselves. The end result can add great strength to the relationships involved. So, when you find yourself in a conflict with someone, don't be surprised, and follow this simple process:

1. Face it quickly.
2. If possible, take the person to lunch to work it out.
3. Take responsibility for your part of the conflict and apologize.
4. Be nice.
5. Keep it contained to the people involved.
6. Together find a solution and commit to move forward.

An ignored conflict today will hinder your success tomorrow, so resolve it now!

Who in your life do you have unresolved conflict with?

Commit to contact them today to set in motion the process above.

January 30
Get Rich Slowly

Scripture for Today: Proverbs 12:11

Do you have a good money plan?

There's a strong emphasis today on instant gratification. One of the main places this can be seen is in the world of money. You don't often hear advertisements on how to accumulate savings over a long period of time. It's more "Do you want cash now?! Call this number!"

What are the benefits of being financially prudent? **It helps us be disciplined in our spending.** If we were given a huge sum of money all at once, it would be incredibly tempting to spend most of it on things we've always wanted! Getting a little at time helps us to be frugal in our spending and teaches us to save more!

It helps us avoid deals that are "too good to be true." We've all seen the ads online for companies that seem to offer a great way to make money while doing hardly any work.

It helps us be prepared for our later years. Build your savings. Invest in your retirement. Your physical ability to work and earn money will go down at some point. Then you will be prepared for such a time when it comes!

How can you begin saving your money to become financially secure?

Take a few minutes and write down all the ways that God has blessed you financially. Thank Him for that!

January 31
Courage

Scripture for Today: Job 1:6–9

Are you facing the challenges of life with courage? We are inspired by the courage of the Braveheart character William Wallace with painted face and prancing horse challenging his men to go into battle. We are inspired by the courage of our own military as they fight on our behalf.

But with how much courage are you fighting your own battles: a battle with cancer, divorce, loneliness, or the fact that you are getting old and dying soon. Perhaps you're a parent, or a leader in business or government with a big decision looming. Some of the greatest battles of life don't happen on a battlefield, but in our own soul!

· I've been inspired many times by those who face their fears and march boldly into the unknown. Courage is not the absence of fear, but the resolve to move forward in spite of it. Jesus said, "I will never forsake you," but will be with you even until the end. So be strong and of good courage as you face your battles. Others are watching!

Are you in the middle of a battle right now? Do you feel like you are losing ground?

Stop and give it to God in prayer, then move forward with courage.

February 1
Habits

Scripture for Today: Jeremiah 22:21, Luke 4:16

What kind of habits do you have? Habits are powerful whether good or bad. It's our habits that determine who we are and where we go in life. We make decisions, then decisions make us.

Here's how it works: a great life is made from many great years. Each great year is made from many great months. Every great month is made from great weeks. A great week is made from great days. And great days are made from great habits!

Success really is that simple. Just repeat good decisions and they will take you there.

But habits also work in reverse. If we repeat bad decisions, a bad habit is developed that becomes a destructive force, driving us to failure.

This is true in all areas of life: how we deal with people, our moral life, spiritual life, financial life, family life, work life, and health life. You might occasionally order a biggie-sized fry, but if it becomes a habit don't be surprised when your clothes just no longer fit. I know that from experience!

What do you find the easiest to establish, bad habits or good ones?

What bad habits do you need to overcome? What good habits do you need to nurture?

February 2
Intentions

Scripture for Today: Jeremiah 29:11

"What are your intentions?" It's a question a father asks his daughter's boyfriend when they've been dating a while—and it's a good question to ask him. It addresses the issue of purpose. He's really asking, "For what purpose are you dating my daughter?"

We should ask ourselves a similar question every morning as our feet hit the floor. What are your intentions? For what purpose are you living today?

God made us so we are the happiest when we live for a higher purpose than ourselves. We must seek to discover that purpose.

You, my friend, are no accident, and you won't find a great life by accident. God made you on purpose, and for a purpose! Don't you think it's a good idea to ask Him what your purpose is? In the Bible, God tells us, "For I know the plans I have for you...plans to prosper you and not to harm you, plans to give you hope and a future." Why not live today to make God thankful He gave you life!

Do you know your purpose for living?

Spend some time thinking and praying through a personal statement of purpose. Write it below or in your journal.

February 3
Communication

Scripture for Today: John 1:1, Hebrews 1:1–2, Matthew 5:37

How well do you communicate? Communication is important on both the speaking and the listening side of things. My dad and I attempted to carry a heavy boat through the thick brush and weeds of the riverbank. Dad led the way and I carried the back of the boat. We had a planned day of fishing together in the Tallapoosa River. Our plans came to a halt when, unaware to me, dad's legs got tangled in a string of briars and thorns. Immediately he yelled, "Whoa!" But I thought he said, "Go!" And I gave him a big push, sinking the thorns deep into his legs. Well, we fished that day with blood oozing down my dad's legs all because of a breakdown in communication.

He clearly said one thing, but I heard another.

If you thought about saying something, it doesn't mean you said it. And just because you said it, doesn't mean they heard it. And just because they heard it, doesn't mean they'll follow through.

I mean, how well are you hearing what God has to say?

Think about a time you had an adventure in miscommunication. Was it harmful or humorous?

God has clearly spoken to us through His word. Are you taking advantage of what God has said to us?

February 4
Growing Up, Growing Old

Scripture for Today: 1 Corinthians 13:11

Are you growing up or growing old? It's hard to know when we move from one to the other. I could hardly wait till I grew old enough to buy my own handgun at age 21. I bought a 44 magnum, Dirty Harry Special. I can still see Clint Eastwood's lip twitch as he says, "Go ahead. Make my day!" That was all a part of growing up. Going to school, graduating, getting a job, getting married, having kids.

But at some point, I'm not sure when, I shifted from growing up to growing old. It's been many years since the Haralson County High School class of '82 walked across the stage. My body no longer grows up, but out. I used to part my hair in the middle, now there is nothing left to part. I'm beyond life's halfway point. It's hard to imagine I'm closer to death than birth. I'm officially growing old, and someday I'll breathe my last breath and leave this world!

But for the believer, the best is still yet to come!

Have you reached the age you've realized you are growing old?

Whether you are still growing up or are now growing old, ask God to help you make every day count for His glory.

February 5
Fear

Scripture for Today: Psalm 27:1–3, 2 Timothy 1:7

What are you afraid of? Fear stalks us every day and threatens to destroy us as we deal with life. It is present whether we are walking onto a battlefield for war, into a new classroom to learn, a new career to work, or down the aisle for marriage! Fear is a brutal beast that lurks in the distance, always picketing our success, displaying signs that read: Fear Failure! Fear Rejection! Fear Disease! Fear Criticism! Fear Dying! The list goes on and on. Fear has been around for a long time, and it's likely not to disappear anytime soon; so, you'd best learn how to face it with great skill.

David, the great King of Israel faced great success and great failure, and in both he faced great fear. How did he do it? He asked and answered one great question: "Whom shall I fear? The LORD is the strength of my life; of whom shall I be afraid?" Can you answer David's question with the same confidence? If not, why not?

Is there anything that has you fearful? Are you being controlled by it?

Ask God right now to turn you from fear to faith in Him in all things you face.

February 6
Vision

Scripture for Today: Proverbs 29:18

How good is your vision? I can remember when mine began to blur and I started wearing glasses or contacts to help me see clearly. Our vision is an essential tool to guide us and help us see where we're going in life. On a deeper level, I've learned that eyesight is no guarantee of vision.

Helen Keller lost her sight as a child. Later in life she was asked, "Can you imagine anything worse than being blind?" She responded, "Yes. To have sight but have no vision." She understood that a person's vision in life is more important than a person's eyesight. Their vision is closely connected to their dreams in life. Helen, although blind, went on to accomplish some great things because of her vision.

The Bible states, "Where there is no vision, the people perish."

What do you dream about? You won't accomplish everything you dream about, but it's likely you won't accomplish anything you don't dream about. So, dream and dream big!

Again I ask, how good is your vision?

Are you currently looking to the future at something bigger than yourself?

What would it take for your vision to become reality?

February 7
Potential

Scripture for Today: Matthew 13:31–32

Are you aware of your full potential? Back in February I planted some small broccoli seeds in my garden. It was exciting to watch the broccoli grow each week as I fertilized it, nurtured it, and kept the weeds out. God and time did the rest. Last week I had the joy of cutting a beautiful massive head of broccoli that provided life-giving nutrition to my family. It took just nine weeks under the right conditions for each small seed to reach its potential to feed several people.

Hopefully you're aware that you have much more potential than a broccoli seed. The broccoli doesn't exist for itself and neither do you. God designed and created you to be an essential ingredient of life that adds great value to the lives of those around you. It's up to you to keep your life nurtured, well fertilized with the right ingredients, and to keep the weeds out. God and time do the rest. Yes, you, my friend, have huge potential. So, live each day committed to reach it to the fullest.

Do you think you have reached the fullest potential you have to offer?

Write down one specific area you believe you could make progress if you focused on it.

What things limit you from fulfilling the purpose God has for your life?

February 8
Refreshing People

Scripture for Today: 2 Timothy 1:16–18, 4:19

Who are your favorite people in life? Recently while working all day in the hot sun I stopped to rest for a moment in the shade under a large oak tree. Soon after I sat down, a welcomed cool breeze began to blow, bringing with it some much needed refreshment and strength to my overheated and tired body. I saw it as a great gift from God at just the right time!

My favorite people are very much like that breeze. Their positive attitude, contagious laughter, and thoughtful actions bring refreshment and strength during the hardest of times. I'm thankful for those kinds of people. More than that, I want to be one of those people.

The Apostle Paul told Timothy about such a man in his life named Onesiphorus. Actually, Paul was in prison in Rome, far away from family and friends. He felt deserted and betrayed, but he was thankful for Onesiphorus who refreshed him often, much like a cool breeze on a hot day. Be a cool breeze in someone's life today.

Who in your life is like a cool breeze to your soul?

Would most people say you are like a cool breeze or a hot summer wind? Ask God to help you be refreshing to more people.

February 9
Deception

Scripture for Today: Proverbs 14:12, Galatians 6:7

Things are not always as they appear to be. I arrived at the airport in Czech Republic in the beautiful city of Prague. As I got off the plane, I was eager to find my driver, but he wasn't there. After several minutes I saw a man in the crowd holding a sign with my last name on it. "W.R.I.G.H.T." I approached him, pointed at the sign and said, "Wright?" He pointed at me, smiled and said, "Wright"? I said "Right." I went with him and made the 45-minute ride to my destination, but he took me to the wrong place. A few minutes later we both realized I was the wrong Wright, and he was the wrong driver. The right Wright and the right driver were still waiting back at the airport. It seemed so right, but it wasn't.

The Bible reminds us, "There is a way that seems right to a person, but the end of that way is destruction and death." Just because something seems right doesn't mean it is.

Have you ever been deceived by a desire, a "gut feeling", or a person? How did you feel when you realized it?

The evil one, Satan, desires to deceive us until the end of our days. Don't let him deceive you away from the truth of God's love for you and His willingness to save you from destruction and death.

February 10
Paying the Price

Scripture for Today: Romans 6:23

Sometimes life can feel like a runaway train and it's essential—but painful—to stop.

When I was a kid I secretly jumped on my brother's bicycle and went for a quick ride down a long hill I'd gone down many times before. I didn't normally ride with just my socks on, and why I did it that day I have no idea. I also had no idea that the brake cable was broken on the bike.

I was enjoying the ride as I rode at break-neck speed, but when it came time to stop, panic quickly replaced joy. I had only two options: ride into the highway and traffic at the bottom of the hill or sink my socked feet into pavement. A week later, my scabbed feet and socks with holes were evidence of my decision; but at least I was still alive!

I'm reminded that sin takes you further than you wanted to go, keeps you longer than you wanted to stay, and makes you pay a price you never intended to pay. Now might be a great time to stop!

Are you in danger of a "sock-feet" stop to your out-of-control life? Did you miss the stop and make a wreck of your life?

Ask God to forgive you for any sins you haven't admitted to, or if you've never received Christ as Lord and Savior receive Him today before the eternal cost comes home.

February 11
Dreaming

Scripture for Today: Joshua 14:12–15

What are you dreaming about? Your dreams are important because they provide a picture of your future. Many years ago, one of my favorite pastimes was to spend the night with my MawMaw and PawPaw on their farm. I still hear the squeaky chain of the porch-swing in the background while PawPaw told stories about the past. I can hear the whippoorwill in the distance as the hot summer sun began to fade for the evening. Then MawMaw would put me to bed and say, "Sweet dreams!"

Well, just as sweet dreams provide the foundation for a good night's rest, our dreams about the future provide a roadmap for an amazing life. The Bible teaches that without a dream, people perish. They wander aimlessly without direction. MawMaw and PawPaw passed away many years ago, but the words, "Sweet dreams" continue to echo clearly in my mind every day.

Every great success or joy in life begins with a dream, so dream big. Your future is counting on it. I'm still dreaming! As you evaluate your life and plan for a New Year, what are *you* dreaming about?

What kind of dreams are you dreaming about in your life? Is it something so big only God can get the credit?

Pause for a moment and consider whether you are expecting God to do too little with you. If you are, ask Him to give you a dream that will honor Him.

February 12
A Name

Scripture for Today: Proverbs 22:1

What kind of name do you have? Your name says something. I recently met a man whose name is GodKnows. We are now Facebook friends. What a name, obviously given to him by Christian parents. I was with GodKnows every day for a week and each time I called his name I was reminded of the great truth that God knows everything.

When people hear your name, what are they reminded of? Your name tells a story.

Since childhood my father has reminded me that, "A good name is better to be chosen than great riches!" It's a principle by which my father lived! He was a devoted Christian, a faithful husband, an awesome father to his four sons, a trusted businessman for 40 years, and a wise mentor to all who would listen. My father lived each day with eternity in mind.

He died in 2011 at his home in Tallapoosa, but the name Alfred Wright will continue to hang around as a reminder of a life well lived. Thanks Dad!

Do you know the meaning of your name? If you have children, did you have specific reasons for the names they have?

The most important name we can know is Jesus, the "name above all names." Why not pause right now and acknowledge the beauty, majesty, and glory of His name.

February 13
Thinking

Scripture for Today: Philippians 4:8

What are you thinking about today? Some people say that success is all about *who* you know. Others say it's *what* you know. But I believe it's about how you think. Bad thinking leads to bad behaviors and good thinking leads to good behaviors. Even the Bible warns us to think about things that are true, noble, lovely, right, pure, and admirable. It also tells us that we become like we think.

Good thinking does not come naturally, especially in today's troubled world. You'll have to work at it. If you are not careful, you'll be completely overtaken with a bad case of stinking thinking!

When I was a little fellow, I hated to take a bath. My parents, however, insisted in spite of my opposition. Bathing has now become a habit for which I'm very thankful. The people around me are thankful for it too!

But your thinking can stink just as badly as your body, so get rid of stinkin' thinkin' by taking a brain bath daily. The people around you will be glad you did!

Do you have any areas of life where you've allowed stinking thinking (negativity) to take over?

A "brain bath" is when you saturate your mind with God's word. If you haven't been bathing in the word, what steps can you take today to make it a priority?

February 14
Be Thankful

Scripture for Today: Psalm 103:1–5

How thankful are you? Thankfulness is feeling like you've been given something you don't deserve, rather than feeling like somebody owes you something you do deserve. These two are opposites and daily we must choose between them. A thankful heart does not overflow with a sense of entitlement, and a heart focused on entitlement is not filled with thankfulness.

Even if you've never been a thankful person, it's an attitude you can develop, and you should.

The Bible records a good conversation David had with himself one day as he talked to his own soul about being thankful. He said, "Bless the Lord, O my soul, and all that is within me, bless His holy name. Bless the Lord, O my soul and don't forget all of His benefits." Now that's a conversation all of us should have.

The next time someone asks, "How are you doing today?" why not respond with a phrase like, "Better than I deserve!" or "Extremely blessed and thankful!"

It will help you and those around you to be more thankful, too.

Do you live in a state of ongoing thankfulness?

The opposite of thankfulness is ingratitude. If your soul is ungrateful, that's a cause for repentance. Stop right now and list five or more things for which you can thank God.

February 15
Jesus is Alive

Scripture for Today: John 20:19–22

Have you ever had one of those moments when you felt helpless or hopeless?

I stood by my brother in the emergency room after his car accident. I prayed and the doctors worked but he was unresponsive. Days later I spoke at his funeral and we buried his body. I felt what Mary the mother of Jesus had felt so many years before when Jesus was crucified, then they placed His lifeless body in the tomb. She felt helpless and hopeless…until three days later when Jesus arose from the dead! That event changed everything!

The resurrection of Jesus provides hope where there is none. My brother had placed his faith in Jesus, and as a result, I will see him again! And while I still miss him, hope has replaced hopelessness.

Have you embraced Jesus as your Lord and Savior? Have you been baptized as a symbol of your faith and a witness to your family and friends? It's the absolute most important decision a person makes in life. Some day you too will leave this world in death. Will your family be left with hope or hopelessness?

If you haven't yet embraced Jesus, what excuses have you used to avoid Him?

The best thing that will ever happen to you is to be brought into God's family through Jesus Christ. If you have not, stop now and surrender your life to Him.

February 16
Tenacity

Scripture for Today: 2 Chronicles 20:17

Do you ever struggle with wanting to quit before a task is finished? It's easy to get sidetracked, frustrated, tired, or lose focus, and all of a sudden that task or goal that was top priority just isn't so important anymore. It's a problem we all face at some point, and we have to dig a little deeper and find something called tenacity.

It's an essential quality on the battlefield, in marriage, in sports, in business, in school, and on the job. Sometimes tenacity is the only thing standing in between success and failure; no one succeeds without it.

Tenacity is about refusing to give up. It means quitting when the job is done, not when you're tired. It means working with determination instead of depending on luck or fate for your success. The most successful people in the world do not have a life without pain, problems, and setbacks, but they do have a heavy dose of tenacity, and you can have it too. Jesus did, and I'm certainly thankful He didn't quit.

You might have heard the phrase "bulldog-like tenacity." Does this describe you?

Remember, no matter your situation, God fights your battles. Be tenacious, knowing the outcome of your efforts is in God's hands.

February 17
Reading Good Books

Scripture: 2 Kings 22:8–10

What books have you read lately? Effective leaders are regular readers! Biographies, history, leadership, or how-to, every book you read can come in handy when you least expect it.

A biography of Winston Churchill might inspire you to continue in spite of difficult circumstances. A biography of Abraham Lincoln might teach you how to make hard, but life-changing decisions. A history of Israel or Denmark will reveal real people and events you never knew existed. Good leadership books by John Maxwell changed the way I think about leadership, putting me on the path to becoming a good leader.

The book that has meant more to me than any other book is the Bible. I truly believe God inspired its words and teaches its truth. Its' Words continue to guide me and transform me. Many times my life has been in turmoil, then I've read something from the Bible, maybe a Psalm or a story about Jesus, and found the peace I so desperately needed..

I heartily recommend reading as many good books as you can! But I recommend the Bible most of all.

When is the last time you read a book that really built your spirit?

Have you ever read much of the Bible?

If not, make a plan to read the New Testament book of Mark, and ask God to speak to you through it.

February 18
Family

Scripture for Today: Colossians 3:18–21

What are you doing with your family this week? Long before a government or school existed, God created the family. Through it we face our deepest sorrows and greatest joys in life. Our family is the most powerful influence upon us. From birth until death they weave the very fabric of our lives. That's why family problems are difficult to work through. So, it's important to build a strong family for the next generation.

We don't get to choose the family we are born into, but we can choose the kind of family we will develop. Building a great family requires time together, so pick up the phone and invite them over. Make a pot of chili, sit around, and talk while the kids play together. I know, some family members are difficult to be around, but I've learned that on occasion the difficult family member is actually me! So, show a little grace, and create a special family memory this week. Your family will be better for it.

Do you have family issues that make it difficult to be around your family or do you have joyful family memories?

Sometimes family issues cannot be addressed until everyone agrees to address them. If that's the case in your family, ask God to get everyone on the same page so problems can be resolved.

If you have joyful family memories, list some ways you can keep them going for the generations to follow.

February 19
Getting Rest

Scripture: Exodus 20:8–10

Are you getting enough rest? There are few things as often talked about and as seldom done as resting! We talk about getting a good night's sleep, but often don't. We take naps because we don't sleep good at night. We sleep all night and wake up tired! It seems like getting rest ought to be easier.

It's good to be busy, productive, and to get things done. There is a good feeling that comes from doing something. But we have to learn to rest in between accomplishments.

If you've ever flown on an airplane, you might remember how the flight attendants show you what to do in case of an emergency. One of the steps they teach is what to do if the oxygen masks are released from the ceiling. They show you how to put on the mask and then they say to make sure your own mask is on before helping others! The best way we can care for others and do our best work is if we first care for ourselves.

So, the next time you want to work, you might need to rest instead!

Do you typically feel rested when you wake up?

Are you tempted to work too much and rest too little?

Ask God to help you realize your need to rest and help you not to feel guilty when you do rest.

February 20
The Importance of Having a Hobby

Scripture: Philippians 4:8, 9

Do you have a hobby? Something you do solely for fun or relaxation? Maybe you are a woodworker in your garage, or tie flies for fishing, or bake wedding cakes, hunt, or tend a vegetable garden. Whatever your hobby, they exist to help us relax!

The co-founder of Apple, Steve Wozniak plays polo riding a Segway scooter! One of the world's richest men, Warren Buffett, plays the ukulele. Churchill painted and so does former president George W. Bush. If these people can have a hobby, so can you!

Three things should be true of the average person's hobby:
1. It should be affordable. No one has to go deep into debt to have a hobby.
2. It should be relaxing. The purpose of a hobby is enjoyment.
3. It should not be all consuming. Several years ago, everyone started collecting baseball cards. The market for them went through the roof! Some people sold investment funds and lost a ton when the baseball card market sank. Let your hobby be a hobby; not your life.

One great thing about hobbies is they can also help you make new friends! So, find something you enjoy and start a new hobby today.

Do you have a hobby? Is it something you truly enjoy?

If you could have any hobby what would it be?

February 21
Fear

Scripture for Today: Exodus 4:10, Isaiah 41:10

What are you afraid of? When I entered high-school I was afraid of getting lost. I was afraid of getting picked on by the bigger guys. But mostly, I was afraid of giving a speech. I was certain I would die if I had to speak in front of the class, so I avoided any subject I thought would require it. Vocational Agriculture was my safety net: cattle, corn, hogs, and horses. I could handle that.

Boy was I surprised when Mr. McGill, on the first day of class, announced that by the end of the year everyone would do a speech on farming. I tried to talk my way out of it, but Mr. McGill insisted. My speech about Angus cattle lasted less than one minute, but I survived!

Now for many years I have spoken to audiences of hundreds or even thousands somewhere around the world almost every week. I'm thankful for Mr. Max McGill who helped me through that fear.

God has not given us a spirit of fear, but of confidence, love, and a sound mind. So live like it!

Do you have a specific fear that is holding you back? A fear of speaking? A fear of crowds? A fear of failure?

Whatever your specific fear, ask God to give you courage to face and overcome it.

February 22
Days

Scripture for Today: Psalm 90:12

What are you doing today? You should approach every day with that question, because every day counts. The life expectancy of Americans has now climbed to 78 years of age. That's 28,470 days.

The Bible wisely reminds us "to number our days, that we may gain a heart of wisdom." Something powerful happens inside of a person when they know how long they have to live. They become real and live each day with a sense of purpose and awareness.

We all know we are going to die, but most of us don't know when. If you knew you would live to the age of 78, how many days do you have left? At the time of this writing I have 10,714 to go. I know I could die tomorrow, or live to be 100, so a more important question is: What are you going to do with today? Smile. Make today special. It just might be your last!

If you knew without a doubt today would be your last, what would you do between now and 11:59pm?

Why not live each day as if it was your last and see what kind of difference it makes?

February 23
Worry

Scripture for Today: Matthew 6:25–34

What are you worried about? Worry is a powerful force, but it's imaginary. Worry is the feeling of fear about what might happen. Or it might not! But in the meanwhile, it steals your dreams, conquers your joy, and removes your smile. It's also extremely contagious, destroying the hopes and dreams of the people around you.

Worry is an age-old problem that Jesus warned us about over 2000 years ago. He said, "Don't worry about your life: what you will eat, drink, or wear. And don't worry about tomorrow. Tomorrow will take care of itself." He said, "Seek God's kingdom first, and then all these other things will come." His words are great advice for all of us in this hectic world. Put God first in life, and He will provide your needs as you live His way. Then you can relax, be happy, and enjoy each day as it comes.

So don't worry! Be happy! You must give up one to experience the other. Which one will you give up today? Worry? Or happiness?

Have you ever been paralyzed by worry?

Pause for a moment and commit your worries to God. Begin to seek His kingdom first and let Him take care of the stuff that you can't control.

February 24
Yes, You Can Change Careers

Scripture: 1 Corinthians 10:31

Have you ever felt trapped in your job or career choice? Perhaps you went to college or received "on the job training" for a certain vocation. You had high hopes of where this career choice would take you! Or maybe you inherited the family business and you expected to do it forever. But after spending some time actually doing the work, you realize you really don't want to do it anymore.

Well, if you have felt like that you definitely aren't the first person to experience it and you certainly won't be the last! People change and their interests do, too. If you have the ability to pursue another career, why not do it? You may find a brand-new passion that will open many doors and take you down a new path.

God gifts all of us with interests and passions that we are to use to further His kingdom! But that doesn't mean we can only pick one to pursue. The Bible says, "whatever you do, do it all for the glory of God." So, whether you stay in the job you've been in or you pick a brand-new career, it's okay! Just make sure you're doing it all for the glory of God!

What are you passionate about? How can you incorporate that into a job if you haven't already?

If you can't pursue another career right now, how can you practice being content where you are?

February 25
Relationships

Scripture for Today: Philippians 2:25–30

Who are you going to talk to today? There are certain people that we work with, eat with, learn from, speak to, and interact with every day. These people help define our lives. We call them relationships. Oh sure, we have relationships at many levels, but in reality, it's the value we add to the people around us that determines how much they value us. What value do the people in your life attach to you? When they look back through life, will they remember you with fondness and appreciation? Or will you be one of those people they remember with frustration and resentment?

God put you in this world with over 7 billion other people. You can't live life alone no matter how hard you try. So, when you look around and see someone looking your way, or their ears are listening to your words, make sure that what they see and hear from you helps make today the best day ever. Go make someone's day today. It's likely it will make yours as well!

What is the most difficult thing for you about having good relationships?

Have you been intentional about adding value to the people around you? If not, why not begin praying about that today.

February 26
Standing Ovation

Scripture for Today: 1 Thessalonians 5:11

Have you ever received a standing ovation? As a pastor, speaker, and leadership trainer I've received several, and it's always a humbling experience. But there is a brief moment of feeling on top of the world. A standing ovation says, "You did an AMAZING job, and I'm deeply grateful for your effort!" "You've blessed me and inspired me!" A standing ovation is the ultimate "thank you."

Most people in this world go their entire lives and never receive one standing ovation, even though they do an amazing job and add great value to our lives each day. The public servant who protects us, the teacher who educates us, the co-worker who helps us, the boss who employs us, the chef and server who feed us, the mom and dad who raise us, the friend who walks with us, the spouse who loves us, and the child who inspires us. On certain days some people deserve one just for tolerating us!

Give someone a standing ovation today and help them feel on top of the world.

Make a quick list of people who need a standing ovation, then carve out the time to walk into their office or room, applaud them, then tell them, "This is your personal standing ovation for the way you _____."

February 27th
God Hates Workaholism

Scripture for Today: Isaiah 26:3

Are you a workaholic? Many people have accepted the idea that climbing the corporate ladder or working 80 hours weeks is the way to success. Being the first one in the office and the last one to leave every day are seen by many as virtues.

The fact is, workaholism is a sin. It's the way we act when we think we are responsible for all of life's needs. When we trust God to meet our needs, we take time to rest. When we rely on ourselves for all our needs, we have to work endlessly. There is a reason God told His people to rest every seventh day.

In one Bible story, God fed all the nation of Israel miraculously. He sent them food called "manna" six days of the week. They could only gather enough for that day or else it would rot. On the sixth day, however, they could gather two-days-worth and it would keep the seventh day. Not only did God teach them He could supply their needs daily, He proved every week they could take a day off and not starve!

Workaholics miss their kids' activities, time with their spouse, church, and a lot of living! Don't work your whole life and end up missing the life God offers you.

Do you think you are a workaholic? Why or why not?

If you've been working too much and it is within your control to stop, make a written plan that gets you into a better working situation.

February 28
Math

Scripture for Today: Luke 12:29–31

What are your priorities today, and where will they take you? I've always struggled with math, but it must be applied to my priorities every day. Priorities require subtracting and adding, and that's partly why choosing between one thing or another each day is so difficult. I can't do everything other people want me to do. I can't even do everything that I want to do! On some days I would love to stay in bed all day, but I haven't found a flying bed yet that can take me to a land where my dreams become reality.

My goals and dreams in life will not happen automatically, so I must choose priorities that will take me there. As a result, each day requires me to subtract some things that might be fun and add some things that might be difficult. And yes, I continue to struggle with this process of adding and subtracting; but it must be done if I expect to accomplish my dreams.

So, choose wisely today because every decision determines your destiny.

What are some things you know you should do that you haven't done? Read a particular book? Take a college class? Reconcile with a friend? Apply for a new job? Submit paperwork for retirement? Join a ministry?

Make a list that reflects God's kingdom priorities and stick with it. List two or three things that need to rotate out of your life so you do the things you need to be doing for the Kingdom.

March 1
Honest and Truthful

Scripture for Today: Colossians 3:9

Have you ever been looked in the eye and lied to? Or lied about? It's a frustrating experience.

Lying and deceitfulness has been a painful part of the human experience since Adam and Eve were in the garden of Eden.

I was lied to some time ago by someone who did the exact opposite of what we had agreed to in detail and in writing. Afterward they acted like it was no big deal.

Honesty and truthfulness are the foundations to a civil society. We sometimes watch the daily chaos in Washington, DC as politicians lie and accuse each other. Then media outlets spread the lies to the public. And when no evidence is found to support the lies, they either tell the lies more forcefully or act as if they never said them at all. But the damage is done. Seeds of mistrust are sown, and civility unravels a little more.

We cannot make self-serving politicians be honest and truthful. But we can be honest and truthful with our own interactions.

Can you remember an instance where you were not treated with honesty? How did you feel when you found out?

Do you practice honesty in your dealings with others? If you want to be treated honestly, being honest is a good start.

March 2
Marriage

Scripture for Today: Ephesians 5:15–33

Are you happily married? Or do you hope to be happily married someday I often say the key is to find someone who can tolerate you and then do whatever it takes to keep them around. I may be oversimplifying things a bit, but I'm close.

Marriage is an awesome gift designed by God to bring fulfillment, and to protect us from immorality. The Bible describes immorality as any sexual relationship outside of marriage between a man and a woman.

Yes, I know such a life can seem strange in our promiscuous culture where many people believe they can decide for themselves what is morally right and wrong. But the creator of the human race established right and wrong so we can live the best life possible. Faithfulness and fidelity in marriage are essential. And refraining from sexual involvement outside of marriage is also essential.

Few things are more destructive to yourself and others than pursuing a sexual relationship with someone who is not your spouse. Keep that in mind if you want a happy marriage now or someday.

Is your life marked more by morality or immorality?

If you are married, commit to be faithful to your spouse. If you hope to be married one day, commit to reserve yourself for your spouse and ask for God's strength to do so.

March 3
Your Eulogy

Scripture for Today: Proverbs 22:1, Acts 11:24

What will they say about you when you die? Did you know that most people will describe your entire life in one sentence? I have spoken at hundreds of funerals over the years, and I've heard a broad range of sentences from people as they stood around and talked. "He or she was trustworthy, a good person, always there when I needed them, changed my life, or, the best friend I ever had." I have also heard things like: "they were always grumbling about something, picking a fight, or mean to the core. They never could get their life together. He died owing me money!"

If you don't like what they'd say about you, why not pick your own sentence and write it down? Then live each day to make it a reality. I've written mine: "I live an adventurous life and I want to inspire others to know Jesus and live amazing lives!"

Life is worth living and you can live it extremely well. What will they say about you when you die? One way or another, you'll decide that.

Have you ever thought about what people will say about you when you die, how you will be remembered?

Take some time to think about a single sentence you want to describe you after you've gone and write it below. If your life isn't currently aligned with what you write, ask God to help you make the necessary adjustments.

March 4
Bad Perspectives

Scripture for Today: Numbers 13:1–3, 25–33

Have you ever caught yourself having a bad perspective? It's a powerful and destructive virus that contaminates our world, our future, and the people around us.

I heard of some boys who pulled a prank on their uncle by smearing some Limburger cheese on his mustache while he was taking a nap. When he woke up, they heard him say, "It stinks in here!" As he walked into the kitchen he said, "The kitchen stinks too!" As he moved through the house, they heard him say, "Every room in the house stinks!"

Then he walked outside onto his porch, took a big sniff, and said, "What is going on? The whole world stinks!"

The moral of the story is: When you have a bad perspective everything does stink, but the stink is usually coming from you. And it follows you wherever you go.

Our faith in Jesus Christ says we have an amazing life and an amazing future. Don't let a bad perspective steal it from you.

Do you tend to have a good perspective or bad perspective about the future?

Sometimes it helps to make a list of pros and cons about reaching our goals. When you work through such a list it can help you see the cons in a better light, giving you a better perspective.

March 5
Change

Scripture for Today: 2 Corinthians 5:17

What needs to change in your life? We struggle to change, but the fact is we must. Too often we don't do the things we should do, and we do the things we shouldn't. Justifying our wrongs will not fix them. It will only lead us to greater failure and misery. We can look into our past and easily see how we need to change and the good news is God made it possible for us to do so.

That's the story of the resurrection of Jesus. Jesus was killed and then raised from the dead so we can have the power to experience a changed life! Through His power we can do what is right, no matter how hard it is. And He has the power to forgive us when we fail.

What needs to change in your life?

Take your family to church each Sunday and celebrate with the millions around the world who've experienced a changed life through Jesus. If you haven't yet joined His amazing journey, maybe this will be your day?

When you think of Jesus or church do you think about rules and regulations or lives being changed by God's power?

If your life hasn't been changed by Jesus, pause right now and ask Him to change you. He will change your life if you ask believing that He can and will.

March 6
Appreciation

Scripture for Today: Romans 16:21–24

Who taught you how to read and write? Whoever it was changed your life. I loved it when my mom read stories to me as a kid.

Then I began school at Tallapoosa Elementary. It was there in 1st grade that I learned to write the alphabet and form words. Reading was a real struggle for me, so learning required lots of one-on-one help from my teacher.

She believed in me and often told me so. Even in my six-year-old mind I knew this was one special lady. When she said "Todd, you can do this," I believed her. She was my teacher and she knew potential when she saw it. She was an amazing teacher. She sent me a personal card and $5 when I graduated from high school just to say, "I'm proud of you!"

I will forever be thankful for Mrs. Littlefield. Her words spoken to my 6-year-old ears, "Todd, you can do this", continue to inspire me. Her love for and investment in the life of a struggling kid made a difference. My life is better because of her.

Who had a big role in changing your life? How did they do it?

Who have you affected in a positive way and you have great feelings about how they are living their life? Why not call, text, or drop them a card today and tell them that. It'll be a tremendous encouragement to them.

March 7
Integrity

Scripture for Today: Philippians 4:1–2

What do you need to fix today? We can all think of people who have done us wrong, hurt our feelings, or disappointed us in some way. We don't like those people, and often our feelings turn to resentment and bitterness. But it could be that we need to fix a few wrongs that we've done to others.

Several years ago, I was at Pizza Hut with my family for lunch. All of a sudden, my memory took me back twenty years earlier when, as a teenager, my buddies and I ate lunch there and we intentionally walked out without paying. Now, I had lost my appetite and was hearing a voice inside saying, "Do the right thing!"

It was scary, but it felt amazing once I confessed to the manager what I had done. I apologized and gave her $30.00 for a twenty-year-old lunch.

The best friend we have is inside us, and we must nurture that friendship every day. What do you need to fix today? It'll help you remain friends with yourself.

Can you think of any wrong from your past that you need to fix?

If it's a quick-fix, take care of it ASAP. If it's a complicated fix—a broken relationship, a legal issue—ask God to give you wisdom and the right steps to take toward fixing it.

March 8
Change

Scripture for Today: Hebrews 13:8

How well do you deal with change? The seasons of life require that we master it. Every year we move through the seasons of winter, spring, summer, and fall. In life, we move from childhood to adulthood. From being single to getting married and possibly single again. From being healthy to facing illness. From being financially broke to financially free, then possibly being broke all over again.

With the advancement of technology, we seem to face a new change in how we live our lives almost every day. We are simply flowing through a series of seasons that take us from life to death. And it's in that journey that we often struggle. Sometimes a particular season seems so brutal it's more than we can take.

Well, I want you to know there is some help out there. God never changes! He is the same yesterday, today, and forever. He is the "God of the times and the seasons," and He will help you through your seasons of life if you will only ask Him.

What change is happening in your life today that you really need God's help to get through?

Pray, acknowledging that God is the same yesterday, today, and forever, and then ask Him to help you through the changes you face.

March 9
Honesty

Scripture for Today: James 5:12

Have you heard the phrase: Say what you mean and mean what you say? Well it's a good practice to have.

Parents often tell their kids to stop misbehaving 8-10 times, warning their kids each time that just one more time and they will be punished. But instead of punishment after the next misbehavior, the parent starts counting: one, two, three, and punishment never comes. And then we wonder where our kids learned to ignore what we say. Even worse, we will wonder where they learned to lie so well! They had a good lying specialist as a parent who trained them.

After a generation of this kind of parenting, these kids go on to run our nation and businesses with the same philosophy.

There's a better way to produce good leaders for the next generation. Jesus said, "Let your 'Yes' be 'Yes', and your 'No' be 'No'! Speak clearly and mean what you say! In a single word, it's called, "honesty."

If you are a parent, have you fallen into the trap of giving your kids endless warnings without following through? Do you see how this works to undermine your discipline?

Commit to being the kind of person whose "yes" means "yes," and whose "no" means "no," and be known for it.

March 10
Today Matters

Scripture for Today: Job 7:6–10

Do you know what today is? It's the day after yesterday, and yesterday is gone forever. Today is also the day before tomorrow, but tomorrow may never come! So, what is today? It's God's gift to you. It's the most important day of your life, because it's the only time you actually possess.

Today is either preparation day for the rest of your life, or it's your chance to finish well with the life you've been given. Either way today is a big deal. Benjamin Franklin said, "One today is worth two tomorrows." Successful people have learned to make right decisions early in life and manage those decisions every day. Real success is not an event, but a journey. And while success can't be reached in a single day, every single day certainly matters if we are going to live a successful life.

Hoping for a great future without investing in today is like a farmer hoping for a great harvest without ever planting a seed!

Do you typically view each day as a gift from God? Do you thank Him for it soon after you awaken each morning?

How can you get the most out of today? (Not worrying about tomorrow is a good place to start.)

March 11
Anchor or Wind?

Scripture for Today: Proverbs 18:21, Ephesians 4:29

What kind of effect do you have on other people? Are you the wind beneath their wings or the anchor beneath their boat? If you're an anchor, you are a problem to people who are trying to aggressively go somewhere in life.

I remember my first big-boy fishing trip with Mr. Ernest Ingram and Mr. Paul Roberts. I was maybe 13 years old. We went to Lake Weiss in Centre, Alabama and those big crappie were biting like crazy!

When they stopped biting, we decided to fish in a different spot. Ernest cranked his big Evinrude motor, pulled back the throttle and away we went… but not for long. Water was rolling into my side of the boat. I had left my basket full of fish hanging out in the water. My basket was now stretched into a tube-like shape, but the fish were still there. I had always left it out in the water as we paddled around my grandpa's pond, and I thought I could do so even with a motorboat. But I was wrong; my great catch was acting like an anchor.

Don't be an anchor to others. Be a wind that propels them along their life's journey.

In what ways can you be an anchor to others? Write a list and commit to avoiding those actions.

In what ways can you be a wind to others? Write a list and commit to putting those actions into practice more often and with more people.

March 12
Loneliness

Scripture for Today: Matthew 27:45–47, 28:18–20

Do you ever struggle with feeling lonely? I can sometimes feel alone with thousands of people all around. It can find me whether I'm at Walmart shopping amidst others, at church with hundreds of people, or working on the farm by myself. I don't think I'm the only one.

Loneliness plays no favorites and obeys no rules. It finds the inmate in prison, the senior adult at home, the student in school, the unemployed mom or dad, and the kid at the ballgame. It also found Jesus on the cross, and no doubt, it was painful.

He clearly expressed the pain of loneliness when He cried, "My God! My God! Why have you forsaken me?" And in the midst of our pain, we are reminded of His. If the greatest leader who ever lived faced the pain of loneliness, you can be sure it will be an enemy for the rest of us. But remember His promise: "I will never leave you nor forsake you." And when He makes a promise, you can count on it.

Do you struggle with feelings of loneliness? Does it encourage you knowing Jesus never leaves nor forsakes His children?

Reading in the Psalms is one way to bring encouragement to a lonely soul. Reading two or three each day is a good strategy.

If your feelings of loneliness have become overwhelming or even debilitating, consider seeing a Christian counselor to get help.

March 13
Expectations

Scripture for Today: Matthew 11:7–10

Well, what do you expect? That's an important question, because expectations are powerful. Without them, we won't be very motivated in life. But if we expect too much, it's likely we will be very disappointed at some point. The real question is, "Who is the object of our expectations?"

We must have high expectations for ourselves and stretch to meet those expectations every day. God gave us the ability to reach a higher potential than most of us imagine.

However, when we expect too much from others, we set a trap that leads to failure and disappointment. It can also lead us into irresponsibility, laziness, and blaming others for all of our failures.

Yes, expectations are a big deal. So, "What do you expect?" Better yet, "Who do you expect it from?" Don't put such high expectations on other people, including your family and friends. Everybody disappoints somebody sometimes. Save those high expectations for yourself!

Have you fallen into the trap of expecting more from others than you expect from yourself?

Make a list of the people from whom you have high expectations. Make sure your expectations are realistic for each person. Ask God to give you patience to work with everyone according to their gifts and abilities.

March 14
Life Appraisal

Scripture for Today: Matthew 6:33

Have you had an appraisal lately? No, not a real estate appraisal, but a life appraisal: an evaluation of your kids, your marriage, your career, and your spiritual life. It's asking questions about yourself and answering those questions with honesty. How old am I? Where have I been? Where am I going? Am I living out the purpose for which God created me? How am I doing?

A life appraisal is necessary to know what needs to change, because a great life doesn't happen by accident.

Doing an appraisal says that you want to live your life to the fullest. You realize you are not going to live forever on this earth, and you want to make sure that when it's over, you have not lived in vain.

Imagine for a moment that your life is a Super Bowl game and you are entering the fourth quarter. What is your score? Are you ahead or behind? What needs to change in your strategy to guarantee a victory? The clock is ticking. Take action today!

If you haven't done a life appraisal recently, there is no time like the present to do one. Carve some time for it out of your schedule.

When you do your life appraisal, make sure to keep God's kingdom priorities as your own so you end with the goals you need.

March 15
Rest

Scripture for Today: Psalm 23

How well do you rest and relax? We live in a hectic world, and we feel the pressure of it. If we don't plan ahead and move quickly, we'll be left behind. But rest is an important part of a successful life; God designed it that way. That's why He gave us several hours of darkness each day; to insist that we rest from our labor. And He gave us a day of rest every week. Certain seasons of the year also provide more time for rest than others. And an occasional vacation is always good for our mind, body, and soul.

Many centuries ago, King David wrote, "He makes me lie down in the green pasture, and He restores my soul."

The need for rest does not discriminate. It's an essential part of life regardless of your age or vocation. It's a basic need in the human race. If you're struggling to get enough rest, remember the words of Jesus who said, "Come to Me, all of you who are tired and weary, and I will give you rest."

When is the last time you've had deep rest for your mind, body, and soul?

We cannot be healthy without rest. If you need to structure rest into your life, do it today. Then rest.

March 16
Love

Scripture for Today: 1 Corinthians 13

How's your love life? Love is a beautiful thing. And it's powerful! It changes our attitude, our habits, and our sense of value. But it also changes those around us. I've seen some rough and tough men become kind, gentle, and patient, all because of love.

Many families struggle, and all they really need is a good dose of love. Love is to the family what blood is to the body. Blood gives our bodies life and energy, and it fights against infection and disease. There is no substitute for it. Blood is an essential ingredient for a healthy life. In the same way, love is essential for a healthy family, and there is no substitute for it. There are three words your family needs to hear every day: I love you. Have you told them today?

Love is a powerful thing. Love caused God to give His own son to die on your behalf, and love caused Jesus to follow through. There's no greater love than for a man to lay down His life for his friends.

Do you really believe God loves you regardless of who you are or what you've done?

Do the people around you know that you love them? Tell them today.

March 17
Consistency

Scripture for Today: 2 Timothy 4:2

How consistent are you? In your actions, performance, attitude, and mood. It's a quality we appreciate in sports, at work, at home, in church, or in business. It's also a quality we likely struggle with at some point.

Consistency says you can be counted on. You're trustworthy. Steady. Reliable. Dependable. Faithful. Rock solid. You deliver. On time. Every day. Every week. You perform with excellence.

Consistency doesn't happen by accident. It's birthed out of patience, discipline, strategy, determination, and strength. It's not affected by the weather, the audience, or other events of the day. And it doesn't know about the Monday blues or holiday hangovers.

In the Bible, it's what Paul was referring to when he told his friend Timothy to "be ready in season and out of season." James called it endurance that would make you complete. It's a treasured quality of Jesus who is "the same yesterday, today, and forever." He's always reliable, and He's never in a lousy mood. How about you?

On a scale of 1–5 with 1 being "Never Consistent" and 5 being "Very Consistent," rate yourself. Are you as consistent as you need to be?

Do people you work, play, and live with view you as consistent and dependable? If not, determine to become the kind of person who can be depended on in every circumstance.

March 18
Knowing Your Value

Scripture for Today: Psalm 139:13–18

Do you know how important you are? There is only one you! And you cannot be duplicated. Your voice, finger print, personality, and smile; your walk, your skin, your handshake, and the features of your face are all unique. Everything about you is found in only one person, and that person is you. And there will never be another. How does that make you feel? Well I must admit that I feel special, because it did not happen by accident. God designed me to be unique, special, and marvelous.

In the Bible, David thanked God for creating him in such a special way. He said, "You made all the delicate, inner parts of my body and put them all together in my mother's womb. Your workmanship is marvelous."

We sometimes struggle with image issues and wish we were more like someone else, but that would only contaminate the awesome person God had in mind when He made us. You, my friend, are somebody special and important. I know this because God does not make junk.

Do you struggle with self-hatred or lack of self-worth? Do you truly believe God created you in a special way for a special purpose?

Remember that any voice of condemnation you hear is not from God, but from the evil one. Ask God to help you view yourself the way He does, then live in that confidence.

March 19
Surprises

Scripture for Today: Matthew 7:7–12

Do you like surprises? Well, that likely depends on what it is! They trigger many of the highs and lows that we experience in life.

When I was in school, I hated the surprise pop-quiz but I loved the surprise ice storm that caused the school to close for a day or two.

I remember one of my best surprises ever when I was just a kid. My dad invited me to ride with him to the Honda motorcycle shop to pick up my brother's motorcycle that was being repaired. As we waited, I sat on every motorcycle in the shop that was close to my size until I found one that was just right, and I dreamed of someday having my own. Then what a surprise when my dad told the salesman to load the one I was sitting on into his truck. He was buying that one just for me. What a great surprise! It reminds me that if our earthly fathers want to give good surprises to their children, how much more our heavenly Father wants to do the same.

What is the best surprise you've ever received? What is the worst?

Stop and ask God to help you react to surprises in a way that glorifies Him. Praise Him for the good surprises He's brought your way.

March 20
Quiet

Scripture for Today: Psalm 46:10–11

Have you had any peace and quiet lately? No TV. No radio. No phone. No traffic. And no people. The fast treadmill of life requires that we plan such times or they won't happen.

On the morning I wrote this, I sat on my porch at 5am enjoying some peace and quiet, along with a good cup of coffee. A few sounds occasionally interrupted: an owl hooting in the distance, a rooster crowing to remind me the sun was soon to rise, the steady chirp of crickets and other insects singing, with the occasional frog hitting a bass-note in the background. But all of these sounds seemed to be ok with my soul. They were sounds that God created to remind me how awesome and trustworthy He is.

It's now 5:49am, and I just heard the call of a whippoorwill. How awesome is that! There's a reason God said, "Be still and know that I am God." It's in the quiet that God speaks the loudest and clearest. Try it tomorrow morning. You'll be glad you did.

How long has it been since you spent 30 minutes in silence, as much as possible outside the presence of any man-made noise?

In a day and age where we are inundated with noise, silence is important. Pursue it frequently to keep a healthy mental state.

March 21
Problems

Scripture for Today: Hebrews 5:6–9

"What kind of problem are you facing?" I know you have one. We all do. Life is difficult. It is often just a series of problems one after another. But there's no reason to complain about them. We cannot ignore them and it's useless to run and hide. If we did, we'd only cheat ourselves. It's actually in the process of solving problems that our life finds meaning and depth.

Problems require us to have courage, wisdom, and endurance. Those are great qualities we would never develop if it weren't for our problems. It's through the problems we face that we grow from average to exceptional. If we never faced a problem, most of us would do very little in life.

Even Jesus was acquainted with grief and problems; He learned obedience from the things He suffered. Problems can become our teacher, mentor, trainer, and friend. On the other side is a better, wiser, more exceptional you. Stand tall and walk forward! If you need wisdom, ask God—He promises to deliver.

Are you facing a seemingly insurmountable problem? How about a series of small problems?

Ask God to guide you through whatever problems you are facing. The strength you gain will stay with you forever.

March 22
Change

Scripture for Today: Isaiah 43:18–19

Do you hope your future is better than your past? I'm sure you do, but you need to know that hope is not a strategy. Many people are sincerely hoping for a better future, but they're going to be greatly disappointed.

A better future requires a dream. A plan. Hard work. And change. No one loves to change, but it's a fact that "If you always do what you've always done, you will always get what you've always got." It's insane to continue in the same behaviors or in the same direction and expect a different result.

This is true in your career, marriage, finances, or spiritual life. I realize more today than ever that I'm not always what I ought to be, and I've not yet reached my potential of who I'm going to be. But I'm thankful, that with God's help, I'm not who I used to be. The fact is, I've changed! You can, too.

What is the number one thing you need to change today to reach the goals you have set?

Most of the changes we need do not require a lot of money or expense. It requires a different approach and that requires change. Commit right now to making the necessary changes in your life to reach the future you've only hoped for.

March 23
Education

Scripture for Today: 2 Timothy 2:15

Are you getting a good education? It's a great question I was asked many times during my youth. Too often we assume that education should be a major priority during our early years. We can't wait to get our diploma so we can move on to more important things as adults. But education must be a lifelong pursuit. Opportunities often come our way, but when they come, it's too late to prepare. Education designs the next options for our journey. If we miss the education, we miss the options, and find ourselves with limited opportunity. Our journey with God, people, careers, and the challenges of life require growth, and growth is not an automatic process.

If what you learned or did five years ago still inspires you, you are not growing. And by the way, your life experience does not make you better; only evaluated experience does. If you don't stop each day to evaluate where you are in life and what you are learning, you're cheating yourself out of a good education!

Have you always thought a formal education is the only kind of education? What are some alternative ways of learning?

If you hope to advance in your career opportunities, what kind of further education do you need? Does it need to be formal? Ask God to give you wisdom about the how and the when of you getting further education.

How much more study of God's word do you need to grow in God's grace?

March 24
Problems and Solutions

Scripture for Today: Colossians 3:17

Do you ever get frustrated at your job? I hear it often as I listen to people complain about every little problem that upsets their perfect little imaginary world. They feel entitled to a life without difficulty. But that's why it's called a "job". Your company or business does not exist to give you a paycheck. It exists to solve a problem of some kind, and you are part of the solution. If not, you don't deserve a paycheck!

Somebody is paying you to deal with the problems so both of you can prosper. So, when you face problems today, don't grumble and complain. Embrace them as your responsibility to solve. It's your solutions that make you needed in the workplace.

The Bible teaches that whatever you do, do it with all of your heart. Do it as if God were watching, because He is. You might dream of a day that your job is absent of problems, but it's likely if the problems disappear, so will the company's need for you.

What frustrates you at work or school? Is it a problem you can solve?

Make a list below of problems you encounter at work and some solutions you can work toward beginning today.

March 25
Investment and Dividends

Scripture for Today: Exodus 24:13; 32:17–19; 33:11

How much do you value the people in your life each day? I know you think some of them are difficult from time to time, and it's likely they are. You should know that some of them think the same about you, and it's likely you are! Yes, life's worst moments usually involve other people, but so do life's greatest moments.

Every great memory and experience in my life I can recall involves other people. If you ignore people to miss the worst moments, you'll cheat yourself from enjoying the greatest moments! It's the people in your life who decorate your journey with depth and meaning. We can trace any success we have back to key people along the way who help us go to the next level.

These people are special to us, and they invested something in us that continues to grow and pay big dividends. Now it's your turn to give back and invest in someone else, and the seeds of your investment will grow long after you're gone. And that is priceless.

What do you usually think of as a good return on investment: 10% a year? 20% a year? 20% over five years?

Do you often think of human investment, the time and energy you give helping others along their journey? It's one of the few investments with eternal returns.

March 26
Faith

Scripture for Today: Mark 9:18–27

Do you ever struggle with faith? The most devout followers of Jesus are often challenged with doubts. The Bible tells the story of a troubled dad who brought his demon-possessed son to Jesus for help. Jesus said He could help the boy if the dad would only believe, and that all things are possible for those who believe. The dad then made an interesting statement and request. He said, "Lord, I do believe, but help me with my unbelief." Then Jesus cured the boy. Jesus obviously saw the dad's unique request as evidence of his faith.

Recently a troubled man seeking forgiveness came to me with a mustard seed. As he placed the tiny seed in my hand he said, "That's about all the faith I have, but I do have that!" I watched with joy as this man received God's forgiveness, and then I baptized him. Then the peace of God entered his life.

Yes, all things are possible for those who believe. Doubts are common, but God can take your small faith and move mountains.

If you are struggling in your faith right now, can you identify the source of your doubts?

Often our doubts are the result of taking our eyes off of God and focusing on some mountain in our path. Ask God to take your focus off the mountain you can't move and look at the One who can move it.

March 27
Out of Control

Scripture for Today: Psalm 115:1–3

Do you ever feel like life is simply out of control? It's scary, is it not? I've been on a frightened runaway horse at breakneck speed, and the power I felt underneath me was terrifying. I've also been in a small airplane during stormy weather, and I wondered if I would survive. Both times, being out of control felt the same, and many times I have had that feeling about the events of life.

But I've learned through the years that God is never out of control. In the Bible, David said, "Our God is in the heavens; and He does whatever He pleases." Has it ever occurred to you that nothing has ever occurred to God? Nothing ever catches Him by surprise. God is neither wringing His hands in despair, nor sweating about tomorrow because of fear. In short, God is in full control and He does what He pleases. He's calling the shots, and like it or not, you can trust Him.

What happens to your emotions when things around you get out of control?

Does it bring you comfort that God is always in control even when things around us are crazy?

March 28
Everything New

Scripture for Today: Psalm 40:3; 2 Corinthians 5:17

Are you aware of the value of springtime? It's best described by the word—NEW. Everyone loves something new. Each year I can hardly wait. After several weeks of bone-chilling wind, snow, and cold weather, springtime brings new leaves, new grass, new flowers, new growth, and much welcomed new warmth.

Last week I saw a new black ball of fur curled in the lush green grass of my pasture. A new calf had just been born. I was reminded of the miracle of new life and new relationships as its mother proudly stood over it. The calf with sparkling eyes gazed at a new world.

Spring is also a time to celebrate Easter as a reminder of the new life and new hope we have through the resurrection of Jesus from the dead. Through Him, we become a new person. Old things have passed away and all things become new. I've experienced the joy of this miracle. Have you?

If you could make anything from your past new, what would it be?

If you haven't experienced a new life in Christ, you can today by repenting of your sins and placing your faith in Christ alone for your new life. Why not do it now?

March 29
Birthdays

Scripture for Today: Psalm 118:22–24

How well do you handle your birthdays? We usually do pretty well until we reach twenty-one! Until then, we are ready for the next one long before it arrives. But after twenty-one, not so much! It's at that point that we realize life is passing rather quickly, much faster than we ever imagined. We then reach 30, 40, 50, 60, 70, and boom…we look back and realize it all happened in a flash.

Just three weeks before my 79-year-old dad passed away, he looked up at me from his bed and said, "Son, if there is anything you really dream of doing, write it down, save your money, then go do it, because just yesterday I was a teenager!" I understood exactly what he meant. I stood there and listened like a little boy, but I was trapped inside of my then-48-year-old body. It was an eye-opening moment.

Don't just celebrate your years on your birthday. Celebrate your days. Every one of them. Today is the day the Lord has made. Rejoice and be glad in it.

Do you know the experience of twenty or thirty years seeming like yesterday?

What can you do to celebrate your days as well as your years so that you get the most out of living?

What are you dreaming of doing? Write it down. Make a plan.

March 30
Storms

Scripture for Today: Mark 4:35–41

Storms! When was the last time you experienced one? Perhaps you are in one now. They are always scary, but there are some good things about storms.

As a kid, when a storm was brewing it was a special time. Our family farmhouse had proven to be a safe haven over and over again. With kerosene lanterns for light and a fireplace for heat, our entertainment was the voices of my parents and grandparents as they talked about the past. A prayer was often heard, "Lord, keep us safe till the storm passes by."

In that room was an awareness that life could change in a moment, as the ones who loved us most held us tightly. And when the storm was over, the community gathered to help those impacted by the storm, and it became an event that defined our lives together. Storms give us a depth and understanding about life that otherwise would be absent. I don't like them, but we need them. I still pray, "Lord, keep us safe till the storm passes by."

Are you in a storm right now? Can you see the end of it yet?

Today's scripture teaches us that storms are no match for Jesus. Why not rest in His strength and power to overcome and see you through it?

March 31
Avoiding Addictions

Scripture for Today: Genesis 15:1; Philippians 4:4

Are you living for something destructive?

Over the last few years before this writing, some in America were reeling from an opioid crisis. Opioids were offered as pain-killers with the promise they were not addictive. Millions of these pills were sold to help people with physical pain, but the problem was, they were highly addictive. Opioids solved one problem but created an even bigger problem!! Thousands have died because of opioids destructive addictive power. I have known several victims myself. What a tragedy!

The fact is, different people are addicted to different things. Sugar, alcohol, tobacco, spending, pornography, or food, but all addictions follow a similar pattern. In the beginning something helps us feel good, but, in the end, we begin to live for the addiction, and it destroys us! Living for God each day has no adequate substitute. It's why we were created!

In the Bible, God once spoke to Abram in a vision: "Do not be afraid, Abram. I am your shield; your reward will be very great" (Genesis 15:1). God offers Himself as the source for the best life possible. Let Him!

If you are struggling with any addiction—if you even think you are—seek help through a professional counselor or attend a local Celebrate Recovery meeting. Your life is too precious to be dominated by an addiction.

April 1
Adventure

Scripture for Today: 2 Corinthians 5:7

Have you been on an adventure lately? As a kid, I loved adventures like a walk to the Tallapoosa River behind our house; a search for arrowheads and Indian artifacts in the field nearby; the first day of school and a new bus route; an unplanned trip anywhere with my granddad.

These adventures here are amazing and added huge value and depth to my childhood. I have often wondered why these times were so special. I think it's because they took me out of the normal routines of life and gave me a new perspective. With anticipation and excitement, they kept me guessing about what was next. I loved that sense of wonder and adventure!

Life can sometimes become a little boring, monotonous, and frustrating, but God didn't intend it to be that way. He makes something unique, special, and exciting about each day: the colors of the sunset, the shape of the moon, the people we will meet, and the challenges we will face. Yes, He gave us today as an awesome adventure! I wonder what's next?

Are you more the adventurous type or the type to take it easy?

Ask God to give you faith for the adventure or adventures ahead of you.

April 2
Heart

Scripture for Today: Deuteronomy 6:5

How's the condition of your heart? Research over the last 50 years has put a bright spotlight on this vital organ of the human body. As a result, people are taught to eat better, exercise, and pay close attention to the heart's condition, because the rest of the body will struggle without a good heart. When something does go wrong, heart experts can often perform procedures to correct the problem and add years to the person's life. I'm thankful for them and their abilities!

But the heart of man is much more than the physical organ. It's also the center of your soul. It's where your conscience lives, and where your rights and wrongs are stored deep inside. It's the very foundation of your character and the real you.

We are reminded in the Bible that while a man judges people by what's on the outside, God looks at the heart. It's important to keep that heart good and healthy. So, I'll ask the question one more time: What's the condition of your heart?

Are you taking care of your physical heart? What about your spiritual heart?

If your spiritual heart is in bad shape, schedule a check-up today with your pastor or a Christian counselor. And remember, the Bible is good for your heart, so take doses of it regularly.

April 3
Easter

Scripture for Today: Matthew 28:1–7

Don't you just love big special events? I remember when Papa Bentley took me to the circus in Atlanta when I was just a boy. He later took me on my first trip to see the Atlanta Braves play baseball. Hank Aaron was getting close to setting a new homerun record and we were hoping we'd get to see him hit one over the fence. As the events got closer, the excitement built. I have felt that same excitement many times through the years as various special events have drawn near. And I feel that excitement each year as we approach Easter each year.

It's a celebration of the most special event in the history of mankind—the resurrection of Jesus Christ from the dead after being crucified. It's because of this one single event that we can be forgiven of our crazy, messed up, and sinful lives. It's this single act of God's love and power that we can have eternal life. Where will you celebrate Christ's resurrection this year on Easter Sunday? If you don't have a church, find one nearby and join them!

What are some big events you remember from your life? A new car? A memorable vacation? A first date? Time with a parent or grandparent?

Have you experienced life from the biggest event in all of history? God is waiting to give you eternal life if you will ask Him in faith.

April 4
Defining Moments

Scripture for Today: Acts 9:1-9

When was the last time you had a defining moment? You know. When you received information or experienced something that changed your life forever? I was in Germany on my way to a speaking engagement when I got the news. My mom had brain cancer, and just 10 weeks to live.

I was always proud of my Mom! She was the most selfless, encouraging, caring, and accepting person I have ever known. She was predictably sweet, kind, simple, and easy to love and talk to. And Mom approached her final 10 weeks in this world with amazing courage, confidence, faith, and humor. She was prepared and ready to go to heaven.

Her goal was to sing and tell others about how awesome Jesus is, until she would meet Him face to face. And she did.

She had inspired me many times before, but once again, she taught me how to walk by faith and face difficulty with amazing courage. She taught me how to live an exceptional life. Now it's up to me to live my own journey.

Many years have passed since I got the news about mom's cancer, but her impact upon my life remains as strong as ever.

Can you think of a defining moment or two in your life?

Write them below along with some thoughts about the impact they have had. Thank God for how He used them to shape you.

April 5
Patience

Scripture for Today: Ephesians 4:31–32

How patient are you with other people? It's an important quality but I must admit, I sometimes struggle with this one. Why won't people just do what I want them to do, when I want them to do it, and how I want them to do it? Especially when it comes to driving. Come on, people: If you're going to go for a walk, don't take your car with you! Either lead, follow, or get out of the way! Ooops. I just lost my patience again, and it can happen so easily in many areas of life.

Patience is a very attractive quality. I've noticed that the people I love and enjoy the most are people who have a great measure of patience. And because of their patience, they can even tolerate me.

I'm really glad God is patient with us too. If God were no more patient with you as you are with others, what would that look like? Be kind, patient, and tenderhearted with one another. Such actions help create a much better world.

In what areas of life do you find it hardest to be patient?

Usually, impatience results from not getting something we think we deserve such as a parking place, or a place in line, for instance. Repenting from selfishness is a good way to start learning how to be patient.

April 6
Stretched

Scripture for Today: Exodus 3:11–15

Do you ever feel stretched? I hope so, because being stretched is a good thing. We are very much like rubber bands. They come in all shapes, sizes, and colors, but they never fulfill their purpose without being stretched.

Too often we try to avoid being stretched. We avoid it because we're afraid of failing while trying to succeed. We avoid it because we're satisfied with our boring little lives. We avoid it because we're lazy and we'd rather just take it easy in life.

If you aren't stretching toward success, ask yourself, why? We have an exceptional God, and He created us to be exceptional in His own image. I know it's scary, but when we look back in life, it's during times of stretching that we've reached our highest potential and grown to a new level of living.

Perhaps it's time to dream a new dream, set a new goal, or start a new project. Don't join the world of half-hearted, mediocre, mundane people who simply wait for each day to go by. God expects more, and you deserve more.

Can you remember a time of stretching that turned out better than expected? Why do people resist stretching?

Sometimes God uses circumstances to stretch us for His purposes. Can you think of a stretching in your life that you can right now see God's hand in it? Thank Him for it and commit to growing through it.

April 7
Loss

Scripture for Today: Isaiah 40:8, Philippians 4:7–10

Do you really enjoy losing? Well, I definitely do not. I hate to lose. I must admit that it bothers me to hear parents scold their children because the child lost a game and didn't smile about it. I realize being a sore loser can be taken a little far sometimes, but I think it's a greater problem if someone loses and likes it.

Loss is always painful. I lost most of my retirement in the economic failure and bank closures of 2008. I'd been saving and investing for many years since I was a teenager, and in a flash—it was gone. It was painful and I didn't like it.

When my parents died, that too was painful; I didn't like it!

But I can handle a few losses along the way, because as a follower of Jesus Christ I know I'm on the winning team. This is not my final home. I'm just passing through this world. I've read the final chapter. We win!

What is a painful loss you have experienced in the last five years?

Some losses are minor and some are tragic. Whatever your loss, God stands ready to see you through. Ask for His strength and grace today to come out on the other side victorious.

April 8th
Tomorrow

Scripture for Today: Proverbs 27:1

Are you ready for tomorrow? Tomorrow is the most difficult day of the week to plan for. It presents a question that no one is smart enough to answer: What is tomorrow going to be like?

On most days, man's knowledge seems impressive: sending people into outer space, building tall buildings, heart surgery, the invention of computers, and the Internet. The list goes on and on. But when it comes to tomorrow, our knowledge plunges to zero.

You may have a PhD in your field of expertise. You might be a genius with an IQ above 170. But regarding knowledge about tomorrow, you're as clueless as the rest of us. Solomon wrote, "Don't boast about tomorrow, because you don't know what another day will bring." We can speculate, dream, and hope, but we don't know what will come our way tomorrow. So, the best way to get ready for tomorrow is to finish well today.

If the best way to be ready for tomorrow is to finish well today, what do you need to do to finish well today?

What are some practical steps you can take to focus on today rather than worrying about tomorrow?

Planning for the future is not the same as worrying about tomorrow. How does focusing on today help you reach your future goals?

April 9
Three Ways to Live Your Life

Scripture for Today: 2 Corinthians 4:17–18

Have you ever met someone who's a hopeless optimist? How about someone who's a constant pessimist? How you view the world matters to you and those around you! I've noticed in my life there are three ways people live their lives, and It has to do with the past, the present, and the future.

Many people get stuck in the past. They've been betrayed, wounded, and scarred. Hopefully you know by now that all people are a little messed up in the head, and you can't figure them out. So just work on being the best you can be!

Others are paralyzed by the present. They wait day after day wondering when something bad is going to happen. They live in fear each day which steals the possible joy they could be experiencing with the people around them.

Too few people live today with the future in mind. Every decision we make today affects our future. Live today and every day with the future in mind. Look forward 5, 10, or 20 years. Dream of the life you want and make decisions that will help take you there. God has given you great potential, but it's up to you to reach for it.

What is the most difficult challenge you face in keeping goals you set? Make a list below.

If you don't know how to overcome those challenges, find a mentor to help you or find a recommended reading list for changing your outlook.

April 10
What to Do When You Don't Know What to Do

Scripture for Today: Philippians 3:12-14

Have you ever faced a dead end in life? I mean, have you ever been on one of life's paths when you've run into a brick wall? Maybe your job stopped progressing? Or your educational progress got blocked? Or that person you thought was "the one" walked away with no explanation?

Many years ago I heard a slogan that has helped me many times: "When you don't know what to do, do what you know to do." It sounds like the same thing the first time you hear it, but here's what it means:

There are certain things we know we should do. We should read our Bibles. We should pray. We should love people. We should encourage each other. We should learn. If we have a job, we should go to work. When we hit a brick wall, these are the things we can do until we decide what we should do about the brick wall!

Not knowing what to do about a specific thing doesn't mean you are out of options! It might mean a short delay, but if you keep doing what you know to do, you might find a way around the brick wall you hadn't seen before.

When is the last time you hit a real dead-end in some area of life?

Did you stall or quit, or did you keep doing things in other areas of life?

It might help to create a visual with the words "When you don't know what to do, do what you know to do" so you can keep it in mind.

April 11
Acting Ethically in Business and Life

Scripture: Luke 16:10

Do you know anyone with a "Do what it takes to get ahead no matter who you have to step on" attitude? It's dangerous to everyone around them, but it's dangerous to them, too!

It is possible to reach the pinnacle of success without ethical behavior; many people have done it. Some tried and got caught and they are now in jail! Being ethical simply means doing what is right all the time, even when nobody's looking. It means staying faithful to your spouse even when someone flirts with you. Being ethical means when you have a chance to close the deal by leaving out information that could kill it, you reveal the information.

Being ethical, really, just means live like God is watching you all the time; because He is!

When Jesus said, "He who can be trusted with little can be trusted with much," He is talking, at least partially, about being ethical. Can you be trusted in every circumstance with handling a little as well as handling much? I hope so, because that's what honors God.

Do you strive to be ethical in all your business and personal dealings?

Would you rather win than be right, or be right than win? Do you ever push the boundaries of the law to make another dollar?

Spend some time evaluating how you treat others, fairly or not, then ask God to help you be ethical in all of your dealings.

April 12
Change

Scripture for Today: Psalm 55:22

Why is it so difficult to change? It's a battle we all face. We face it every day as we attempt to improve our lives. We face it when we try to get rid of an old bad habit that's threatening to destroy us. And we face it when we get married and begin to adjust to a very weird person living in our home.

It was many years ago, but I remember my new bride hitting me across the back with one of those massive wooden spoons she had just yanked off the wall. To this day, I don't remember what I did wrong, but it's obvious we were struggling with change! It wasn't funny at the time, but today we laugh.

Good change is always an uphill battle that requires a daily pursuit. In part it's difficult because change is a lot like experiencing death. We must let go and say goodbye to the way things used to be. It's an emotional exercise and we feel the loss, but until we let go of the past, we *cannot* grab hold of the future.

Is there anything in your past that is keeping you from your future goals?

Pause right now and pray, casting your burden on God, believing He will sustain you.

April 13
Greatness

Scripture for Today: Matthew 23:11

Do you think about doing great things? Having a great marriage, a great career, a great life. Every child dreams about greatness, but often, as we become adults, we allow the pressures of life to kill those dreams. Too often we surrender to discouragement and begin to settle for mediocrity. Hardship and disappointment are powerful enemies, but we can defeat them. Everyone gets knocked down from time to time, but the great ones are those who continue to get back up.

The example of Joseph in the book of Genesis is a great one. His mother died in his childhood, but he lived to honor his father. His brothers sold him into slavery, but he worked hard for his master. He was falsely accused of rape and sent to prison for many years, but he chose to not be bitter. Ultimately, he became Prime Minister of Egypt and saved his nation and family from starvation.

Greatness is not developed in a day, but daily. So, keep doing the right thing. Greatness is on the way.

What are some things in your life that could possibly add up to greatness?

Ask God to help you see the things He's doing around you and continue doing the right thing on the way to becoming great.

April 14
Relationships

Scripture for Today: Proverbs 18:24

Are you the kind of person others are proud to be identified with? Are you a trusted friend? A dependable parent? A respectful son or daughter?

We usually apply such questions to the "Other" person in our lives, but you should apply such questions to yourself.

Relationships are powerful. Everything we know, we learned from someone else. Every great memory we have includes someone else. And every great dream we have involves someone else. That's the power of relationships.

When we are young, we define our existence by our family: our parents, grandparents, brothers, sisters, aunts, uncles, and cousins. Then we have friends, neighbors, co-workers, a husband or wife, with children to follow. Finally, there are grandchildren.

Everything we do from birth till death is linked to the relationships in our lives, but they are also linked to us.

So be a person that people are proud to be identified with. You are responsible for half of every relationship in life, so make sure your half is the better half.

Do you think your relationships are stronger because you are in them?

If there are any strained relationships in your life, what can you do to improve them?

April 15
Hurt, Hate, and Forgiveness

Scripture for Today: Matthew 5:43–47

Have you ever heard the advice to: "Just be yourself"? Well that may be the worst advice ever for some people. There are many wounded and hurting people in this world. Wounded people can be a lot like wounded dogs...they growl and bite! Be careful, because as a result of their own pain they can hurt you. They are angry and bitter over something that happened in the past and they just can't let it go. They refuse to forgive. It's changed them, and it is not a pretty sight.

I know what it's like to be wounded; during those times you would not want me to be myself! You might not have survived.

We must reach deeper and rise to a higher level of living. We must heed the words of Jesus to forgive those who hurt us, love those who hate us, and do good to those who spitefully use us. In the process we heal our own wounds and protect our own hearts from the greatest disease ever—the disease of hate.

It can be hard to admit that we truly hate someone. When we do, it puts us on the road to healing. Is there anyone in your life you truly hate?

Your hate is doing damage to both of you, but it's a disease within you that will kill you from the inside. Ask God to forgive and deliver you from hate, then, as much as it lies with you, reconcile with any person you've hated.

April 16
Learning

Scripture for Today: Luke 2:52

What did you learn today? It's a question I was asked by my parents every day after school. I didn't always have a good answer. I had learned some things so gradually I didn't even know I'd learned them. At other times I didn't have a good answer because I simply did not pay attention or pause to think about what I was learning.

When I was a kid I was being forced to learn by others, because they knew it was best for my future. My parents made me go to school. My teachers made me go through a process of learning one concept after another. Sure, I had to apply myself, but they owned the process. But once I became an adult, nobody was there to make me learn anymore.

As an adult I have to own my learning process. Learning is a choice I have to make every day. And now at the end of each day I have to ask myself," What did you learn today?" And I'd better have a good answer!

Can you name the last book you read to learn something you didn't know? Can you name two?

What have you learned about God lately? Ask Him to lead you into a deeper relationship so you can know Him better each day.

April 17
Respect

Scripture for Today: Genesis 1:27

How much respect do people give you? A better question is, how much respect do you give other people? Respect means to "take a second look" at a person. It's about recognizing their God-given value.

As a kid I remember one of my mentors, Mr. Ernest Ingram, giving other people respect. He was really good at it: Rich or poor, young or old, famous or unknown. He gave it for no apparent reason except that the person was breathing. I watched him stand and take his hat off to a lady or tip his hat when a man walked by.

On other occasions I watched my dad show respect by greeting someone with a handshake and then work hard to call them by name when he'd see them again. These acts of respect are not by accident. They are intentional and they require constant effort.

We should give respect to others, not because of who *they* are, but because of who *we* are.

To be respected is to be noticed and heard—and every human deserves that.

What does it feel like to be respected? To be disrespected?

Since respect means to "take a second look," how can you regularly show respect to those around you?

April 18
Difficult Times

Scripture for Today: Psalm 23:3–4

How do you make it through those difficult times in life? You know, when something terrible happens and it catches you by surprise: A death, a disease, or a disappointment invades your otherwise tranquil life. I hate it when that happens! At that moment it's hard to see any hope for the future. Our faith in God is trampled by fear and our confidence turns to questions, even questions about the character of God.

Well there are some facts that I have to be reminded of from time to time. With over 7 billion people on the planet, God still knows me by name. Though I may not understand a lot of things in this life, God is always trustworthy and never makes a mistake. He created me to fulfill a unique purpose in this world. Even the disappointing events of life play a role in that purpose. And God will never forsake me and will be with me until I see Him face to face! You and I can trust Him even in the most difficult, darkest days of life.

Does it encourage you to know that the difficult time you are in did not catch God by surprise?

Difficult times are simply the way of this life; no one gets around them. Pause and ask God to help you through your difficult time and have faith that He is with you in it.

April 19
Love

Scripture for Today: Romans 5:8, 1 John 4:7–8

Love is a beautiful thing. As a matter of fact, some would say, "All you need is love." Well, I tend to agree, that is if we use the right definition for love. Love is powerful as it transcends culture, language, gender, and age, but it often means different things to different people.

In the music and movies of today's pop culture, it's presented as a selfish feeling of happiness that is void of any personal responsibility. But true love requires lots of responsibility, whether the feelings of happiness are always present or not.

The words, "I love you" are important, but love is much deeper than words. It requires kind actions and deeds toward a person, even when that person is functioning at their worst.

God has taught us how to live that way. He demonstrated His love towards us by sending Jesus to die for us while we were still sinners. By His actions we are challenged to love others not only when they behave the way we want them to, but even when they don't.

Who in your life is easy to love? Who in your life is difficult to love?

Make it a point to let the people you love know it by telling them frequently.

April 20
Evaluating Our Aging

Scripture for Today: 2 Chronicles 1:8–10

How well are you aging? I'm not talking about physical features such as wrinkles, loss of hair, sight, hearing, or hair color. I'm talking about things that really matter. Is your purpose in life more clear? Is your heart more thankful? Is your spiritual life in order?

As I look back at my life, there's been something special about the big birthdays I've had. You know: age 21, 30, 40, and 50!

We don't automatically get better and wiser with age. I've met some really wise old people, but I've also met some really dumb ones. King Solomon was extremely wise in his youth but became foolish in his old age.

As you approach each major season of life, it's important to evaluate yourself more closely than ever. It's a great time to make some much needed adjustments. Your success tomorrow is counting on your adjustments today!

Can you remember any big changes on your milestone birthdays? What's your next milestone birthday? What adjustments need to be made in your life?

Regardless of your age, commit to growing wiser as you grow older rather than simply growing older.

April 21
Children

Scripture for Today: Psalm 127:3–5

Do you have any kids? If so, you know it's a game changer. Few things serve as a wake-up call more than the phrase, "We're having a baby!" I've heard it twice, and a thousand questions bombarded me. Will I be a good dad? Will the baby be healthy? Will it be a boy or girl? Who or what will they look? What should I do next?

We're reminded in the Bible that children are a heritage from the Lord. They're an awesome gift from God and at the same time, a massive responsibility. Children were never intended to raise themselves—they must be loved, trained, disciplined, and cared for until they become adults. It takes a man and a woman to create a child, and both should be involved in raising them. I'm inspired by the devotion of single parents who do it all, but if you help bring a child into this world, you should also invest in them. When your child succeeds, it should be partly because of you, not in spite of you.

If you have kids, do you view them as burdens or blessings?

Is there any area where you can more intentionally invest in your child? If so, ask God for wisdom, then make a plan for intentional investment.

April 22
Family Reunion

Scripture for Today: Mark 10:13–16

Have you gotten together with your family lately? The busyness and routines of life can take over and isolate us from the people we love the most: Brothers, sisters, moms, dads, aunts, uncles, cousins, grand maws, and grand paws. Some of my greatest childhood memories happened at family reunions, which was the only time I saw some of our family. Some of them traveled for many hours to come. I loved eating the food of the old ladies as we heard the old men tell stories about the past.

Our dreams and our jobs are important, but not nearly as important as our families. It's sad that the most common time for families to come together is when one of them dies. We then wish we could visit with them just one more time, but it's too late!

It's now springtime, which is a great time to have a family reunion and a cookout. You might be waiting on your invitation for the next family gathering, but this time, perhaps you do the inviting.

Are you in the practice of putting your family before your career and hobbies? If so, they will appreciate it until the day they die.

If you have family members who are distant from you either geographically or relationally, why not reach out to them today? Plan a time to get together.

April 23
Purpose

Scripture for Today: Hebrews 9:27

What's your purpose for daily living? Too often we begin each day without any thought of making it count for something significant. And at the end of the day we look back and find out it didn't.

If you do that day after day, there will come a time when you look back at your life and wish you could do it over again differently; but you can't. We only get one shot at it, and then after that we stand before God to give an account.

The pressures of life often cause people to lose focus of the most important things in life: God, family, morality, integrity.

You need to know that today matters, and you need to know why today matters. You can live your life any way you want, but you can only live it once. It's best to get it right one day at a time!

What are you doing today that will last beyond your lifetime?

Have you knowingly aligned your purpose with God's purpose for you? If not, make it a priority beginning today.

April 24
Temptation

Scripture for Today: 1 Corinthians 10:13

Did the Devil really make you do it? We often think about doing something foolish. On occasion our thoughts are so bad we are surprised and even ashamed. How could a fine person like myself think such a thought? At other times we become delusional and embrace them as the way things ought to be. Then we turn them into actions. Failure, devastation, and chaos are soon to follow.

No one, and I repeat no one, is exempt from this possibility, and we can't blame it all on the Devil. All of us have a sinful nature at the core of our being, and we are constantly flooded with temptations to do wrong. These temptations are common for everyone, but we don't have to put them into action. If we do so, it's because we choose to. But God will give us wisdom and strength to do the right thing, if we'll only ask. The Devil won't make you do the wrong thing, and God won't make you do the right thing. You have a choice!

Do you have temptations that sometimes seem overpowering?

In Jesus Christ no temptation has ultimate power over you. If you don't have a relationship with Jesus, ask Him to save you.

April 25
Good Character

Scripture for Today: 1 Corinthians 15:33

What are you doing to develop and maintain good character? It's important because your character serves as a compass to point you in a certain direction every day. As you know, a good compass always points north so a traveler can make good decisions to direct the journey that lies ahead. If a compass is not working properly, the traveler can get lost, all the while thinking they are going in the right direction. And once they arrive, confusion, frustration, and anger are soon to follow.

If you don't develop and maintain good character it will, just like a faulty compass, lead you to a place where you never intended to go, keep you there longer than you intended to stay, and make you pay a price you never intended to pay. But if you take good care of your character, your character will take good care of you. And someday you'll look back on your life as a life well lived. So, once again I'll ask: What are you doing to develop and maintain your character?

Do you see yourself as a person with good or bad character? How do others perceive you?

Reputation is what people think you are, but character is what you actually are. It's also the most important. After a minute of self-reflection, ask God to help you have the kind of character that honors Him.

April 26
Trust God

Scripture for Today: 2 Corinthians 5:7

Do you trust God completely? On some days it's easy, especially when we get that new job or an increase in pay. It's even easier when we get a good report from the doctor or someone survives when we thought they would die. But it's a little different when the news isn't quite so good. We wonder for a moment if God has forgotten us, or if He's not as trustworthy as we thought. I've been down that path a few times myself. You know, when God did not do what I thought He should have?

But I've learned that God is wiser than I am. Imagine that! His plans are perfect. The sunrise, sunset, rain, and rainbow are simple reminders of His consistent goodness, wisdom, and brilliance. He is perfectly wise, and perfectly good. He is always trustworthy. I must trust Him, especially in things that are beyond my control. It's called "faith." I trust Him with my life, my family, and my eternity. Do you?

Why is it sometimes difficult to trust God?

Is there anything in your life right now you should surrender to Him?

April 27
Seasons

Scripture for Today: Ecclesiastes 3:1–8

Have you learned how to flow with the seasons of life? Doing so will help you live with less regrets. God made the times and seasons to provide for us a sense of rhythm in life. It's in the great "time" chapter of Ecclesiastes 3. You know, "There is a time for this and a time for that!"

Every year flows through winter, spring, summer, and fall. Each has its own purpose.

Every segment of life is seasonal: our childhood, adulthood, and marriage. Each flows from one season to the next. And there are specific things that must be done in each season if we're going to live without regrets. In the seasons of parenting we are often unaware that our kids are changing. We think they will always be small, sitting in our lap, or giving us a tight squeeze around our neck. But, they won't. It's a season that passes too quickly.

What season are you in? Make the best of it, because a new season is on the way!

If you are a young person in the spring of life, how can you keep your focus on God during the upcoming seasons of your life?

If you are an older person in the winter of life, you may have regrets, ask God to help you keep your eyes looking forward rather than behind.

If you are in the summer or autumn of life, ask God to keep you focused on the purpose He has for you in each season.

April 28
Motivated

Scripture for Today: Romans 8:28

How well do you stay motivated? You know, that sense of drive and purpose that gets you going each day and helps you face it with enthusiasm and excitement. The challenges we face can certainly take it out of us, and it fluctuates throughout the week. Yeah, we're usually a little more motivated on Friday and Saturday than we are on Monday. And we're certainly more motivated to go on vacation than we are to get a root canal.

But as followers of Jesus Christ, our motivation flows from a much deeper understanding of life. For the believer, there is God's promise that all things work together for good for those who love Him and are carrying out His purposes. He has begun a good work in us and will continue that work until we stand before Him face to face. Every day, every challenge, and every victory is a time when God can shape us as we prepare for eternity. Yes, we're just passing through this world, and for the believer, the best is yet to come!

Do you find it hard to be motivated for your daily tasks? What things easily motivate you? What gives you tremendous motivation?

We experience motivation from God when our purposes are aligned with His. Are you aligned with Him right now?

April 29
Faithfulness

Scripture for Today: Hebrews 11:1–2

How faithful are you? Your faithfulness is a quality that shows up every day of your life. It's a character trait that identifies your dependability and trustworthiness. It identifies whether or not you can be counted on when it counts. When the ball is put into your hands, what do you do with it?

We live in a day of excuses and blaming others for our own failures. It's happening in our families, churches, and the workplace. Even our government leaders at the highest offices seem to have mastered it and we suffer as a result. Since our leaders behave in such ways, many in society think it's justifiable for them too. But it's not.

If the quality of faithfulness is not held high in a society then that society is in trouble.

Will you take care of your family? Will you go to work every day, and be on time? If you're a leader, will you lead with diligence, honesty, and integrity? The ball is in your hands. Be faithful.

Are you the type of person who wants to take the last shot or make the last pass, or the type who'd rather be watching from the sidelines or the stands?

It is important that we own our own failures rather than blaming others. If you have blamed someone for your own mistakes or misdeeds, go to them today and make it right.

April 30
A Proper Perspective on Money

Scripture: 1 Timothy 6:10; 1 John 2:15

Have you ever heard the old saying, "Money is the root of all evil?" Some even say it's in the Bible. That's almost true.

The Bible does say, "The love of money is the root of all kinds of evil." It isn't the presence of money itself, or even having a lot of it that's the problem. The problem is when we love having money, that's when we have things turned upside down!

In another place the Bible says, "Do not love the world or the things that are in the world." Jesus warned, "You cannot love God and mammon," an old word for stuff or possessions. In those verses we see again possessions are less a problem than if we love them.

It is dangerous to love things! A tornado or house-fire can take them away from you in an instant. If you place all your love in stuff and then the stuff gets destroyed, what do you have?

So, be careful what you love! It's always right to love God first and foremost, then love family, friends, and neighbors. But don't love money or the stuff it buys. It just won't last.

Have you ever caught yourself saying, "I just love my _____"?

Take some time to evaluate what it is you really love. If you love any of your things more than you love God, ask His forgivenesss, then rearrange your "love life."

May 1
Sinners and Winners

Scripture for Today: Romans 3:10, 23

Why do good things happen to bad people? Oh, that's usually not the question is it? No, we usually ask, "Why do bad things happen to good people?" And we always assume that we are the good people. It's those other people who are the bad people. We each have our own sense of self-righteousness that puts us into the highest percentage of the human race. I mean, we are the cream of the crop, aren't we?

Even if we were, that's not saying much. It's like saying, "I'm the best rotten apple in the world." The Bible clearly teaches that we are all sinners at the core of our being. And even our righteousness is as filthy rags in the sight of God.

No, we aren't quite as good as we'd like to think and the history of our behavior proves it. And that, my friends, is why Jesus came. Our sinful nature guarantees failure before God. Then Jesus stepped in and made it possible for us to become winners. And because of Him, that's exactly what I am!

In your mind, what is a winner? Do some people win who should be losing?

To reject Jesus Christ is the ultimate losing decision. If you want to be an eternal winner, pray right now and ask Him to save you from your filthy rags.

May 2
Nicknames

Scripture for Today: Acts 11:22–26

Have you noticed how easily offended people are today? We should strive to be caring and encouraging to others, but we should not wear our feelings on our shoulders either.

I grew up in the south where lots of people have nicknames. I remember Buck, Ajax, Knob, Shorty, Doomer, Zeke, Cooney, and Scratcher. Today, even a nickname is considered offensive to some people, But as I recall, those with nicknames were amazing people who, in many ways, seemed larger than life. Their name was a term of endearment that identified them as uniquely special and greatly loved.

Whether you know it or not, the name "Christian" is actually a nickname. It was not intended as a good word, but was used by observers to describe people who were trying to live and behave like Jesus. Instead of being offended, they embraced it and wore the title with honor. Today, one third of the world's population uses it to describe their faith in Jesus Christ. If someone observed your life, would they possibly give you the nickname, "Christian"?

When someone tells you they are a Christian do you respond positively or negatively?

If you are a Christian, commit to living a life that honors rather than dishonors that nickname.

May 3
Rhythms of Life

Scripture for Today: Ecclesiastes 8:6

Do you ever feel like your world is spinning a little too fast? Or maybe at the moment it seems a bit boring!

I remember when I was just a kid we had a hill near our house that we played on and around. That hill was a place where we played Army games, cowboys and Indians, and experienced some of the great thrills of life. We rolled 55-gallon barrels to the top, climbed inside, and rolled at terrifying speeds all the way to the bottom. Once inside, we couldn't wait for the barrel to stop rolling, but once it stopped, we couldn't wait to do it again.

That's often the way life feels. We feel trapped somewhere between the adrenaline rush of too much going on, and the frustration of being bored. We need times of rest, but most of us need a little excitement too. It's what develops for us the rhythm of life. And a pretty amazing life can be had if we can only learn how to flow with that rhythm.

As you read these words, how would you describe the rhythm of life you are currently in?

Sometimes the "too fast, out of control" rhythms are our own doing. Take a look at your calendar or to-do list and see if anything needs to go.

May 4
Where's Your Margin?

Scripture for Today: Exodus 20:8–11

How well are you doing with the KISS method of life? You know: Keep It Simple Stupid. I learned it many years ago, but sadly I still struggle putting it into practice. When we violate it, we soon feel the pressure of an over-complicated life. Too much to do in a short period of time. A long way to go and a short time to get there. Too much month at the end of our money.

Such statements describe a life without margin. Margin is that extra time we build into our schedules to handle the crisis of life. It's the extra money we set aside for unexpected expenses like medical bills and car repairs.

While we should hope for a life without incident, we know by now that unexpected challenges happen to everyone. Therefore, a simple life can be developed if we expect the unexpected and plan for it. Such a plan helps reduce stress and create a much better life for you and the people around you. Ignoring such a plan is insanity.

Have you ever thought of the Sabbath Day as God's divinely ordered margin for our lives?

What decisions will help you create the margin you need to maintain mental, emotional, physical, and spiritual health?

May 5
Shelter

Scripture for Today: Psalm 31:19–20

A good shelter is always a great thing to have. I recall a hot summer day when I was riding through the pasture to check on my cattle. It's something I tried to do every day. When I found them, they were tightly packed under a large sheltering tree, enjoying the shade. I've watched them gather under that same tree during the wintertime and rainstorms, too. It seems to be the "go to" place for them when life becomes a little too unpredictable.

Well those cattle are a lot like we are. We too need a good shelter to run to when life becomes unpredictable. We sometimes find that shelter in our homes, our families, and our friends. But if you've been around for a while you know that sometimes these shelters fail. Sometimes they are actually the problem!

King David in Psalm 31 spoke of the good shelter he turned to. He said, "In You, O Lord, I have taken shelter." That good shelter is available to all of us, and He never fails.

Do you need to seek God's shelter from something you had not predicted or anticipated?

Ask God to help you trust Him for shelter rather than finances, position, or other things that are not as powerful and dependable as He is.

May 6
Can You Handle Truth?

Scripture for Today: John 14:6

"You can't handle the truth!" It's the famous statement by Colonel Jessep, Jack Nicholson's character in the movie *A Few Good Men*. It's a riveting exchange, but his assumption is that society can function better being told lies by their leaders, instead of being told the hard truth; that people are too shallow, simple-minded, and incompetent to face the facts.

This philosophy has invaded our society and is spreading like an epidemic and destructive virus. History bears record that lying is not a new thing. We are flawed by sin, and if confronted with difficult consequences men, women, boys, and girls have been known to try to lie themselves out of trouble. But just because it's been done in the past does not mean it's okay. Lying is destructive whether it's by a child, a parent, a pastor, the IRS, or a politician.

There will come a day when each will stand before God, and we won't be able to lie our way out of the consequences of our actions. Just the truth please. Just the truth!

Why do people sometimes turn to lying?

Have you made truth-telling a habit? Ask God to help you be truthful because He is truthful.

May 7
Book

Scripture for Today: Psalm 119:33–40

Have you read a good book lately? In the sixth grade I read *Where the Red Fern Grows*. It's a story about two Redbone coonhounds and a boy hunting in the Ozarks. It was the only book I had read in its entirety—by choice, that is. I was so moved by the relationship between Billy and his dogs, Old Dan and Little Ann, that I saved some money and bought some coonhounds of my own. Through my teenage years, coon hunting was a regular pastime for my buddies, Rodney and Kevin, and me. When I moved back to West Georgia I bought another coonhound and hunted for several years so I could give my daughters the same experience. I have lots of great memories all because of a good book. As a gift for my 50th birthday, a good friend gave me a copy of the book signed by the author. I consider it a great treasure.

However, my Bible continues to be my favorite book of all time. And its Author is brilliant.

What is the first book you remember reading? What is the best book you have ever read?

Is the Bible among the books you read regularly? It is inexhaustible in its depth, so make a plan to read it every day.

May 8
Wounds

Scripture for Today: Job 24:12

What kind of scars do you have? As boys, I recall comparing scars with my buddies. We wore them as badges of honor. We told stories about our bravery or stupidity that had produced them. But as we get older, we take on scars of a different kind and the events that produce them are often too painful to talk about. They are scars of the soul. It's been a dark reality of our human existence since the beginning of time.

The ancient character Job, writing in chapter 24 verse 12 of his book in the Bible, said, "From the city men groan, and the souls of the wounded cry out." These are secret wounds and silent cries, but they are real nonetheless. They are scars from our soul being stabbed or cut. Perhaps by our own sin or failure, or we've been misunderstood or treated unfairly. Someone we love has died, or perhaps we feel rejected by a friend. And silently, our heart breaks and our soul bleeds. But there's just one Physician in town that specializes in that. His name is Jesus.

Are you suffering from a soul-wound? Does it feel mortal? Has it been hurting you for decades?

Pause right now and ask the Great Physician, Jesus Christ, to heal your wounded soul.

May 9
Stillness

Scripture for Today: Psalm 46:10

Have you enjoyed some silence lately? In today's world of constant noise, entertainment, and quick travel from one place to another, times of silence, peace, and quiet are far and few between. The quality of our lives shows the evidence. Too often our emotions are like bombs ready to explode. Such explosions often injure those we treasure the most.

Silence, peace, and quiet are powerful medicines that help heal our soul, in part because that's the right environment to get to know God. We often imagine God speaking loudly, maybe like thunder. But more often than not His voice comes as a whisper in the depths of our soul. In the Bible, God tells us to "Be still and know that I am God." The fact that we are always busy and on the move is a problem that must be addressed for each of us. We must slow down, gear down, and quiet down, and in that silence we can hear and feel the voice of God as He speaks new life into our soul.

Does your life more resemble resting beside a mountain stream or being on the front row of a NASCAR race?

What are some steps you can take to get away from the noise of life and experience life-saving peace and quiet? Where might you go?

May 10
Mother's Day

Scripture for Today: Exodus 20:12

I love springtime for lots of reasons, but for one, it's a time we set aside to honor our moms. The gratitude shown on Mother's Day should be carried over into everyday of the year, but I'm glad we have that day set aside to send a clear message. Moms are awesome!

They are not always perfect. They are not always happy. They sometimes make mistakes. They can't remove every pain we face in life, and yes, occasionally, they might be the cause of it. But at the most basic level, none of us came into this world without a mom. And there are many amazing moms who couldn't or didn't give birth, but they've chosen to be a good mom to someone anyway.

My mom has already passed away, and I miss her terribly. But I'm more thankful than ever to have had such an amazing mother to love me and shape my life. In the Bible, God said we are to honor our mother and father. Yes, doing so is a big deal!

What are some ways your mom helped shape you?

If your mom is still alive, does she know how much you love her? Why not send her a card or text this week and remind her?

May 11
Joy

Scripture for Today: Matthew 5:3–10

Are you joyful? You'll notice I did not ask if you're happy. There's a big difference between joy and happiness. Happiness exists because of what happens in our lives. If something good happens, we're happy, but if something bad happens, well, we're not happy. That's why some people have such massive mood swings. Their feelings are connected to the latest events that happen in life.

Joy flows from a much deeper place than what happens or doesn't happen. Joy flows from a firm confidence that your heart is connected to the heart of God, and that regardless of what happens in life, God is always trustworthy. Joy flows from a deep, abiding peace in the depths of your soul. It comes from knowing that you don't have to understand or control everything that happens in this world. You are confident that God can handle it. You can relax. You're not in charge of the universe, and if you were, you'd likely mess it up!

Have you grown to understand the difference between happiness and joy?

Are you experiencing God's joy right now?

May 12
Pharisees

Scripture for Today: Matthew 23:13–17

Are you a Pharisee? Pharisees were religious leaders in Jesus' day, but He was pretty tough on them. They created strict do's and don'ts that were based upon their own opinions and cultures. They made rules that God did not create, but the Pharisees taught them as if He did. And along with the rules came a self-righteous and arrogant attitude that was sickening. They thought they were the perfect examples of a godly life, but they were not.

Jesus was obviously sickened by them. He compared them to a grave where people decorate the outside to look good, but the inside is full of death. He even called them snakes! They wanted others to be impressed with their religious devotion, but Jesus was not impressed at all. He called them hypocrites as He warned them about their attitudes and actions. It's a good warning for us too.

We must identify more with Jesus who showed love to people in the kindest and most humble of ways. Are you a Pharisee or a Christian? They are not the same thing.

The Pharisees acted as if they were close to God, but they didn't recognize God when He stood before them. They were frauds. Do you know any modern Pharisees?

Find some time for a deep inventory of yourself to make sure you aren't a Pharisee, because God isn't fond of them.

May 13
Apathy

Scripture for Today: Ezekiel 12:2

Do you ever struggle with apathy? No, apathy is not an old friend you once went to school with. And it's not an old girlfriend or boyfriend you used to date. It's actually one of the greatest enemies and threats to your success. If anything, apathy is an old enemy you've faced since birth, and it's likely to return from time to time until you die! It can attack you in your family life, your career, and your spiritual life. These three areas of life are the most important treasures you have and must be protected from apathy at all cost.

To be apathetic means to lack emotional connection, to be indifferent to something, or to simply not care. That may sound like a good place to be, to simply not care; but it's not. You need to know that when you're apathetic, you're just one letter away from being pathetic. To be pathetic means to be pitifully unsuccessful and that's an awful place to be!

When you think of apathy, who or what comes to mind?

Are you apathetic about anything that you should be focusing on? Ask God to give you the right vision and motivation so you aren't apathetic about something He wants you to do.

May 14
Crackpots and Integrity

Scripture for Today: Proverbs 11:3

Are you a crackpot? If someone is called a crackpot, then we usually think they're a little on the crazy side. But the term crackpot is actually connected to a person's integrity, not their emotional stamina.

In the ancient days, the potter would make a pot, and from time it would crack during the drying process. If the potter had integrity, he would throw the pot away and start over. But if he did not have integrity, he would spread wax over the crack to hide it from the naked eye. Then he would sell it as a good and wholesome pot. When the buyer later heated the pot so they could cook some soup, the wax would melt away and they were well aware they had a crackpot on their hands, all because the potter lacked integrity.

There's no doubt that we all have flaws. But the real issue is, are we covering our flaws or fixing them? Honesty, confession, forgiveness, and restitution may be painful and frightening, but they repair our flaws really well.

Do you have any flaws you are trying to hide with insufficient means, like wax on a cracked pot?

Rather than covering flaws, ask God to fix them with His character which has no flaws.

May 15
Valuing Your Employee

Scripture for Today: Ephesians 6:9; Colossians 4:1

Who is the best boss you ever had? Chances are he or she was a person who taught you, complimented you, corrected you, but most of all valued you as a person and an employee.

If you're an employer, do you make an effort to make your employees feel valued? Do you feel certain that your employees feel encouraged and needed each day? This is an important question to ask yourself as an employer!

Each day, you have the ability to lift your employees up or bring them down. Will you create an environment that is filled with respect, compassion, and appreciation for those who work for you? Or will you be unfair, mean, and insufferable?

The Bible makes it clear that people in authority are to treat their employees "justly and fairly, knowing that you also have a Master in Heaven." When you start to wonder how you should treat those who are under your leadership maybe examine how God treats you! Is He cruel and punishing, or does He approach you with patience and kindness? You have the perfect person after which to model your behavior.

Do you work hard to show your employees they are valued? If not, what are things you can do to change that?

Can you think of an employer from your past who valued you? What stands out to you about them? Take some time to thank God for good leaders and ask Him to help you be one!

May 16
Depression

Scripture for Today: 1 Kings 19:1–4

Do you ever deal with depression? It's not something most of us want to talk about. But with the death of comedian Robin Williams, the discussion of depression made it to the headlines. How could someone who laughed so much on the outside be so sad on the inside? One of his friends said, "He could make everyone happy, except himself."

Depression can be a disease from a body that isn't functioning well, the result of a lack of rest or grief, lost hopes and dreams, lost health or wealth, or lost relationships that were once held dear. And yes, it can even attack the most devout in the family of God. Moses, King David, the Prophet Elijah, and the Apostle Paul, struggled through depression.

You might seriously need to go to a doctor to get some help. Or it might be as simple as taking some time off, feeding your soul through Bible reading and prayer, developing a new circle of friends, or starting a new project.

Encourage someone today. You never know what's going on behind the smile.

Do you ever struggle with depression?

Sometimes depression comes and goes, but if you are constantly beset by it, please seek help through counseling or seeing a doctor.

May 17
Contributing

Scripture for Today: Matthew 5:16

Are you doing something that contributes to the lives of others? Doing so is much more powerful than you might think.

On a trip to Connecticut, I walked out of my hotel toward my Uber driver who would take me to the airport for my flight home. The driver was smiling from ear to ear as I opened the car door. As I got in, he welcomed me with kindness and grace.

In casual conversation, I asked, "So how did you become an Uber driver?" He told the story of losing his business a few years earlier, and of the bankruptcy that followed. He drew his unemployment for a brief period, but depression set in. He said, "I became an Uber driver because I needed to contribute something. A man needs to contribute something to feel good about himself and about life!"

It was a great reminder that God designed us this way—to do good works and to be a blessing. And to contribute something of ourselves to make life better for others. Well, do you?

What kind of contributions do you make to other people's lives?

Sometimes the problem is we aren't looking with eyes to see what's happening with other people. Ask God to help you see the opportunities around you so you can do good works for other people.

May 18
Willpower

Scripture for Today: Proverbs 21:5

Do you ever struggle with willpower? I've heard it said, "Where there's a will, there's a way." But is that always true?

It was the year 1936 when my granddad and his friend named Will planted a large field of corn and cotton.

Everything was looking great until his mule died before the plowing was complete. He and Will scrambled to borrow one from a friend so they could finish. Then the rain began. At first they were thankful, but their gratitude turned to frustration when the rains continued for several days. The Tallapoosa River arose from its banks and flooded the entire crop! All of their efforts had been in vain.

In disgust he and Will sat on the porch with my grandma. He gave her a cockeyed grin and said, "Well, this is one time I had a Will, but there was just no way!"

Sometimes life is simply hard and things don't turn out the way we hoped. But as a follower of Jesus Christ, I know Heaven is awaiting around the corner.

Have you ever faced a failure even though you had planned well?

What do you do when things don't turn out the way you hoped?

May 19
Commitment

Scripture for Today: Ephesians 5:25

"All you need is love." At least that's what the song says, referring to that special bond between people. But the song is wrong. Yep; I said it! It's wrong.

In a marriage or friendship, it isn't feelings of "love" that hold it together. No, it's true commitment! It's a commitment to treat each other with honesty, dignity, and respect, even when the feelings of love are not present. It's a commitment to honor a person with your presence, loyalty, and companionship. It's a commitment to add value to the other person's life, attempting to make their life better. It's a choice we make to work through our frustrations with each other, spend time together and share the special moments of life.

Oh love is a powerful thing, but all "true love and true friendship" rests on the power of commitment. But that commitment cannot be one-sided. It's required on both sides of the relationship. Maybe someone will write a song about commitment, but I won't hold my breath while I wait to hear it.

Have you heard the sentiment, "They fell out of love"? What does that describe in your way of thinking?

Commitment is the decision to do the things that keep us in love. Who do you love that might require more commitment that you've been giving?

May 20
Psalm 119

Scripture for Today: Psalm 119:1–16

Have you spent any time reading Psalm one hundred nineteen? It's the longest chapter in the entire Bible with one hundred seventy-six verses. One hundred seventy-one of those verses have a direct mention of the value and power of God's word. This psalm instructs us how to live the best life possible.

"Happy are those who keep God's word." "How can a young man keep his way pure? By keeping God's word!" "God's word is a lamp to our feet and a light to our path."

God's word gives us direction and understanding, protects us from sin, provides for us wisdom, shields us from deceit, brings comfort in times of affliction, and renews our spirit when we are discouraged.

But it only does so if we read it, meditate on it, trust it, embrace it, and surrender to it. A simple process to follow is: Learn it, love it, and live it. Today and every day!

It's been said that sin will keep you from your Bible or your Bible will keep you from sin. Which will it be?

Is Bible-reading part of your daily life?

God's Word has often been likened to daily bread for our spiritual life. Do you normally go longer without spiritual food than physical food? It's impossible to grow as a follower of Jesus without a regular diet of scripture.

May 21
Legacy

Scripture for Today: Proverbs 13:22

How well are you living your life? What will they write in your obituary? It does matter. It's your legacy I'm talking about! Perhaps you could make an imaginary visit to your own funeral. Just go into the chapel, have a seat, and listen to the preacher. What's being said about you?

Alfred Nobel was a chemist who invented dynamite and numerous other explosives used as weapons of war. When his brother died, Alfred read the newspaper to see what they wrote about him. To his surprise, they thought it was Alfred who had died and had mistakenly written his obituary instead of his brother's. What an eye opener! They wrote, "Alfred Nobel—He became rich by inventing explosives that have killed many people." Alfred did not like what was written about him, and he was determined to change directions. He decided to use his wealth to award people who had benefited humanity. And that's why we have the Nobel prizes. He changed his legacy, and you still have time to change yours.

If you died right now, what kind of legacy would you leave? Is it the kind of legacy you want to leave?

If you need to make any life changes to change your legacy, begin to work toward them today.

May 22
All In

Scripture for Today: Matthew 16:24–26

Are you the kind of person who dabbles, or do you go "all in"? It's the difference between success and failure.

Over a century ago there were some missionaries called the "One Way" missionaries. They bought "One Way" tickets to their destinations, and they never bought the return half of the ticket. Instead of packing their suitcases, they packed their few earthly possessions in a coffin, boarded a ship, and sailed to their destinations never to return. The message was clear: they were "all in." Turning back was not an option.

This attitude is a powerful force that gives us an edge toward success whether it's applied to marriage, business, education, or our spiritual life. It's the same attitude Jesus applied when He said, "You cannot be my disciple unless you pick up your cross and follow me." Pick up your cross? Yes, it was a clear message that being "all in" was His way of living. So, go "all in" and don't dabble. Your success is counting on it.

Are you "all in" in life? If not, what's holding you back?

More importantly, are you "all in" with Jesus? If not, get rid of whatever is holding you back and go "all in" with Him.

May 23
Failure

Scripture for Today: Exodus 2:11–22

How much do you learn from failure? I hope it's a lot, because you'll have much more failure in life than success. We all do.

Failures come in all shapes and sizes-from a failed grade on a test to failed business ventures, moral decisions, and marriages. Our first instinct is to blame someone else, but if we'll look closely, some problems can always be traced back to our own foolishness and stupidity.

There's always something we can learn from each one that will help us if we'll only be honest with the person we see in the mirror each day. One of the most important lessons is that failure is not final unless we make it so. If we actually learn from our mistakes, our greatest days can be just around the corner.

We remember Moses for standing up to Pharaoh, and for leading the Hebrews out of captivity and into the Promised Land. But most people forget that 40 years earlier, he had murdered a man and fled for his life. He obviously learned from His failure. Will you?

Even when failure feels final it is not final unless you refuse to move forward or learn from it. Is a failure from your past limiting your future?

Is someone around you paralyzed by a failure? Help them see how moving beyond it can help their future.

May 24
Giving Our Best

Scripture for Today: Colossians 3:23

Are you doing your best? As a kid I was challenged to do my best, whether playing ball, preparing for a test, or working around the house. It's a voice I continue to hear every day. That's right, I hear voices! Voices from the past like those of my mom and dad and pastors and teachers. I even hear the voice of God, challenging me to do my best. It's a good challenge that I need to hear often. Without it, I've been known to get a little slack.

It's those voices that cheer me on during the most challenging times of life.

The Bible reminds us, "Whatever you do, do it as unto the Lord." And we are to do so with all of our heart. In other words, do it as if God were watching because He is. He created us, and there's no doubt He is cheering us on and loves to see us succeed. Are you doing the best you can, right where you are, with what you have? Someone is counting on it!

Do you tend to give it your best all the time or do you tend to slack off when things get tough?

Think about people from your past or in your present who consistently encourage you to give your best. Pause to thank God for them, then give your best to this day and every day!

May 25
Missing Out

Scripture for Today: 1 Peter 1:3–5

Could it be that God has a much better life for you than you're aware?

I read about a family that was planning a 4-day trip. The wife booked the hotel. When she told her husband the details, he was extremely frustrated over the high cost of the hotel and wanted to cancel. The wife was frustrated too, but she assured him she would save some money by taking their own food for meals instead of eating out. So, he agreed.

For the first three days, as they went out for adventure, they bypassed the beautiful dining hall filled with people smiling eating the best food money could buy. They, instead, ate fruit, sardines, peanut butter crackers, and the like. As they prepared to checkout for the final day, the desk clerk asked them if they would like to schedule their final breakfast for the next morning, since all the meals are INCLUDED in the price!

Could it be that you're making the same mistake? Don't miss out on the best life possible simply because you're unaware of God's promises.

When is the last time you asked for something in prayer based on a promise in the Bible?

If you are guilty of missing God's promises, dig into His Word today and come away with riches you've been missing.

May 26
The Faith of Job

Scripture for Today: Job 1:13–22

Do you ever feel like your whole world is crumbling? How does it affect your faith in God? Perhaps you lost your job, your house, your marriage, your retirement, or a family member.

Few in history have endured more loss in less time than the biblical character Job. He lost his children, his wealth, and his health in a matter of days. It's understandable that he felt alone, depressed, and forsaken by God. He said he looked everywhere, but he could not see or feel the presence of God anywhere. He had been a man of great faith in God, but nothing was working out the way he had planned. As he sat in pain, nursing open sores, broke, and weeping for his dead children, his angry wife told him to curse God and die. His friends blamed him for his own tragedies.

But Job's faith in God took center stage as he said, "The Lord gave and the Lord has taken away. May the Name of the Lord be praised!" Job was a wise man!

What is your response when bad things happen? Do you complain or trust God?

When we truly trust God in times of trial, we can say with Job, "The Lord gave and the Lord has taken away." Ask God to open your eyes to that truth so you too can say, "May the Name of the Lord be praised!"

May 27
Rich People

Scripture for Today: Matthew 19:24

What are your thoughts about rich people? Rich people have been greatly demonized by some of our leading politicians, as if being rich is a crime. I'm thankful for those rich people. Every hard-working American is paid by a rich person. If you have a job, you can thank a rich person. I've never been given a paycheck by a poor man. Rich people gave birth to our hospitals, universities, museums, and many of the national parks and vacation spots we enjoy. Besides, you, my friend, are a lot richer than you'd like to think.

Now for those who are rich, the Bible gives a warning. It's easier for a camel to go through the eye of a needle than for a rich man to go to Heaven. Impossible then, you say? "But with God," Jesus said, "all things are possible!" Both rich and poor go to heaven the same way: through faith in Jesus Christ. Because of Him, I'm so rich I'll be walking on streets of gold someday. How about you?

Do you think of yourself as rich? How many genuinely rich people do you know?

Regardless of your net worth, are you trusting in your wealth for what only Jesus can do? Have you turned to Jesus alone for salvation? If not, do that now. Earthly riches can never save.

May 28
A Healthy Soul

Scripture for Today: Psalm 62:5, 131:2

What's happening on the inside? Do you have a healthy soul? There are some things you can do to build and maintain a healthy soul.

Practice humility toward God and other people. You will need to practice it, because it won't happen automatically. We tend to lean toward pride, thinking we are smarter than God and better than other people. But practicing humility will add strength to your soul.

And don't play God. You are not in control of everything. There are some things you simply cannot do. There are things you will never understand. Let it go. Simply trust Him. Don't try to be Him and you will feel the stress and pressure dissipate. It will be good for your soul.

And calm down. We really do live life today at a faster pace than ever before. Instead of walking, sailing, or riding a horse, we travel in cars and planes at breakneck speed. Our schedules leave little room for the simple things of life. Stop. Sit down. Be quiet. Calm down. It will be good for your soul.

Do you think your soul is healthy or unhealthy?

What is your biggest obstacle to a healthy soul? Ask God for the power and wisdom to address it so you can enjoy quiet and calmness in your soul.

May 29
Slow to Anger

Scripture for Today: Ephesians 4:2

Have you ever felt like you were in a slow cooker where the heat and pressure were gradually breaking you down like a tender piece of roast beef? That process is not a good feeling while it's happening, but it's necessary to help us become the best person possible. Being tender, gracious, kind, and sweet are amazing qualities in a person, but they are not easy qualities to attain. Neither are they easy to keep once you have them.

They are directly connected to our level of patience. Patience is our ability to wait without getting angry. Little patience means quick to get angry. Much patience means slow to get angry. We are all too familiar with the battle between those two extremes.

There's no such thing as quick or instant success. The best things in life are going to take a while.

So, the next time you find yourself in a slow cooker situation, just remember, God is increasing your level of patience. He's helping you become more tender, gracious, kind, and sweet.

How do you usually respond under pressure? Do you cook like a roast to tender perfecting or blow your top?

Patience can be a hard lesson, but it is worthwhile. Ask God to help you to respond well when it comes.

May 30
Racial Unity

Scripture for Today: Ephesians 2:11–22

How well do you connect with people who are different than you?

With over 7 billion people in the world today, you won't have to go very far to find someone who's vastly different. That shouldn't frighten you; it should excite you.

As a follower of Jesus Christ, I'm reminded that Jesus died for the sins of the whole world. He commanded believers to go throughout the whole world and make disciples of Jesus. Red, yellow, black, and white, they are all precious in His sight. The Bible describes heaven as a place where a multitude of believers from every nation, tribe, people, and language will worship Jesus together.

Yet, for some reason, even most churches still huddle together each Sunday with people who are racially the same. Often, they are fearful of the day someone from another race joins them for worship. In a country such as ours, there should be no such thing as a black church, white church, or any other exclusively racial church. If we're going to worship Jesus together in heaven someday, why not today?

How many friends of different races do you regularly engage with?

How do you think God sees churches that reject people based on race?

Ask God to help you live a life that demonstrates love and grace for all people.

May 31st
Memorial Day

Scripture for Today: Colossians 3:15

How will you observe Memorial Day? It's not about a long weekend or family cookout. It's about the highest sacrifice possible for our freedom.

A few years ago, my family and I went to visit some friends in Europe. It was inspiring to visit historical sites and memorials about the events and people of the past: the last port of departure for the Titanic in Ireland, or Waterloo, Belgium where Napoleon was defeated.

After a quick drive to Germany, my Flemish friend said, "There is one more place you should see before returning home." He took us to the Henri-Chappelle American Cemetery in the hills of eastern Belgium. There rest the remains of 7,992 American soldiers who said goodbye to their families, left for war, and never returned. Its large American flag flying high over the distant land is a memorial of the cost of freedom. We wept as we walked through. There are twenty-four such American cemeteries on foreign soil around the world with almost 125,000 graves. Memorial Day is a day to remember and say, "Thank You!"

Have you thanked God recently for living with the freedoms you enjoy?

If you know someone who is related to a fallen servicemen or servicewoman, express your appreciation to them today because there is a strong chance they are still hurting.

June 1
Love Someone

Scripture for Today: John 3:16, 2 Corinthians 5:14

Why not just love someone today?

It seems like so many people are looking for someone to hate, resent, be jealous of, or be contrary toward. Too many seem to need an enemy! Someone they can argue with, be mad at, and despise.

There are two big lies in today's culture. The first is if you disagree with someone's beliefs, actions, behavior, or lifestyle, then you *must* hate them, fear them, or treat them with contempt and disrespect.

The second lie is to love someone means you *must* agree with everything they believe, say, or do.

I'm glad God chose to love me in spite of my sin. In more ways than we can count, God blesses the just and the unjust, the people who follow Him and the people who choose not to, the people who love Him and the people who ignore Him. He does not change His mind to conform to a person's sinful lifestyle, and neither must we.

So just love someone today, whether you feel they deserve it or not.

Is there a group of people you find harder to love than others? Why do you think that is?

The love of Christ compels us to love others. Ask Him for that kind of love to flood you today.

June 2
Better

Scripture for Today: Proverbs 27:23–24

How well are you doing? You know, with those New Year's resolutions you made six months ago? Have you lost any weight? Planning to be in church again this weekend? Are you still giving your best at work and at home? Spending more quality time with your spouse and kids?

All the decisions made as New Year resolutions each year can be summarized with one phrase. They are *decisions to get better.* Better at something that will improve your life and the lives of those you love. And "better" is always a good thing, because "better" is the bridge to being great!

Most people desire to have a better life, and many will make the decision to do something about it. But getting better is found in how we live today, and every day that follows. Following through and developing better habits is the only way to get better. Yesterday ended last night, so don't think too much about what might have been, should have been, or could have been. Simply learn from it so today and tomorrow can be better.

Do you tend to focus on what might have been rather than what might be?

What decisions can you make today to help you be better tomorrow?

June 3
Idiot

Scripture for Today: Ecclesiastes 2:13–14

"Everything happens for a reason!" You've heard that before, haven't you? Well, it's true. Everything does happen for a reason. We often use the phrase to explain things we don't understand. You know, it makes us feel a little better if we believe God was involved and we can see a higher purpose—and there's no doubt that sometimes that's the case. God is involved, and He does work in our lives through the events we face each day.

But there's another side of the story that I heard recently. Everything does happen for a reason. And that reason is sometimes because you're an idiot and you did something really stupid. And as a result of that really stupid thing you did, something bad happened. God doesn't need to get the blame for that! It was your mouth, your actions, your betrayal, or your bad behavior that caused it. Take responsibility and try to fix it if possible.

God will help you learn from it and become a little wiser for the next time.

What is the most idiotic thing you've done recently? Are you still feeling the effects?

The next time you are tempted to make an idiotic choice, look for what God's purpose might be in the happening, then ask Him for strength to live out His purpose.

June 4
Simplicity

Scripture for Today: Hebrews 4:9–11

Does your life feel chaotic and complex? I've learned to appreciate the simple things of life: a pretty sunset in the evening, a cup of coffee in the morning, a round of golf with a friend, or a warm fire on a cold day. In each moment I find a sense of rest, and I'd often like to stay in that moment forever!

But like many of you, I live a busy life and my responsibilities are very demanding. I feel the pressure. I have a large team of employees and a church who rely on my guidance. A wife, kids, and grandkids who are counting on me. Decisions must be made. Plans for the future must be developed. Bills must be paid. I'm tired just thinking about it!

But I find great rest in my relationship with God, in keeping a clean heart, and in appreciating the simple things. Because rest is the result of what's on the inside, regardless of how busy we are on the outside.

How much complexity in your life needs to be simplified? Are you wearing yourself out spinning plates?

Have you come to experience God's rest He makes available for His children? If not, why don't you surrender to Him now.

June 5
Today Matters

Scripture for Today: James 4:14

Is it that time already? Yes, the year is almost half-over and it seems like just yesterday we were celebrating as one year came to a close and a new year began.

When I was a kid, I recall older people talking about how time flies, how it seems to go faster as we get older. Now I know exactly what they were talking about! Life really is like a vapor. We are here for a little while and then we vanish away as a new generation takes our place. That's why today matters.

Every action you take today and every interaction you have today matters: the people you meet, the choices you make, the attitude you have, the commitments you keep, and the character you develop. These things matter today more than we can imagine because they contribute to who we'll be tomorrow. And yes, we can experience God's forgiveness for even our worst failures in the past, but we will never forget those failures as we move into the future. So today, be wise and live well.

Does it seem like time is going by faster and faster?

What decision have you been delaying that you can make today so tomorrow will be a clean slate when it arrives?

June 6th
Jump Start Your Finances

Scripture for Today: Proverbs 27:23–24

Are you preparing well for your financial future? In his helpful book Start Late, Finish Rich, author David Bach gives some great advice.

He gives three practices you can start early that will pay dividends in the long run: finding your "Double Latte factor," pay yourself first, and make saving automatic.

The Double Latte factor refers to those things we spend money on that we don't have to. They bring us enjoyment, but if we didn't have them we'd still be alright. If you don't buy a $3.50 latte a day how much can you save in 10 years?

Paying yourself first means to prioritize savings while using the tax advantages you can to get more of your money for yourself!

Make saving automatic by having a certain amount automatically deducted from your salary and deposited in an IRA or a 401(k). Keeping some money inaccessible prevents us from easily misspending it.

Not everyone will be rich and that's okay. But everyone can be better prepared financially. Why not you?

What are some indulgences you can cut back on and still enjoy life?

Strike a balance between spending and saving that better prepares you for the years ahead. You won't be sorry.

June 7
Joseph and Doing the Right Thing

Scripture for Today: Genesis 45:7–8

How do you respond when life doesn't turn out so well? Especially when you've tried so hard to do the right thing?

We can learn a lot from the story of Joseph in the Book of Genesis, the first book of the Bible.

He honored his parents, but his brothers sold him into slavery. He worked hard for his master, but was falsely accused of attempted rape and thrown into prison. He helped his fellow prisoners, but was forgotten and left there to rot. Finally, at the age of 30, he interpreted Pharaoh's dream and as a result, was made the Prime Minister of Egypt. In that role he not only saved Egypt from starvation, but his family as well, including his brothers who had sold him into slavery. Joseph wisely explained, "What you intended for evil against me, God intended for good, that He might preserve our family." The truth is, God is wiser, and He sees farther than the rest of us. So, relax, and keep doing the right thing!

What "right thing" have you been doing that has felt pointless?

Ask God to help you continue doing the right thing even when it looks like you aren't making any progress.

June 8
Priorities

Scripture for Today: James 4:13–17

Do you ever struggle with knowing what to do and when to do it? Sometimes, with so many people wanting something from us and so many things requiring our attention, it's hard to know what to do. The pressure can be too much to handle and we begin to feel overwhelmed. At that point we retreat and do nothing.

I often remind my leadership team, "If you don't plan your life, someone else will!" You must establish your own priorities and get them on your calendar. It's much easier to say "No" to other people's agenda if you have a clear agenda of your own. There are three words that will help you in your process of discovering what's important each day.

Number one is Requirement- What's required of me, by God, by family, and employer?
Number two is Return- What effort will give me the greatest return toward my goals?
And number three is Reward- What gives me the greatest satisfaction and reward?

Remember, if you don't plan your life, someone else will!

If you use a calendar app, put a daily reminder with the words "requirement," "return," and "reward." Use the reminder to reflect on the concepts often.

Ask God to make your priorities line up with His priorities.

June 9
Flip-Flop Faith

Scripture for Today: John 14:6

How long will you hesitate between two opinions? That was Elijah's question to his fellow countrymen who now worshipped pagan gods instead of the true God of the universe. Their ancestors had been fully devoted to the true God, but the new generation struggled to make a clear concrete decision of faith. They flip-flopped back and forth between gods. They did not want to declare themselves, leaving their options open.

I remember a man who wanted me to baptize him. As I talked to him about sin, forgiveness, and salvation, he interrupted and said, "Let me make this clear. I've been baptized as a Mormon, a Catholic, a Methodist, and Church of Christ. I also want to be baptized a Baptist. I'm just trying to cover all my bases to make sure I get into Heaven!" I informed him, that's not how it works. Jesus is the one and only Savior, not some denomination.

Don't hesitate or flip-flop with your faith! Jesus is the way, the truth, and the life. No one goes to heaven except through Him.

Are you trusting in something like baptism, church membership, your good reputation, or something else for eternal life?

If so, you need to turn from those things because they will not save. Repent from your sins and believe in Jesus alone to save you from your sins and make you right with God.

June 10
Bible Verse

Scripture for Today: Psalm 119: 1–2

Do you have a favorite verse in the Bible? I call it a Life Verse. You know, it's that verse you turn to time and time again when life seems to go haywire; when things happen you don't understand; or you face a decision that requires the greatest wisdom and discernment. God's Word is always a good "lamp for our feet and a light for our path." There's nothing like having that Life Verse that seems to help get our feet back on solid ground.

For me it's Proverbs 3:5-6, "Trust in the LORD with all your heart, and do not rely on your own understanding. Think about Him in all your ways and He will guide you on the right paths!" The entire Bible is important, but I love having that Life Verse that has been my faithful and wise friend through some of my most difficult journeys. What's yours? Take a fresh look at it today.

Do you have a Life Verse? Try to share it with someone this week and explain to them why it is your Life Verse.

If you don't have one, read the Bible more slowly than usual over the next few weeks, asking God to impress you with a verse you can lean on the rest of your days.

June 11
Spiritually Dry

Scripture for Today: John 7:37–38

Have you ever been truly thirsty with no water in sight? Nothing makes us more aware of our need for water than going through dry barren places. I have spent days in the Sahara Desert, serving the people there. I baptized many people who responded to the gospel, giving their lives to Jesus. It took several hours to fill the baptism tank one bucket at a time. The water pump was over a mile away. It was the first and last time most of the people ever had their heads under water. All of them have known what it's like to be truly dry and thirsty.

But at least now, they have living water flowing through their life. Jesus promised, "If anyone is thirsty, let him come to me and drink. Whoever believes in Me will have rivers of living water flowing out of his heart!"

You may be going through a dry, barren, and difficult time in your life. You don't have to remain thirsty. Jesus can turn you into a mighty river, bringing life to others.

Are you in a spiritually dry period right now? Have you come out of one recently?

Jesus is the Living Water. Pause and ask Him to refresh you with Himself.

June 12
Stand Tall, Fall Hard

Scripture for Today: Ephesians 6:10–18

What's your next move? As you take it, will it cause you to stand tall or fall hard? Life is full of choices and decisions that, once made, lead us to do one or the other. When we make the right moves, we stand tall. We feel bigger than life, almost superhuman. Batman, Superman, or Wonder Woman come to mind!

But when we make the wrong moves, we fall hard. We feel like a failure, a little like the scum of the earth.

I know very well what it feels like to do both. No one plays the game of life perfectly. About the time we figure out how to play it well, it seems like some of the rules are changed, or we face an unexpected storm that gets us sidetracked. The game of life is not played in a stable environment where everything stays the same, allowing us to simply do what we've always done. It's an adventurous journey of faith that is best lived with our heart being guided by God's Word and God's hand.

Did your last big decision end with standing tall or falling hard? Which decision was it?

Do you consider your daily life to be walking in faith? God's Word will increase your faith empowering you to stand tall. If you haven't been spending much time in the Bible, plan to do so in the days ahead.

June 13
Kindness

Scripture for Today: Galatians 5:22–23

Can you think of an act of kindness that someone has shown you recently? Our selfish and ungrateful nature can easily recall our disappointments from the past, but an act of kindness...? Well, we'll have to think about that for a moment. But there are plenty of them: a smile and a kind word to brighten our day; someone treats us for lunch; another sends a Facebook message to see how we're doing. These are all simple things but they should be met with a sense of gratitude. They did not have to do these things, but they did.

The greatest act of kindness ever shown to humankind was when Jesus suffered and died to pay for my sins and yours so we could be forgiven and have eternal life. He did not have to, but He did. Our selfish and ungrateful nature will remind us of disappointments for which we should blame God. But reach a little deeper and instead be thankful for His kindness. Be grateful enough to go to church this week to celebrate His gift of eternal life!

Do you typically find it easier to be kind or not? What most often brings out kindness in you?

Kindness is a fruit of the Spirit. Submit to His guidance to bring from you the kindness needed to bless the people around you today.

June 14
The Tongue

Scripture for Today: James 3:3–12

Have you ever seen a delivery package that reads: "Caution! Handle with Care"? I always wonder what's on the inside of that package.

We all have something similar inside us and we need that warning every day. You know, Caution: Handle with Care!

That dangerous thing on the inside is our tongue. The Bible gives us a clear warning. Our tongue pollutes our entire body. It sets the course of life on fire. We can tame the beasts of the forest, but no man can tame the tongue. It's a restless evil that is full of deadly poison. With it we try to bless God one minute and curse man who was created by God the next. This is not the way it should be!

Our tongue, though it's a small part of our body, can have a profound impact. Much like how a small fire can burn an entire forest, or a small rudder can control a massive ship. Yes, my friend, your tongue is a powerful item! So, Caution: Handle with Care!

Has your tongue gotten you into any trouble lately? Has it set any fires? Damaged any friends?

Scripture teaches us that those who control their speech are able to control their entire body. Ask God to bridle your tongue so your speech reflects His glory.

June 15
Fathers

Scripture for Today: Proverbs 23:24

How's your relationship with your father? Every year, Father's Day is a reminder of this powerful relationship.

Being a father is complex, stressful, and overwhelming. Provider. Protector. Teacher. Corrector. Our father's voice is the loudest in our soul. It can be a voice of blessing or cursing, but it's always there. There's no "how-to" manual that guarantees success. Even if someone's an outstanding father, there's no guarantee their kid will heed their instruction.

My father died several years ago, but his words of wisdom still speak loudly inside me. I have great memories and plenty of stories to tell my grandkids about their great-grandfather.

Every kid longs to hear two phrases from their father: "I love you!" and "I'm proud of you!" So, if you're a father, let your kids hear that from you this week.

Most fathers feel undervalued and unappreciated. If your father is still around, show them some love this week. You wouldn't be here without your father.

How would you describe your relationship to your father? If you are a father, how would you describe your relationship to your children?

Our heavenly Father sets the example of how we are to love our children. Was your father a good example of this to you? If you are a father, do your children see God's love in you?

June 16
A Good Attitude

Scripture for Today: Mark 12:35–37

Does your attitude attract people or repel people? We have bad days from time to time, but we have to make sure our attitude is one to which people are attracted. We are not in this world alone. We must work together with other people in every area of life. God designed it that way.

My wife walked across the street to get our mail out of the mailbox as I waited in the car. As she opened the box door, her reaction and refusal to reach in and get the mail told me something was wrong. As a prank, someone had put some sugary food in my mailbox. Its' power of attractional sweetness had caused at least a billion ants to climb a post and work their way into the mailbox. The inside of my box, along with my mail was completely infested. Yes it was a scary sight, but it was also a beautiful reminder of the power of attraction. So be nice, friendly, kind, and sweet. To do so is a powerful thing!

Be honest with yourself: does your normal attitude attract people or repel people?

Having the mind of Christ will lead to having an attitude like His. Submit yourself to Jesus, allow His mind to fill yours, and have an attitude that draws people to yourself and to Him.

June 17
Determination

Scripture for Today: Philippians 3:12–14

How much determination do you have? Toddlers have it in abundance as they continue to reach for things we don't want them to have, long after we've told them "NO." They stay focused and continue to find a way to get what we thought was out of reach. And to our dismay and frustration, they often succeed.

Why can't we seem to find that determination when we need it as adults? You know, when our dreams, goals, and ambitions continue to be just out of reach, or a new obstacle keeps getting in the way. It's a fact that life is hard, and the challenges and pressures we face can easily take us to a place of discouragement and despair. Maybe we should go back to our childhood and find determination. We must take responsibility to overcome our own challenges. We can and should pray during such times, but God's answer might require us to simply dig a little deeper and try a little harder. Don't simply cry about it like a baby; be determined like a toddler.

In what area of your life (work, marriage, school, ministry) is determination needed right now?

Considering today's scripture reading, do you have the spiritual determination of Paul? Are you making every effort to pursue spiritual growth?

June 18
Halftime

Scripture for Today: Luke 14:28

Has it sunk in that the month of June has officially arrived? It seems like yesterday we were celebrating and setting goals for the New Year! We wrote down things like: lose some weight, go back to school, read through the Bible, and go to church every Sunday. Well, how are you doing with all of that stuff? It's more than just stuff. It's your future we're talking about!

June is what I call the halftime month. It's a time to stop and evaluate. And if you're not doing so well, it's a time to get back on track before the month of July! If you don't adjust now, it's likely you won't! And it's likely you'll get to the end of the year, look back, and blame God, the government, and everyone else around you that your miserable life is right where it was a year ago. But instead you can just look at your stubborn lazy self in the mirror and blame that person. Or better yet...you can get back on track this month. It's just the month of June! You still have time to have an amazing year!

Do you re-evaluate yourself at halftime or plow on through?

Take some time this week to see where you are on your goals for this year and adjust your plans as necessary.

June 19
Gratitude and Generosity

Scripture for Today: Exodus 20:17, Hebrews 13:5

Do you ever struggle with having nice things? Sometimes we dream of having a nice home, a new car, a boat, a motorcycle, or to go on a nice family vacation, but we're broke. We've had a hardship, or simply don't make enough money right now to support some of those dreams. As we see others enjoy the things we would like to have, misery, resentment, and jealousy set in. Regardless of what we have, somehow we feel entitled to have more, even if we cannot afford that lifestyle.

And others who have such things often feel guilty, even if they can afford them. And they struggle to enjoy them. They think somehow that it's wrong to have nice things, and that God is opposed to people enjoying life.

The answer to both of these struggles is to live a life of gratitude AND generosity. Nowhere in the Bible does God condemn or condone poverty or wealth. But we are clearly challenged to have a grateful and generous heart, regardless of our current economic status.

Do you struggle more with having more than enough or envying those who do?

Think back through the past few months. How generous have you been in giving to others or giving to God?

June 20
Memories with Family

Scripture for Today: Acts 10:1–2

Are you making some good memories with your family? God designed the family to be a positive guiding force in life. Together we explore the mysteries, learn our heritage, dream of the future, celebrate accomplishments, and mourn losses. Families are the first people to embrace us when we are born, and they are usually the last people to say goodbye before we die. And in between birth and death, we experience things that become memories that either bless us or haunt us until it's our turn to die.

So I'll ask you again. Are you making some good memories with your family? I remember hunting and playing golf with my brothers; fishing, plowing, or hanging out with dad in his store; working on the farm with MawMaw and PawPaw; and cutting grass and eating a good meal with mom. I remember simple vacations at Coleman's Lake or Panama City Beach as a family. Many of them are gone now, but I greatly treasure the memories. Now it's my turn to make some new ones with my family. How about you?

Do you have good family memories from when you were young? Take a second to thank God for them.

Sometimes family memories are not good. Some people have to work through them before they find joy on the other side. Does that describe you?

What kind of memories can you be making with your own family right now that will bless them for years to come?

June 21
Being a Nibbler

Scripture for Today: 1 Peter 2:2

When it comes to eating, are you a nibbler? The reality is that nibblers have a tendency to weigh a few more pounds than non-nibblers. It may not seem like a small bite here and there will make much of a difference, but over time, it definitely does.

The same is true with reading your Bible. When taking in God's Word, nibbling would be reading just a verse or two. It takes less than 30 seconds. It may not seem like a verse or two here and there will make much of a difference, but over time, it definitely does. Using a free Bible app and its verse for the day, it's easier to be a Bible nibbler than ever before!

So often we think we just don't have time to get the spiritual nourishment we need. We think we have to have a full course meal, which might be a chapter or two. But in reality, a little nibbling can make a big difference in your spiritual journey. And a nibble is always better than nothing!

The most popular app for Bible reading is simply called the Bible App. Check the app store for your smartphone to find it, then use it to constantly nibble God's Word.

June 22
Togetherness

Scripture for Today: Psalm 133:1–3

Together! Now that's a beautiful concept, is it not?

"They've been together for 50 years."
"That team really works well together."
"Now they have their act together."

Anytime we hear such statements, we are reminded of deep commitment, intentional unity, and meticulous discipline. And we are inspired, because we all know that working together is hard work, but it leads to success.

Togetherness is always inspiring to watch: an engine that's working on all eight cylinders, a team of which every member is working for the win, a man and woman working through the hardships of life to have an amazing marriage, or a Triple Crown race horse like Secretariat or American Pharaoh as all four legs and feet flowed in perfect harmony and rhythm crossing the finish line. There's nothing left but the celebration!

Are you working together with your team, your staff, your family, and your church to bring about success? Togetherness is always a beautiful thing.

Do you normally prefer to work with teams or alone? Are you willing to submit your preferences to the best outcome for your team?

Ask God to help you work with the people around you for the success of the teams you work with.

June 23
Competence

Scripture for Today: James 1:56

Have you ever dealt with someone who is supposed to be competent in a particular job, but it just doesn't show? A singer who can't sing. A speaker who can't speak. A preacher who can't preach. A chef who can't cook. A leader who can't lead. Such experiences are always frustrating.

Incompetence is sometimes a matter of lack-of-giftedness, such as singing. All of the lessons in the world can't make a great singer out of someone who can't sing.

But more often than not, competence is a skill that's learned through hard work and discipline. It begins as an attitude and mindset for how everyday life is to be approached.

Competent people are always committed to excellence, and they never settle for being average or mediocre. They pay great attention to detail, especially in the little jobs they face. And they're committed to do their best, all the time, every day.

Yes, a mindset of competence virtually forces success in your direction, so be competent and get ready for a better life!

About what subjects or skills do you feel competent? Incompetent?

If you need to raise your competence level, read a book, talk to an expert, or enroll in a class. But, most of all, ask God to give you the wisdom you need to excel.

June 24
Bumper Stickers and Forgiveness

Scripture for Today: Colossians 3:13

Bumper stickers have some great sayings these days, don't they? "Warning: Don't drive close. Driver chewing tobacco!", "Don't laugh. It's paid for!", or "You mean, I left the womb for this?"

People are always trying to communicate a message that's humorous or important to them, but sometimes our driving style gets in the way.

I had one on my car that read, "God on Board!" Then someone said, "The way you drive you're going to kill Him," so I removed it.

One bumper sticker reads, "Christians are not perfect, just forgiven." It's a true concept that sounds simple but is hard to comprehend. Many who first begin to follow Jesus are surprised when they mess up and sin after doing so. Many who are not followers of Jesus are quick to point out the sins of those who are, as if they will be perfect. It seems impossible that through faith in Jesus my sins are forgiven, but that's the miracle of salvation that guarantees I'm going to Heaven someday. You can too.

Do you know of God's forgiveness of sins?

If not, turn from your sins now and turn to Christ. He will forgive you and bring you into His family forever.

June 25
Adaptability

Scripture for Today: 1 Peter 5:8–9

How adaptable are you? Adaptability is essential to have a winning strategy for reaching your goals, especially if you're working with others to accomplish a major task. Sometimes we have to change roles on the team or quickly change strategies in order to bring about success.

A few years ago I visited Waterloo in Belgium, the site where the famous General Napoleon Bonaparte was finally defeated. While Napoleon had an Army of 72,000 men, his defeat had required an allied force of almost twice that many.

What had been the real strength of Napoleon's success? He loved to be on the battlefield so he could see the movements of the enemy and adapt his strategy. The Duke of Wellington, one of Napoleon's fiercest enemies said he considered Napoleon's presence on the Battlefield equal to 40,000 men!

The Bible warns us "our enemy walks around like a roaring lion, seeking to devour us." But our heavenly Father will lead us to victory every time if we'll adapt to His plans.

Can you think of a time you've had to adapt yourself to a change in your life?

How about adapting your life to keep following God? Sometimes that means moving or shifting our daily patterns to be obedient. Ask God to help you always be adaptable so you can always be ready to advance the Kingdom.

June 26
Disillusionment

Scripture for Today: Psalm 74

Have you ever been disillusioned with God? Over 50% of church members don't go to church regularly. At one point they were baptized and went to church every weekend; but something happened. A death, a divorce, a financial crisis, or a disappointment when God did not answer a prayer the way they thought He should.

Well I've been there! I prayed for a young mother to be healed of cancer, but weeks later I stood and faced her two little girls at her funeral service. I prayed for God to let my brother live after his car accident, but he did not. I invested financially for many years and prayed that God would multiply it, but it vanished. Soon thereafter my dad died and then a year later my mom died after a 12-week battle with brain cancer. Was I disappointed with God? Absolutely! But I will still be in church each weekend to gather with other believers to tell God how awesome He is; because I don't have time to list all the amazing blessings He has given me.

Have you ever caught yourself focusing on the bad things that have happened to you rather than God's blessings? It's a trap.

The old song says, "Count your many blessings name them one by one." If you haven't done that recently, write down specifically as many blessings as you can remember, then praise God for them. It's the cure for disillusionment.

June 27
Jesus

Scripture for Today: Psalm 16

Who is Jesus? Jesus Himself first asked the question, "Who do people say that I am?" Then he asked his disciples, "Who do you say that I am?" It was an important question and it's just as important today.

The prophets in the Old Testament had clearly described him several hundred years before his birth. Isaiah said, "When a virgin girl gives birth to a son, you can call him Immanuel" meaning "God is with us." He also wrote that "he would suffer for our sins." Micah said he would be born in the city of Bethlehem.

Around 850 years before the event, Psalm 22 describes details about the crucifixion of Jesus: that his hands and feet would be pierced, some would gamble for his garments, and He would feel forsaken even by God the Father. In Psalm 16 we are even told of his resurrection. Jesus fulfilled every indicator just like it was written. Jesus Christ is the Son of God, the one and only Savior of the world. You'd better get that one right.

Have you already come to know Jesus as the one and only Son of God?

He is the promised King, the Lamb of God, and the Savior of the world. If you haven't already, yield your life to Jesus and trust Him to save you as He has billions of others through history and today.

June 28
Loving Your Neighbor

Scripture for Today: Leviticus 19:18; Matthew 19:19

Do you ever find it hard to love someone else? The Bible tells us to love our neighbor, but it isn't just talking about the person who lives on the property beside you. It means anyone you come into contact with!

"Love your neighbor" is one of the most quoted verses in the Bible but can be one of the hardest commandments to obey! There is a reason that loving your neighbor is listed as the second greatest commandment right after loving God with all your heart!

Part of loving God with all your heart is learning to see everyone else as people who reflect the image of God. You and I were made in the image of God, but so was every person on Earth! Your coworker, your children, that person in traffic, but also that person who looks differently than you, lives differently than you, and believes differently than you were all made in the image of the God of the universe! Isn't that amazing? When you commit to loving God, you are also committing to loving the people made in His image. You are committing to love everyone!

Do you struggle with seeing people as being made in the image of God? Why or why not?

What are practices you can implement in your day to day to help you remember to love your neighbor?

June 29
The Sifting of Peter

Scripture for Today: Luke 22:31

Are you feeling the pressure of being tested? I never enjoyed being tested!

A few days before Jesus went to the cross, He gave some startling information to Peter, his most passionate follower. "Satan desires to sift you like wheat!" It was sort of like saying, "Satan wants to put the squeeze on you" or "put you through the ringer" or "lead you astray, turn your life upside down, confuse you, ruin you, and make your life miserable through failure!" Yeah, that was Jesus' message to Peter and it's a warning for us today.

But then Jesus said, "I have prayed for you that your faith may not fail. And when you turn back to me, strengthen the others."

The testing and temptation of Peter are reminders of our own battles with sin, and of our need for a Savior. At some point, all of us have been sifted, put through the ringer, gone astray, become confused, and feel ruined. We have felt forsaken by God, but it was we who forsook Him!

Pick up your faith again! Jesus knows our journey and is eager for us to walk faithfully with Him!

Do you know what it feels like to be sifted by Satan?

Do you realize that Jesus stands with you and protects you? Call on Him as soon as the sifting starts so His strength can be yours.

June 30
Life Is Short

Scripture for Today: 1 Chronicles 29:15, 1 Peter 1:23-25

Do you ever sit back in amazement at how fast time goes by? Wow, it seems like just yesterday I was in the birthing room where my kids were being born. Now both of them are married and now I'm a grandpa!

I remember sitting in my grandpa's lap as he read me a story. Now I'm the old guy who is doing the reading!

The Bible reminds us that life is short! It's like the beautiful green grass that flourishes in one season, but soon withers away in another.

Life is not only short, but it's also uncertain. And when those two thoughts are put together, it should drive us to live every day with a sense of awareness and commitment to make each day count for something good. It should also drive us to deal with the most important issue of all: where we will spend eternity. I've already dealt with that issue and I'm ready to live to be an old man or to die today, whatever God chooses. Are you?

Does it seem like time goes faster as you get older?

We only get one try at life, so it's important we live it as God wants. That includes being in a right relationship with Him through His Son, Jesus Christ. If you do not know Him, ask Him today to bring you into His family.

July 1
Sufferings

Scripture for Today: Romans 8:18

Have you ever been angry with God over the sufferings you face?

Suffering, pain, and hardship are the foundations of greatness! A life of ease, coddling, comfort, and privilege often lead to being a spoiled brat or an adult without character.

Two famous men once lived in Rome, the capital of the Roman Empire. One was the Emperor and the other a prisoner. One was Nero. The other was Saint Paul. Nero was given the empire at the age of severnteen, and had every indulgence imaginable. Paul had been lied about, beaten, shipwrecked, stoned, and left for dead, and was in prison awaiting his death sentence by Nero. Then it happened—Paul was beheaded. A few months later Nero committed suicide.

Who was great between them? Well, thousands of parents have named their children Paul or Pauline, but I've never heard of another child named Nero. And there are no St. Nero Cathedrals in the world, but there are several named after St. Paul. Don't be angry about your sufferings in this world. Embrace them and let them take you to greatness.

What sufferings have you faced in your life? Are they more or less severe than those listed about Paul above?

Ask God to help you see beyond the sufferings of this present time to the glory He will reveal in you.

July 2
Problems

Scripture for Today: Proverbs 13:4

Do you have any problems? Well that's a joke of a question isn't it? We all have problems. The real question is: Do we face them and deal with them, or do we ignore and run from them? We tend to do the latter and that's an even bigger problem!

Solving problems brings meaning and depth to our life. Problems are the edge upon which we discover failure or success. They force us to choose between being wise or foolish. They require us to either rise with courage or sink with fear and cowardice. They are the stimulus for all of our mental and spiritual growth. It's through confronting and solving problems that we learn and rise to a new level of living. As much as we resent and run from problems, they are often some of God's greatest gifts designed to stretch us, teach us, and deepen our walk with Him.

So, the next time you have a problem, deal with it; growth and wisdom are waiting just around the corner.

Is your tendency to run from problems or deal with them?

Running from problems tends to increase our anxiety because they are always waiting around the next corner. Set aside some time to plan how to deal with any problems you've been running from.

July 3
Nobody

Scripture for Today: Romans 10:9–10, 1 Corinthians 1:26-29

Do you ever feel like a nobody? Like everyone in the world is famous, rich, happy, loved, special, or good looking - except you? Well you're not alone in your thinking. Lots of people feel that way at some point, and usually for all the wrong reasons.

That kind of thinking is based on the flawed human desire to feel elevated above other segments of society. And the fact is: regardless of our wealth, heritage, education, race, or giftedness, we have all sinned and are in desperate need of salvation through Jesus Christ. No one is so special, rich, or gifted, that they can get into heaven on their own. Actually, you *must* become a nobody to get there. To some people's dismay, God has chosen what this world thinks is foolish to shame what this world thinks is wise. And He has chosen what this world thinks is weak to shame what this world thinks is strong.

So, if you feel like a nobody, keep in mind that when we are weak, He is strong!

Some people struggle with feelings of superiority (better than others) and others struggle with feelings of inferiority (worse than others). Are you in either of those groups?

We shouldn't think of ourselves as better than others, or worse than God has made us. Pause and ask God to help you have an accurate view of yourself and live in faith that He sees you that way.

July 4
Erosion

Scripture for Today: Hebrews 2:1

Do you have an erosion problem? I was mowing my lawn and I noticed a new root showing above ground. It was large, and had been under the surface for many years, providing life to the towering oak tree that hovered above it. Now it was bare, and open to the destructive elements of the sun, rain, and lawnmower blades. Over time, erosion had removed it from the safety and coolness of the soil; now it was facing new dangers that were never intended.

Erosion can also impact our physical and spiritual health. Erosion doesn't happen suddenly. It happens slowly over time, as the seasons of life often bring one challenge after another. Age will certainly erode our physical health at some point.

However, our spiritual life can actually get stronger and deeper as we get older, but it's not a guarantee. We fight against spiritual erosion as we walk with God through daily prayer, Bible reading, and worship. And regardless of what life brings on the outside, we can be strong and stable on the inside.

Can you see erosion happening in your soul right now? Are you sliding in your relationship with God?

The deepest soil for every human is to be in the Word of God and in regular prayer. If those things have eroded away from your life, stop right now and renew your commitment to them.

July 5
Clean Up

Scripture for Today: Ephesians 4:32

Have you cleaned up after yourself lately? It's painful, is it not? Many years ago, an old man asked me to visit his wife as she neared death. I told him I'd be glad to make the visit and would do so that week. However, I got busy with other things, and simply forgot. I had good intentions, but I failed to do what I said I would do, and his wife died. In addition to the pain he felt from losing his wife, he was also angry and disappointed with me, and rightly so. A part of me wanted to go hide somewhere. As a matter of fact, he told someone he never wanted to see me again, but I knew I had to face my failure at some point. Knocking on his door was one of the hardest things I had ever done, but I'm thankful my sincere apology was met with forgiveness, and we embraced.

Have your actions caused pain in someone's life? It might be time for you to clean up after yourself!

This is a tough one, isn't it? But it's necessary. Is there anyone in your life you've caused pain for?

Maybe it's time to face up to it and do what you need to do to make it right. Remember: whenever possible a face-to-face conversation is the best.

July 6
Shobane, the Kind Soul

Scripture for Today: Genesis 40:14, Colossians 3:12

Have you considered the impact of a kind-hearted soul? A few years ago, I met a man from the kingdom of Swaziland. His name was Welcome Shobane Matsebula. His name was fitting for his character. Within a few minutes I felt welcomed into his life, his family, and his world. We developed a friendship of love and respect that easily flowed from this kind-hearted soul named Welcome. He was not a wealthy man, but he started an orphanage to feed, house, and educate children without parents. He raised pigs to share with neighbors in his poverty-stricken village. He became a partner in ministry with my church as we taught and trained leaders together in Zimbabwe, Swaziland, and South Africa.

When I received news that Welcome had died from complications with diabetes, I was deeply saddened. We were supposed to teach together the next February in Zimbabwe. Although separated by over 8,000 miles I immediately felt grief over his absence in this world; and, as I wept, I was reminded of the impact of a kind-hearted soul. In honor of Welcome, be a little kinder today!

Who in your life reminds you of Welcome Shobane Matsebula?

Pause and pray for them now, then ask God to work the depth of kindness in you.

July 7
Listen and Learn

Scripture for Today: Proverbs 8:33

Are you listening and learning?

We all know that person who acts like they are the smartest person in the room! We've all been around someone like that before, and if you haven't, maybe that someone is you! It's human nature to want to be the person who has all the answers, but it's not possible for us to know everything without listening to people who have gone before us!

The book of Proverbs is filled with verses about wisdom and instruction and how important it is to let those guide you. Proverbs 8:33 says, "Listen to my instruction and be wise; do not disregard it." To truly be a wise and knowledgeable person means listening to the people in your life who offer you advice and wisdom. Maybe it's a grandparent, a pastor, a boss, a friend, or a spouse. People have different life experiences and the beautiful thing about that is each person can teach us something from their own personal journeys.

We cannot learn lessons that we don't listen to. If we want to be as knowledgeable as we think we are, we must also be teachable! God gave us two ears and one mouth, so listen more and speak less!

Who are people in your life that you look to for wisdom and instruction?

Who in your life looks to you for wisdom and instruction? What are ways that you can teach them?

July 8
Arrogance

Scripture for Today: Isaiah 2:12

Do you ever struggle with arrogance? You know, exaggerated feelings of self-importance. Arrogance is always self-imposed, but it can develop from a variety of sources. Arrogance is no respecter of people. It flows freely from the rich and poor, male and female, religious and irreligious!

But when a person becomes a follower of Jesus Christ, arrogance is one of the first attitudes that must be conquered by God's amazing grace, because following Jesus requires humility. Saul of Tarsus, whom we know as the Apostle Paul, is a great example. Before his conversion, Saul was religious, but he was arrogant, cocky, and aggressive in his dealings with others. He was fearless and brutal as he persecuted followers of Jesus Christ.

Then Jesus transformed his life, and soon his name was changed from Saul of Tarsus to Paul, which actually means "small" or "humble." From Arrogant Saul to Apostle Small and Humble! Wow, what a change! Lose the arrogance, my friend. You aren't that important.

Who is the most arrogant person you know? Is it you? Have you ever asked anyone if you are?

Arrogance is directly opposed to everything God wants to do in us. If God has shown you to be arrogant, ask His forgiveness right now and seek humility instead.

July 9
Happy Times

Scripture for Today: Proverbs 16:20

Do you ever feel like it takes too much to make people happy these days? Some of my greatest memories of happy times have also been simple times. Not extravagant. Not expensive. Not impressive. But happy!

When I was a kid we went camping at Coleman Lake in Fruithurst, Alabama with the Morris family. We fished, threw rocks in the water, sat around the campfire, and listened to Dad and PeeWee tell stories. Then a storm moved in and the rain came. To get out of the rain, both families—all ten of us—piled into the back of Dad's pickup for a fish fry. That's right: fish, hushpuppies, French fries, coleslaw, and tartar sauce!

It was not Disney World or an exotic island somewhere, but as I've traveled the world as an adult, I realize it's one of my favorite memories of happy times. Perhaps because I was with the people I loved. And I knew they loved me. So create some happy times for your kids. Even after they're adults, they'll be glad you did.

How long has it been since you've had a happy time? Was it a long-awaited trip, or a spur-of-the-moment hike, or an unexpected invitation to a concert or game?

It is important to our mental well-being to be happy, and our mental well-being is important to our success. True happiness comes from God alone. Ask God to help you stay focused on Him as the source of all happiness.

July 10
Sacrifice

Scripture for Today: Hebrews 10:12–14

How thankful are you for those who've sacrificed so you could have a better and longer life? Parents, grandparents, military, educators, law enforcement, doctors—the list goes on.

I stood at a riverbank with my wife near the Amazon in Brazil. I had taken her there to celebrate our 10th wedding anniversary! The water was infested with piranhas. We caught some and cooked them for dinner that night. It was also cowboy country, and earlier that day we rode through a large herd of cattle being driven by some rough looking cowboys. They were headed toward the river and would soon have to cross. I asked, "How will they get the cattle across the river without them being wounded or eaten by piranhas?" The answer? "They will drive sacrificial cows into the water upstream and downstream from the herd and shoot them. As the piranhas swim to the blood to devour the sacrificial cows, the rest of the herd can safely cross the river." Wow!

Lots of people have sacrificed so we could live better and longer. But none have had a greater impact than Jesus so we can live for eternity.

Who can you think of right now who has sacrificed for you? Do you know anyone who has actually given their life to protect you?

Jesus' sacrifice is the greatest because it was for the sins of the entire world and because it is for eternity. Have you accepted for yourself what Jesus did for you on the cross?

July 11
Tragic Loss

Scripture for Today: Psalm 18:2

How well do you face difficult challenges in life? You know, disappointments, tragedies, heartaches, betrayals, and such. It doesn't matter who you are, sometimes life really does not seem fair. I recently read that life is ten-percent what happens to us and ninety-percent how we respond to it. I'm sure it's not a scientific statement, but I tend to agree.

Bad things happen to all of us at some point. For some, it's the end of the world, while for others it's the beginning of the most inspiring and adventurous life imaginable. I think of Todd Beamer who on 9/11 fought the terrorist high-jackers of Flight 93 after making a phone call to his wife Lisa. It was their last conversation. His and the other passengers' heroic actions saved the lives of many on the ground, but all their lives were lost in the process.

When Lisa was asked how she felt about her husband's courageous act, she said, "It made my life worth living again!" Wow. In her tragic loss, she found purpose and strength, and you can, too.

Have you ever faced a loss so big you weren't sure you'd ever recover? Have you?

Scripture often uses the imagery of God being our rock. He is our fortress, a place to run for help. Ask Him for His help any time you are in a time of loss.

July 12
Multiply

Scripture for Today: 2 Timothy 2:2

By what mathematical formula are you living through? Adding, subtracting, dividing, or multiplying?

Once I played golf at Farmlinks at Purcell Farms, in Sylacauga, Alabama. While I was in the clubhouse, in walked 85-year-old Jimmy Purcell. Through Purcell Technologies, Jimmy became wealthy developing controlled-release-fertilizers used on golf courses around the world. He spoke as if we were lifelong friends and began to poke at my wife and me, about how blessed I was to have married such an awesome lady! Then he said, "Have you read my book?" I had not, but since he reminded me they were on sale in the clubhouse, I knew I would have to get one.

I'm glad I did. Its title? "Finding The Ultimate Multiplier." He believes that giving his life to Jesus Christ and doing business God's way is the key to his success. If Jesus can take five loaves of bread and two fish and feed thousands, He can take a simple businessman in Sylacauga, and multiply every area of life and reach thousands with the good news of Jesus. I agree with Jimmy!

Are you living your life as a multiplier?

If you are a follower of Jesus, multiplication is foundational to reaching people for Christ; everyone is to reach people. Ask God to help you avoid subtraction and division, then move beyond addition to multiplication.

July 13
Excellence

Scripture for Today: Philippians 2:19–23

What do you do for a living, and do you do it with excellence? Excellence is an attitude long before it becomes an action. It's a commitment to full awareness, to detail, to focus, and to be "all in" to carry out your daily duties.

While making a dinner reservation at a restaurant, I was recently put on hold for six minutes in the middle of the afternoon. I had to wonder why.

At a drive through window, I was recently ignored for an extended period of time. I had to repeat parts of my order several times. When I arrived at the window, they were telling personal stories and I felt like an intruder messing up their punchlines.

I admit there have been times when I was the one who got sidetracked or lost focus, and in every case, it created either frustration or disappointment for someone else.

All of our actions or inactions always affect other people. If someone pays you to do a job, do it with excellence. It's just the right thing to do.

When was the last time you interacted with someone professionally who didn't try to be excellent in their work? Was it frustrating for you?

Commit to do everything with excellence since giving your best honors God.

July 14
Three Keys to Leading in Tough Times

Scripture for Today: Jeremiah 32:27

How well do you lead through tough times? Every leader has a double challenge: not only do you face tough times, but you must lead yourself and others through tough times.

Here are three keys to leading your people in tough times:
1. Keep their heads up.
2. Keep their eyes forward.
3. Keep their feet moving.

Keeping their heads up refers to motivation or their emotional state. Like a coach keeping players motivated during a squeaker of a ballgame, encourage your people so they aren't chins down, but heads up.

Keep their eyes forward by reminding them of your organization's mission and goals. Tough times have a way of blinding people to what is important. Keep their focus on the mission.

Finally, keep their feet moving. Tough times sometimes call for pivots, pauses, or changes of pace. You'll need to lead through all of these at some point, but it's important to keep their feet moving so they can follow your leadership.

What are some ways you can keep your people's heads up?

What are some ways you can keep their eyes forward?

What are some ways you can keep their feet moving?

July 15
Trusting God

Scripture for Today: Proverbs 3:5–6

Do you struggle with trusting God? You can trust me when I say God is trustworthy. He is God and makes no mistakes. That does not mean He works everything out the way we want, but He does work everything out the way He wants, and that's what matters. Life is all about Him, not about you and me! We exist to serve Him, not vice versa. We are here for His pleasure. Not the other way around.

There are four words that help keep me in line with trusting God.
Whatever. Whatever God wants me to do or be, He can count me all in. I trust Him.
Wherever. Wherever God wants me to serve him, He can count me all in. I trust Him.
Whenever. Whenever God wants to interrupt my life or require something of me, I trust him.
And, However. However God wants to work in or through my life, I trust Him.

Has it ever occurred to you that nothing ever occurred to God? You can trust Him!

Do you find there are some things easy to trust God through and some more difficult? Can you identify the line where easy becomes hard?

Remember to make Him known in all your ways and not rely on your own understanding. Trust Him in what you don't understand and let Him make your way straight.

July 16
Looking Back

Scripture for Today: John 14:26

Have you taken a look back lately? No; we should never attempt to live in the past, and we must work to let go of those things that are behind us. But it's a healthy thing to look back from time to time. It can be very beneficial for our future.

Looking back is how we remember the special people in our journey, many of whom have already passed away. That's how we develop gratitude.

Looking back is how we learn from the failures, mistakes, and difficulties in our journey, to prepare us for a better future. That's how we foster wisdom.

Looking back is how we're reminded that time flies by swiftly, whether we have a good plan and attempt our dreams or not. That's how we create a sense of urgency.

Looking back is how we compare the person in the mirror today with who we used to be and who we hope to be. That's how we begin to change. So, take some time to look back. You will be better for it!

How often do you intentionally look back to what has happened in your past to evaluate how you have responded or grown?

Looking back should not always bring grief or sorrow. Ask God to help you be intentional about looking back to develop gratitude, foster wisdom, be urgent, and begin to change!

July 17
Moose Hunt Uphill

Scripture for Today: Isaiah 43:2

Have you figured out yet that life doesn't get easier as we move forward? I was in Alaska with a friend on a moose hunt. We stood on a mountain and saw a bull moose across the valley about two miles below. Our bush-plane pilot had said it should take us a couple of hours to hike down the mountain to the valley, but he was wrong.

To me, a couple of hours means two! But instead, hiking down the mountain was so difficult, the two hours became eight hours. And we were confident it would get much easier when we reached the floor of the valley, but instead it got even harder. Underneath the waist-high grass in the valley was a foot or more of water, making it a massive swamp. The journey was all down-hill or flat, but it was the hardest physical journey of my life! Yes, I killed a nice bull moose, and it was an adventure of a lifetime, but I was reminded that life is like an uphill climb every day, even when it's downhill!

When is the last time you entered a period you thought would be easy that turned into a swamp-slog?

Sometimes the best thing we can do is be determined to go forward whether uphill or downhill. Ask God to keep your terrain from holding you back.

July 18
Look Forward

Scripture for Today: Proverbs 6:6–8

Do you live your life with intentionality? It's important to look back and evaluate where you've been and to look around and see where you are, but it's even more important to look forward and write down your dreams for the future. Really great dreams don't just automatically happen. They must be intentionally planned—a goal set, a strategy developed, and then we must follow the strategy day-after-day until our dream is reached.

And when we do reach the dream, observers all around us will stand and talk about how lucky we are! And they will often wonder why they are not as lucky as we. But they are the ones who will treat this week as every other. They will not look back. They will not look around. And they will not look forward. They will write no dream, make no plan, set no goal, and develop no strategy.

God did not create you so you could hope to be lucky while being lazy. God created you to be intentional and strive for excellence.

What are some of the differences you have noticed between people who are successful and people who aren't?

What are you doing intentionally to make sure your goals come to pass?

July 19
Our Book

Scripture for Today: Matthew 5:16

If your life were a book, what kind of book would it be? Typically, at this time of year we're focused on the "beach books" to read, the blockbuster movies to watch, or the new and healthier habits we decide to embrace after seeing ourselves in a mirror in our bathing suit!

But if your life story were the book being read, would it focus on success or failure, faith or history, adventure or mystery, business or health, or perhaps even horror? As people read the book, what would they learn? Would it inspire them or discourage them? Most importantly, as they approached the bottom of each page, would they be excited to turn the page and read the next to continue the story?

I have found that many people don't like their life. They don't like their past. And they don't like their present. They think their story is not interesting, inspiring, or helpful. If you're one of them, you should know your book is not yet complete. As long as you're living, your story continues. So start writing the rest of your story the way you would love for it to be.

If you are blessed with an average life-span, are you in the early chapters, middle chapters, or later chapters of your book of life?

Regardless of where you are, you can begin writing better chapters than the ones you've already written. Why not ask God, the Divine author, to help you write better chapters for the rest of your life?

July 20
Write Your Own Obituary Now

Scripture for Today: Proverbs 22:1

What's your reputation?

I've attended plenty of funerals in my life and spoken at so many I can't count them. Sometimes, if someone hasn't particularly lived a good life, I've struggled to do the eulogy. I'm usually limited to things like: he or she loved baseball, football, cars, motorcycles, cats, or dogs!

If you think about it, we are writing our own eulogy every day. The way we live, the way we treat people, how we love our families, how we conduct ourselves at business. All of these form our eulogy; it is what people will say about us after we have left this life. What do you want them to say about you?

I want them to say I loved God, my wife, that I loved my kids and grandkids, and that I loved my friends and church.

The Bible tells us to choose a good name more than "great riches." You can have great riches and still have a terrible name. You can amass a fortune but have nobody to say good things when you die, because they don't have a reason. Write your obituary now, and if you live well you will write it well!

Take a few minutes to write the obituary you have written so far in your life. Be honest.

Now, take a few minutes to write the obituary you want your life to write. Be hopeful.

July 21
Hungry

Scripture for Today: John 4:31–32

"Are you hungry?" You might respond with, "I'm starving!" But are you really? I'm not talking about food; I'm talking about life. Being hungry for life is about that gnawing pain in your gut to excel, succeed, and to reach your full potential. Some people have it and some people don't, but all people can and should if they expect to succeed.

God created you for a purpose, to succeed so others can see what an amazing creator He is. Being hungry is all about the desire to find that purpose and give it all you've got. Anything short of that is to settle for less than God created you to do.

You may have accomplished much or feel like you've accomplished little, but either way your future waits for you to discover, "What's next?" Always pause to enjoy the present, but don't pause so long that you forget to ask God, "What's next?" Your future and the people around you need you to be hungry. The world is a better place when you're hungry, so I'm wondering, "What's next"?

Do you ever find yourself hungry for life? Is there a "holy discontent" about your situation?

Stop and ask God "What's next?" for your own life so you can continue moving in the direction He has for you.

July 22
Bravery

Scripture for Today: 1 Samuel 17

Are you hindered by a lack of bravery? We love a good story of adventure, especially when the main character overcomes fear, takes a risk, and as a result enjoys victory! Oh yes, occasionally, bravery leads to death instead of victory. And that's the tension we face everyday in life. If we're not careful, we will allow our fear of failure and death to hold us back, to settle, or to accept the status quo.

One of my favorite Bible characters is the teenage shepherd boy named David. He was filled with bravery, having killed a lion and a bear, and finally conquered the Philistine giant warrior named Goliath. He did all of that in his teenage years! He went on to become the most revered King Israel has ever known.

Bravery is not the absence of fear. But it's the willingness to take a risk, step forward, and do the right thing regardless of the consequences. If God is for us, who can be against us? So be brave. If you walk with God daily, nothing else really matters!

When was the last time you exhibited bravery? Write a summary of it below or in your journal. When is the last time you could have been brave, but were not?

Reading about brave people and brave actions can increase our own. Read in your Bible the stories of David, Daniel, and Esther. Read biographies of strong leaders who bravely withstood difficult challenges. Finally, ask God to give you courage to face the difficult circumstances in your life.

July 23
Life Direction

Scripture for Today: Proverbs 3:5–6

Do you struggle with where you're going in life and what road will take you there? It's likely the most common struggle of all: am I on the right path?

We dream about the future and wonder how things will turn out. We dream about success and we worry about failure. We dream about happiness and worry about disappointment. We dream about the best and worry about the worst. With every decision we make, we wonder if that decision will keep us on the right path to success with our marriage, our family, our career, and our spiritual life.

In the Book of Proverbs, the wise King Solomon gave his solution to this enduring problem of humanity. He said, "In all your ways acknowledge God, and He will direct your path." According to Solomon we are focusing on the wrong thing. We are trying to direct our own path and guarantee a certain outcome. Instead, we must simply acknowledge God, salute Him, concede to Him in all of our ways, and He will direct our path. Sounds like a good plan to me!

As you read these words, do you believe you are on God's path for your life or off of it?

If you are off of it, take a few minutes to review when you left the path, ask God to forgive you and ask Him to get you back on the path He has chosen for you.

July 24
Learning

Scripture for Today: Luke 2:52; 2 Timothy 4:13

Are you still committed to learning? The desire to learn is a quality that begins to fade with aging. As we get older it's replaced by the desire to be respected for how much we already know. It's easy for even the most successful people to get mentally lazy, to resist being challenged, to resist the need to change. We begin to settle into a comfortable way of life. We begin to think the world will somehow freeze and stand still, allowing us to remain on the cutting edge. But it won't, and we won't!

We have big responsibilities as parents, grandparents, employees, and community leaders. And as followers of Jesus Christ we must excel. The God we serve deserves our absolute best!

The great Hall of Fame basketball coach John Wooden gave some of the best insights on this subject I've ever heard. He said, "A leader who is through learning is through. And so is the team such a leader leads. It's what you learn after you know it all that counts!"

Have you ever thought about the fact that even though Jesus Christ is the Son of God, when He lived on earth He learned?

Even the Apostle Paul, late in his life, asked for scrolls so he could continue learning. Regardless of your age, commit to being a lifelong-learner so you never stagnate.

July 25
Motivation

Scripture for Today: Proverbs 18:10

Do you ever struggle with being motivated? That struggle is real. We sometimes lack the drive to go to school, to go to work, to go to practice, to finish a project, to study, to exercise, stay on the diet, go to church…and the list continues!

Motivation does not just happen. It has to be nurtured, especially when times get tough. It's so easy to just throw up our hands and quit. But you can be filled with motivation to get out of bed every day and tackle the goals you've set with a kick in your step and joy in your heart. How? It's all about understanding the, "why". You need to remind yourself, "What happens if I do?" and, "What happens if I don't?" Once you answer those two questions, you'll begin to understand the "why" and motivation is not very far behind.

"Why" is one of the first words kids focus on when they begin to speak. They want to know "why" about everything. It's a great word for adults, too.

Do you often ask "why"? Why or why not?

Asking "why" can reveal obstinance, but more often it reveals a desire to learn. Never hesitate to ask "why," then be ready to use the answer to move forward with more clarity and new motivation.

July 26
Humility

Scripture for Today: Proverbs 16:19

How high on your goals list is humility? I doubt you've given it much thought or developed a strategy for that one! And there's no school that offers a humility certification! Yet it's one of the character traits that people most admire in their leaders and relationships at every level.

Humility is directly connected to our self-awareness. It's about knowing who we really are, not the fake image of who we want people to think we are! Humility is an understanding that, even with successes, we still have many flaws to work on. Sometimes our diplomas, awards, titles, and success can lead us into a fairy tale world where we are always the center of the story. Such a world will lead us to become an arrogant know-it-all who no one wants to be around. It's a dangerous world to live in.

Know who you are. Treat people with respect. Be faithful and walk humbly before God and man—and be real. People prefer to follow a leader who's always real, instead of one who's always right.

Why is it difficult to be humble?

Ask God to help you aim toward authenticity and humility rather than hiding your true self and arrogance.

July 27
Stick-With-It

Scripture for Today: Isaiah 50:7

Are you good at sticking with something once you commit to it? It's one of the key qualities for the path of greatness, so if you don't have it you'd better get it.

Robert Madu said, "In a culture where quitting is normal, be crazy enough to stay committed, foolish enough to be faithful, and stupid enough to stick with it!" I agree with Robert.

Sticking-with-it requires discipline to apply such a principle to our family, career, and spiritual life. We must commit to do what needs to be done, when it needs to be done, and how it needs to be done. And we must do that every day until we die. Because greatness is not a place at which we ever arrive. It's a journey that must be lived until death takes us out of here.

Perhaps you have some challenges, decisions, and frustrations staring you in the face today, and you'd really like to throw up your hands, quit, and walk away. But now is the time to be a little abnormal and stick with it!

What has proven to be your greatest personal challenge to sticking-with-it?

Will it help you stick-with-your career, education, family, spiritual growth if you view life as a journey rather than a destination?

July 28
Blessings in Burkina Faso

Scripture for Today: Ephesians 5:4

Do you ever look around and ask, "Why does everyone seem to have a better life than I do?" "Why are they so lucky and I'm not?" We live in a world of comparisons, and, as a result, we often see ourselves as having gotten the short end of the stick. But if we look around, we'll see that we might not have it so bad after all.

Several years ago, I was with some African friends in the country of Burkina Faso. It's one of the poorest countries in the world. They are a gracious and kind people, but the Sahara environment in which they live is an extreme place that can push the body, mind, and soul to its limits.

It had not rained in four months. The airborne dust could be tasted with every breath. The heat from the desert sun pierced through every possible shade. At mealtime, the fear of an intestinal parasite accompanied every bite.

Yet, every day my friends who live there began by giving thanks to God for their many blessings.

They knew that gratitude was the key to feeling good about life, not comparing their life to someone else.

Do you ever play the comparison game with people around you or people on social media? Do their successes make you ungrateful for your own blessings?

Every good and perfect gift comes from God. Have you thanked Him lately for how He has blessed you without comparing to someone else's blessings?

July 29
Bridges

Scripture for Today: Philippians 3:12–14

What do you know about bridges? They come in many styles and sizes. Some are complex while others are simple. Some have great eye appeal while others are rugged and raw. But we are greatly impacted by what we do with each bridge.

The key is to know which bridges to cross, which ones to burn, and which ones to build.

There have been some awesome people and places in life that have added great value and joy to your journey. Make sure you keep those bridges open and cross them often into the *land of gratitude.*

Life is full of unfairness and disappointment. You'd better burn those bridges quickly and keep them burned because they will reappear often and take you to the land of *misery.*

But regardless of where you are right now, there is a *land of opportunity* that waits in the distance. You see it, and dream of a better future, but it seems you just can't get there. Well that's a bridge that you've got to build. So, stop whining and start building today.

Bridges to burn usually have to do with bad relationships, bad decisions, and bad memories. Do you need to burn any of those bridges so you don't return to the land of misery?

What bridge to the land of opportunity can you begin building today? Ask God for wisdom equal to the task.

July 30
Don't Play Favorites

Scripture for Today: Matthew 7:12

Do you treat everyone the way you want to be treated? Have you been treated unfairly yourself, or as a lesser valued person than someone else?

It can happen at school, at work, and in other social groups of life. People pair up, group up, and almost always someone is on the outside. It seems unfair because it is unfair!

A big leadership challenge is treating everyone well even if you have to give more attention to someone you are training. Leadership always involves getting others ready to lead and sometimes helping them adjust to bigger responsibilities. But you can't let that turn into personal favoritism.

When you begin playing favorites, those who aren't favorites are hurt and feel ignored. Would you constantly give your best only to be ignored?

Provide good leadership in your organization and family by treating everyone fairly, and by refusing to play favorites. Employees, volunteers, and family members deserve equal respect. It's what we all want and should be what we all give!

Have you ever been in a situation where there were favorites and you weren't it?

The Bible reminds us to treat others the way we want to be treated, so think about how to treat everyone around you with decency and respect.

July 31
Worship

Scripture for Today: Exodus 20:1–2

Where do you channel your worship these days? You may or may not consider worship a big deal. You may not think you worship at all, but we all worship someone or something. We were made to worship, and worship we do! We are great worshippers, but we don't always worship great stuff!

Worship does not simply take place at church. True worship takes place in your spirit, inside of you! From there we choose to focus our gratitude, love, affection, commitment, time, energy, devotion, and emotion toward the thing, person, or people we value most. And whether you know it or not, your worship—and where it goes—is a big deal to God.

God's first commandment of the Ten Commandments is, "Have no other gods before me." When Jesus was asked, "Which is the greatest commandment?" He said, "That you love the LORD your God with all your heart, mind, soul, and strength!" Don't waste your worship on a hobby, job, family, spouse, money, status, or yourself. Give it to the only One who deserves it!

What does the word "worship" mean to you? It comes from a word meaning "to declare the worth of something." How does that explain the value you place on God?

Ask God to help you worship only He who is worth worshipping and recognize that everything else is only a blessing from Him, a blessing that should lead us to worship Him even more.

August 1
Thankful for Teachers

Scripture for Today: Proverbs 9:9

Are you ready for school to start back? When I was a kid, I was asked that question a lot about this time of year and I was always ready. I usually got some new clothes, a new pair of shoes, a new lunchbox, a new notebook, and a new haircut. I felt like a million bucks! But the greatest thing was reconnecting with my old friends, meeting some new friends, and getting to know my new teachers. Starting back to school was my biggest social event of the year; I loved it! And the education I received was okay too. Throughout the journey, going to school helped prepare me for life, and the things I learned have made me who I am.

Today, I'm more thankful than ever for my teachers, administration, lunchroom workers, and custodians from my school days. All of them played a huge role in my personal growth and development. If you are a parent, encourage, pray for, and help a teacher succeed. They are shaping your child's future.

Who are the teachers who formed you into who you are?

If you have kids in public or private school, how can you honor and bless their teachers to keep them encouraged?

August 2
Fresh

Scripture for Today: Acts 3:19–20

Are you struggling with staying fresh? You know, a fresh perspective, a fresh attitude, and a fresh outlook on life? Life's difficulties and pressures make it easy to lose that sense of freshness. I've been there on many occasions.

But things can be different and you can see a turnaround! What's the key? You have to make a fresh new commitment to your family, your friends, and your faith. They serve as three different water-wells from which you can draw during the driest of times.

Your family, though flawed, is a foundational structure for a stable life. Your real friends, though not perfect, will energize you to see a better future. And it's your faith in Jesus Christ that will take you into the greatest realm of living possible. Each of these take time and effort, but if you ignore them, don't expect much in return. As you make regular deposits into your family, friends, and faith, they will make deposits back into you, and you will soon be feeling fresh again. God designed it that way. Make a deposit today.

When is the last time you've made a significant deposit into your family? Your friends? Your faith?

Take a few minutes to evaluate where you can best invest yourself this week and plan how to do it.

August 3
Posture

Scripture for Today: Philippians 3:13

How good is your posture? When I was a kid I began to slouch and slump at one point, losing any resemblance of having good posture. My dad quickly addressed it as a problem. He made me practice walking with my shoulders back and head high. He said my posture was linked to my attitude about life. It showed if I was confident or fearful. He was right, and as a result I still work at having good posture many years later.

But posture is more than physical. It can be mental, or even spiritual. For instance, when you pray about your future, is the posture of your spirit one that leans forward or backward? If and when God gives you direction, are you in a position to run forward in that direction or are you leaning away from it. Your spiritual posture is either one of faith or fear. If your posture has begun to slouch and slump, you need to fix it. A bad posture soon begins to negatively affect every other area of your life.

How would God evaluate your spiritual posture right now, straight or slumping?

Faith in God's character and plan is what straightens our posture. Spend some time in His word today so your faith may be increased.

August 4
Pursuing

Scripture for Today: Psalm 42:1

What exactly are you pursuing? If you're tired and worn out, you are obviously running after something. And that's ok. Pursuing is a part of living! It's what keeps us moving from one day to the next and from one goal to the next. But if we're not careful, our desire to pursue can be tricked to pursue empty promises and short-lived happiness. Too often people like the pursuit more than actually reaching the goal. And they too quickly move on to pursue something or someone else.

It's true with relationships, careers, cars, houses, and other stuff. And another broken heart and disillusioned soul is born.

But there is one pursuit that's worth the journey and effort. It does not make you tired and weary but gives you peace and rest. It does not get old and stale but is fresh and exciting every day. Pursue a daily relationship with God who created you and loves you unconditionally. I love that God loves me. He pursued me long before I pursued Him.

Whatever you pursue, make sure it's worth reaching!

Have you been pursuing God as a thirsty deer looks for water?

Can you identify pursuits that interfere with pursuing God? Prioritize your pursuits today so that God has top spot.

August 5
Servant

Scripture for Today: Mark 10:45

Are you striving to be a good servant? Let's be honest: Being a servant is not at the top of the priority list for most of us. Instead, today's culture places emphasis on being served. The great people of the world are served, cared for, catered to, and revered to such a degree they often begin to feel they deserve such treatment. Arrogance quickly begins to take over. And yes, this problem moves far beyond the politicians of the world. It's found its way into everyday life.

Jesus taught His disciples the greatest among them was the servant of all. Then He explained servanthood by washing their feet. Jesus said He did not come into the world to be served, but to serve. Learn to serve your spouse, parents, coworkers, customers, supervisor, and employees. Serving others helps produce a better life for everyone involved. If Jesus, God's Son, can serve others what makes you think you're better than He?

Is serving easy for you or difficult?

When you think of servanthood, does any person come to your mind?

Ask God to help you serve like Jesus today and every day.

August 6
Listening

Scripture for Today: 1 Samuel 3:7–10

"Did you hear that?"

It's a question I heard many times as a teenager when I rabbit hunted with Ernest Ingram and a few other older men. The dogs were barking off in the distance as they chased the rabbit. The old men, with hand cupped behind their ear, listened to every bark, smiled at each other, and occasionally gave quiet commentary about each dog and about the rabbit. The constant barking was often interrupted by moments of silence. And that meant something too. The old men seemed to know exactly what was going on just by listening. To me, it was just noise in the background as I looked for the rabbit. To the old men, the noise was like music in their ears. I simply didn't know what to listen for, that is, until I bought my own dog to join the pack. Then I too became an intentional listener and enjoyed the music.

Listening is an essential part of learning in your relationship with God and with people. Do you hear noise or music?

Did you hear that?

Do you find it difficult to hear God because of all the noise in life?

The best place to hear God speaking to us is in His holy Word, so to hear more from God make it a bigger part of your life.

August 7
Overwhelmed

Scripture for Today: Isaiah 6:1–5

When was the last time you were overwhelmed with the goodness of God? It's likely we more clearly recall our frustrations with God. We all experience tragedies, heartaches, and disappointments in life and God gets to hear how it's all His fault!

But I'm absolutely certain you also have some amazingly good things in your life. Does God get to hear how awesome He is for giving you those? Too often we forget that part.

When you see the work of His hands, are you overwhelmed? I am.

When you consider your own sin and mess-ups in life, and understand that because of God's mercy you can still have a relationship with Him, are you overwhelmed? I am. Pause for a moment today to say, "God, thank you for your goodness in my life! You are amazing!" And it's ok to become a little overwhelmed.

Have you ever been truly overwhelmed by God's goodness to you?

Sometimes we aren't overwhelmed by God because we simply don't think about all He's done for us. Pause to praise God right now and be overwhelmed by Him.

August 8
Partnership

Scripture for Today: Isaiah 41:8

Are you aware that you're living life in partnership? There was a time when I thought life was whatever I made it to be. Period. But at some point I learned life is made better through partnership.

Great partnerships make you better than you are. They take you where you could never go alone. They help you do what you do best while you help others do what they do best. And they give you someone with which to celebrate, brainstorm, and work to accomplish your goals and dreams.

I have some amazing partnerships: My wife and family, my staff, our leadership team, and members of Midway Church. And most of all, I'm thankful for my partnership with God. We all share the same values, goals, and dreams, and we can do more together than we could do alone. And together, the journey is simply more fun and rewarding.

With whom are you in partnership? I hope they want what's best for you, and can help you become better. That's why God should be your first partner!

Have you entered a partnership with God through faith in Jesus?

All life's relationships are better when God is our partner because He helps us develop them when we let Him. Think about the important partnerships in your life and ask God to make all of them the best partnerships they can be.

August 9
Leading in Uncharted Territory

Scripture for Today: Joshua 1:1-8

There have been several times in my life I had to lead into uncharted territory. It was uncharted for me, anyway! I've had to lead through financial difficulties I had never faced, organizational difficulties I had never faced, and personnel difficulties I had never faced. It was all uncharted territory at the time!

One of the best leadership books I've ever read is Canoeing the Mountains: Christian Leadership in Uncharted Territory, by Tod Bolsinger. In it, he draws leadership principles from Lewis and Clark. What was their uncharted territory? Everything west of the Missouri River! What people thought about the terrain was wrong.

He says that when you are facing uncharted territory, first reframe the moment. Wherever you have been isn't where you thought you were going. Create a new way of looking at the future. Second, recover your calling (or mission). Ask these questions: Why do we exist? What are our goals? How do we reach them now? Last, discover—the uncharted territory around you and your own capacity to lead.

Whatever change of territory you are facing, don't worry that you don't have a map. Start leading and map it as you go!

What is the biggest "uncharted territory" challenge you have faced? How did you get through it?

Take some time to imagine an uncharted territory scenario and use the purposes above to plan what you would do.

August 10
Grit

Scripture for Today: Romans 2:7

Do you have what it takes to finish your journey? The Bible calls it perseverance. It's the long-term tenacity to keep moving forward in spite of difficulty or pain.

I love the childhood story about the Little Engine that Could. Children in a poor village would get no toys unless a locomotive could pull the train of toys up and over a mountain to get to the village. No engine was willing to try. Then a small lighter engine heard about the poor children without toys; it volunteered to go. The big engines laughed and scoffed, but the little engine hooked up to the train cars with toys and headed up the mountain. He put forth all of his effort and began to huff and puff, and say, "I think I can, I think I can, I think I can!" And as the little engine finally pulled into the village of poor children, with a train full of toys, he said, "I thought I could, I thought I could, I thought I could!"

You can, too, so keep moving!

Do you most often see yourself as the Little Engine that Could or the Little Engine that Quit?

What things motivate you to keep going? A complimentary word? Enough rest? Time in prayer? Pleasing God by doing well should be our greatest motivator. Ask God to help you please Him today even in the most difficult things you face.

August 11
Alone

Scripture for Today: Psalm 32:8

Do you feel like you're all alone as you face life's most difficult challenges? It's one of the common struggles of humanity in every generation since the beginning of time. Right when we feel we need a friend the most, not one seems to be found. That is not reality, but it sure feels that way. At such times it even feels like God is nowhere to be found. But that's not reality either. We're reminded in Psalm 32:8 that God will instruct us and show us the way to go. With His eye on us, He will give us counsel.

I love the old song, His Eye is on the Sparrow:
Why should I feel discouraged?
Why should the shadows come?
Why should my heart feel lonely
And long for heaven and home?

When Jesus is my portion,
A constant friend is he.
His eye is on the sparrow
And I know he watches over me.

Regardless of what we've done, or what we're going through, we are never alone!

Pause right now and think about the fact Jesus cares for you and watches over you at all times. Spend a few minutes thanking Him for it.

"His Eye is on the Sparrow," by Civilla D. Martin and Charles H. Gabriel. Public domain.

August 12
Drifting

Scripture for Today: Hebrews 2:1

Are you drifting? Do you find yourself automatically moving in a direction you never intended to go and you're not sure how to get back on track?

Drifting can be scary. Several years ago, while floating at the beach, I closed my eyes for just a minute to relax. I guess it was a little longer than I realized. When I awakened, I didn't even recognize where I was. It was very unnerving being somewhere I never intended to be and not knowing how I got there.

It can be that way in life sometimes too! You're not sure how your life, your marriage, your finances got where they are. You never planned it to be this way. Well, getting on track and staying on track requires knowing where you want to go, and then taking the right steps every day to get there. And yes, to stop drifting is hard work, and often feels like you're swimming against the current, because you are. If life gets easy, you're likely drifting in the wrong direction.

Have you ever heard the saying, "Any dead fish can float downstream, but it takes a live one to go upstream?" It's true. Anything can float downstream: a leaf, a twig, or a corpse.

Do you feel like you are drifting professionally or in your family or maybe spiritually? If so, ask God to re-orient you to the direction you need to be heading.

August 13
Weights

Scripture for Today: Hebrews 12:1–2

Are you hauling things around that you should have dumped a long time ago?

The Bible teaches "we should lay aside the weights and sins that so easily hinder us, so we can run with endurance the race that's ahead." When we were kids in junior high school, my brother, Richie, wanted to try out for basketball. I remember his deep commitment to practice and to play. Every day at home, he put weights around his ankles and ran. With those weights on, he would jump around our yard like a kangaroo. And when it was game time, he would take the weights off, allowing him to run and jump like never before. Taking the weights off was the only way he could effectively play the game. To play the game with the weights on would have sabotaged his effectiveness and that of the team.

If you're holding on the hurts, disappointments, and wounds from your past, you're trying to play the game with the weights on. Dump your baggage from the past and begin to play like a champion.

Have you ever noticed marathon race winners don't run weighted down? They run in lightweight clothing designed for maximum speed. Are you living life that way?

Stop for a few minutes and identify anything that is weighing you down. Ask God to help you put it down, then don't pick it up again.

August 14
Mission

Scripture for Today: Matthew 18:11

Are you on a mission? If not, you should be.

When I was a kid my missions were simple and shallow. I wanted summer to arrive so I could get out of school. Or I wanted Christmas to come. Or I wanted to get my driver's license.

I wrote this on my 52nd birthday, and through the years I've come to understand my mission more clearly. Yes, it continues to evolve a little along the way, but in general I know my mission in this world, and I'm committed to live it to the fullest. Do you know yours?

Your mission is the filter through which you make every other decision in life. Your mission helps you live each day with a sense of purpose. Your mission forces you to choose to do this or that. And yes, your mission, if lived well, will live long after you're gone. In short, your mission is how you'll be remembered when you die.

Jesus knew His mission and He lived it well! As a result, we can have eternal life.

Have you ever thought about the fact that Jesus' mission on earth included you? He came to seek and save the lost.

If you haven't responded to Jesus' invitation, consider doing that now. Believe that Jesus will forgive your sins, ask Him to change your life, and He will!

August 15
Stubborn

Scripture for Today: Psalm 32:9

Have you ever heard the phrase "Stubborn as a mule"? When we hear it, it's usually in reference to a particular human rather than a mule. For me, "Stubborn as a mule" was the title of my very first sermon in 1983! King David warned us, "Do not be like a horse or a mule, without understanding, that must be controlled with bit and bridle." In other words, you should not have to be forced to do the right thing; don't resist doing the right thing! Don't be stubborn about it. Stop fighting against God. It's a fight you cannot win.

At the age of 19, I understood it was I who had been "stubborn as a mule," and I vowed to change. It was a change from being stubborn to being teachable. It's a change I've never regretted. Rather than stubbornly resist, I now ask God, "Lord teach me the right way, and give me the courage to do it!" It's a much better life. I don't know why I kept being stubborn about it.

What is the difference between determination and being stubborn?

Can you think of some areas where you've been stubborn in the past and now regret it?

Ask God to help you be determined toward good, helpful things, and not be prideful and stubborn when you are wrong.

August 16
People Adding Value

Scripture for Today: Exodus 17:8–16

Who are those people in your life who make you better?

Their strength helps your weakness and together you become better than you are alone. If you lead a team, you know how important this is. Every effective leader has a few people behind the scenes with a unique set of gifts and abilities with which the leader does not possess. But without those gifts and abilities on the team there would be no success.

In the Bible, Moses had Aaron, Joshua, and Caleb. Each played a key role in the journey of taking the Hebrew people out of Egypt and into the promised land. Moses could not have done it alone. He had too many weaknesses, as do most of us. But with the right people around him, he became known as one of the greatest leaders in history.

At Midway Church I have an amazing team of people who help me. And I'm thankful for each one.

Do you have a team around you as you lead or are you trying to forge your way alone?

Who are those people in your life? Have you thanked them lately for their investment in your journey?

August 17
Reset Button

Scripture for Today: 1 John 1:9

Don't you just love a good reset button? You know, that moment when everything goes haywire on a piece of electronics, or the power goes out and you don't know what to do next? Then you see it—a reset button! With reluctance you press it, and *voila*! Everything works correctly again.

I wish everything in life had a reset button to help things get back to normal. It does not; but our spiritual life does. "If we confess our sins, God is faithful and just to forgive us of our sins and to cleanse us from all unrighteousness." And *voila*! He makes everything right again.

I don't know why, but for some reason we are reluctant to press the button. We choose to live in chaos, guilt, and darkness instead. As a result, life continues to go haywire and normalcy seems to go further out of reach as the days go by. For once, take a step in the right direction; press the spiritual reset button today. You'll be glad you did!

When is the last time you hit the 1 John 1:9 Reset Button for your spiritual life?

Take some time soon, preferably right now, and confess as many sins as you can remember. God will forgive them and give you the reset you desperately need.

August 18
Chaos Perspective

Scripture for Today: Psalm 37

What's your mindset during times of chaos, evil, and injustice, or when you're personally offended? It's easy to join in with a mob mentality, to be filled with anger and resentment, and to look for ways to strike back and get even. Too often we do and say things that, at the moment, might make us feel better, but hurt and destroy innocent people who had nothing to do with our original offense.

God's advice from the Bible is, "Don't be agitated by evildoers. Their destruction will come quickly. They will wither like the grass."

As for you, "Trust in the Lord and do what is good. Delight yourself in the Lord and He will give you your heart's desires. Commit your way to the Lord and He will act."

God is the ultimate judge who will make all things right. Vengeance is not ours to take; it's His. Stay on the right side of His laws! And when you stand before Him face to face at the judgement, you'll be glad you did.

Can you think of a time you took revenge on someone? What was the result?

God demands we leave revenge in His hands, because He's the only one who can carry it out perfectly. Pray right now and commit anything to Him that you are tempted to avenge, then trust Him to do what is right.

August 19
Rain

Scripture for Today: Joel 2:23

Do most summers seem unusually dry or am I just imagining things? As a farmer I may be a little more sensitive about it than some, but it's difficult to grow grass for cattle without a steady flow of rain. During one dry spell I thought I actually felt a raindrop, but it was just a bird flying over! I pray in such times for some rain to help bring new life to our dry and crusty soil.

Our spiritual lives can get a little dry and crusty also; but it's not from a lack of rain. No, we can't blame that on anyone but ourselves. We can freshen our spiritual life anytime we get serious about it; it's our choice. We can choose to read our Bible every day. We can choose to pray and give thanks to God every day. We can choose to go to church every week. We can choose to be an encouragement and serve others. And when we do, it's like a good refreshing shower on our dry and crusty soul.

Do you feel dry and dusty at the moment?

God used the image of rain to illustrate His blessings. Pause and ask Him to bring rain on you today. Asking for rain isn't selfish; it's life-giving.

August 20
Giants

Scripture for Today: Hebrews 10:38

Did you know we're being invaded by giants? Sounds like a fairy tale does it not? But it's true!

We can all see the increase of terrorism, the empowerment of radical nations, the tension of racism, the open assault on law officers, and the fact that many have to work harder and longer only to earn less than they once did. But these are not the real giants.

The real giants are inside us: fear, worry, anger, resentment, hatred, jealousy, doubt, and bitterness are the real giants we face. They secretly torture us when we're alone or in crowds, on vacation, at our jobs, or with our families around the dinner table.

As a follower of Jesus Christ, I know who holds my future. I am not afraid. I am not afraid to travel. I am not afraid to die. Therefore, I am not afraid to live, and live confidently. This world is not my home; I'm just passing through. True faith can kill the giants. Be brave. Be bold. Be a giant-killer!

Which inner giant has proven most difficult for you to overcome?

No giant, no matter now strong, can stand against God's power. Ask God for the strength to overcome them today so you can live free from fear.

August 21
Relationships

Scripture for Today: 1 Thessalonians 5:11

How's your relational life these days? I'm sure you have felt used and hung-out-to-dry a few times by other people, as have I. Such experiences can make us a little distant, skeptical, and confused. But life's worst and best moments involve other people. If you avoid people to miss the worst, you'll cheat yourself from enjoying the best! Remember, you are only one half of a relationship or friendship. And yours is the only half you can control.

With that thought in mind, John Maxwell gives several ways to add value to others.
1. People are insecure...so give them confidence.
2. They want to feel special...so compliment them.
3. People desire a better tomorrow...so give them hope.
4. They need to be understood...so listen to them.
5. People are selfish...so speak to their needs first.
6. They get emotionally low...so encourage them.
7. And people want to succeed...so help them reach their dreams.

And when the sun goes down each night, you can know you've made someone's life better.

How often do you experience one or more of Maxwell's seven ways?

How often do you practice them on others?

Write this list on an index card or app. Refer to it as often as it takes until practicing these becomes part of your daily routine.

August 22
Growing

Scripture for Today: Colossians 2:6–7

Are you growing in your faith? Growth is a key part of our success in everything we do, including our spiritual life.

It's a fun process for kids to indicate their height by putting a mark on the wall at the top of their head every few months. After a while their growth becomes obvious, and after a few years they can look back and see how fast or slow they grew in some seasons.

Is now a good growth season for you in your spiritual life? Growth is often painful and confusing, but God can use it to grow us. I love the childhood song I learned in Vacation Bible School as a kid:

"He's still working on me, to make me what I ought to be.
It took Him just a week to make the moon and the stars,
the sun and earth and Jupiter and Mars.
How loving and patient He must be!
'Cause He's still working on me!"

I'm glad He is. I'm still growing. Are you?

Are you still relying on God for your spiritual growth?

Tell God that you trust His wisdom, to help you become rooted and built up in Him.

"He's Still Workin' on Me" written by: Joel Hemphill
Lyrics © Universal Music Publishing Group

August 23
Disillusionment

Scripture for Today: Psalm 27:14

Do you ever get disillusioned and sarcastic with God? Sometimes as hard as we try, life does not make sense. And yes, even for believers, it can seem like God is nowhere to be found.

I know people want to believe we pastors have all the answers; but the fact is we too face major challenges and struggle to understand. I went through a period where, within a few weeks, several close pastor friends faced major challenges. It was devastating!

One died after a long battle with cancer. Another fell and damaged his spine. We're not sure yet if he will ever walk again. Another whose wife was diagnosed with breast cancer and just had surgery. Another whose wife had a brain tumor and major surgery. None of these are old people; they all have teenagers. They live their lives to serve God and other people. I admit I don't understand. It does not make sense; but it's a reminder that I don't have to have all the answers. It's a reminder that my name is Todd, not God!

Do you ever become disillusioned with God? Are you right now?

Often, disillusionment comes from feeling God has somehow mistreated us. Stop and ask God to strengthen your faith as you wait on Him.

August 24
Bad Circumstances

Scripture for Today: Matthew 28:19–20, Romans 8:31

What do you do when you find yourself in a flood of bad circumstances? When you look in every direction and all you see are problems, many of which you did not create, but they impact your life nonetheless!

Some people simply quit. They quit trying, working, and living. But quitting is a permanent solution to a temporary problem. As a result, they never move forward in life. They're stuck!

Other people pretend there are no problems. They live in denial, attempting to function in a "make-believe" world. As a result, they're unhealthy on the inside, and a mental or emotional breakdown is a constant threat.

Other people have learned it's best to face the problems; they attack them head on. They rely on God's promise that He will never leave us nor forsake us; He will be with us until the end of the age.

If God is with us, it does not matter how big the bully is—he has a big defeat headed his way. And so does the big flood of problems.

What do you normally do when facing problems?

Ask God to help you look forward so you can rely on the promises He's given you in His word.

August 25
Training Kids

Scripture for Today: Ephesians 6:4

Have you learned how to raise your kids without raising your blood pressure? Parents must train their children to do what is right, but we will train them to have bad habits if we don't have a plan.

Every kid must learn clear communication, boundaries, and the consequences of not learning them.

They must learn the difference between yes, no, and maybe; that training begins before they're one year of age.

We've all seen the battle between parent and child at the store. Child says, "I want that." Parent says, "No!" Child gets angry, screams, cries, and begs. Parent says, "Ok, you can have it!" That parent just trained the child to get angry, scream, cry, and beg to get what they want in life. They can expect more of the same behavior in the future.

Think. Plan ahead. Communicate clearly. Say what you mean and mean what you say. Make sure they understand, but never count to three. You said it, they understood, they disobeyed, there must be consequences. Period. Your kid will be a better adult if you are consistent in your training.

Were your parents consistent or inconsistent in training you when you were a child?

Pray and ask God to help you be consistent so your kids learn what is good and not good for them.

August 26
Real Faith

Scripture for Today: Matthew 16:24–26

Is your faith in Jesus for real?

During China's Boxer rebellion of 1900, ninety-nine students were having Bible study and worship when the insurgent militants arrived. Knowing they were Christians, the militants laid down a cross in front of them and said, "If any of you will trample this cross you can go free. If not, you will be shot!" The first seven students walked forward, trampled the cross, and walked free. The eighth student, a girl, walked forward, knelt before the cross and prayed as she trembled. She stood and carefully stepped around the cross to the other side. Then she was shot to her death. The remaining 91 students followed her actions, and they too were killed. It's obvious their faith was for real.

Jesus said, "You cannot be my disciple unless you pick up your cross and follow me." Have you? Will you? Does anyone else know? Can anyone else tell? Gather with God's people this weekend and every weekend and worship Jesus. That's just the starting point. Don't pretend; keep it real!

The cross was an instrument of death like the electric chair. Have you taken up your cross and died to yourself?

Jesus' death on the cross paid the penalty for our sins. Taking up your cross means dying to self and living for Him. Each day, acknowledge your life in Christ and demonstrate a real faith to a watching world.

August 27
Generational Anger

Scripture for Today: Ephesians 4:26–27

Have you ever been sucked into an issue by another person's anger? Be careful because it can be dangerous for many generations to come.

With the Hatfields and McCoys, the offense is traced to the Civil War days. Resentment built. Kids from one family were taught to mistrust, dislike, and be angry with the kids of the other. The kids became adults and then passed their anger to the next generation. Many men, women, and children died as a result of generational anger and resentment. Historians and family members disagree about the reason for the hatred, but it was deep. In May of 1976, almost 100 years after the original offense, Jim McCoy and Willis Hatfield, the last two survivors of the original family, shook hands in a public ceremony. They wanted to bury the generational curse.

The roots of resentment, anger, and bitterness run deep. Don't talk openly about your frustrations and offenses in front of your kids. You might give them a generational curse that lives long after you're gone.

Are you in a family suffering from multi-generation anger toward another family or about some past event?

Anger both arises from and causes bitterness which is like poison. Ask God for wisdom if there is a generational curse you or your family needs to bury.

August 28
Giving

Scripture for Today: Psalm 24:1–2

Are you a generous giver?

I heard about a wealthy father who took his son to McDonald's. The son ordered a Big Mac combo and biggie-sized it. Dad ordered a quarter pounder and drink. Then dad pulled out his wallet and paid the bill.

During lunch the dad reached over to get a couple of fries from his son. The son quickly defended his fries, refusing to allow dad to have any. The son refused to be a giver.

Several things ran through the dad's mind:
"There are some things my son doesn't understand about me or French fries. I'm the source of those fries. I paid for and gave the fries to him. I'm bigger than he is; I can take those fries away from him if I want to. I have enough money to bury my son in French fries. I don't need his fries, I have enough money to purchase my own. I really just wanted his willingness to share them."

God is the wealthy Father, and too often we are like this selfish son.

What do you have that you feel is owed to you? Do you feel like you have earned everything you have?

Scripture makes it clear that God owns everything, that all we have comes from Him. Take some time this week to thank God for what He has allowed you to manage for him and repent if needed for acting as if He owes you something.

August 29
Lies

Scripture for Today: John 8:44

Have you ever made a decision based on false information? False information leads to bad decisions. Occasionally we get a "do over" to make it right once we get good information.

The Bible refers to Satan as the Father of all lies. Here are some common lies that get people in trouble.

Satan wants you to believe that the Bible is not always true. *It is.*

He wants you to believe your sin is your business. *It is not.* It impacts lots of other people. He wants you to believe God will make an exception in your case. *He won't.*

He wants you to believe there are many ways to God. *There aren't.* Jesus is the only way. He wants you to believe there will not be a judgment day. *There will be.*

He wants you to believe you cannot be happy living a Christian life. *You can.* He wants you to believe you have plenty of time. *You don't.*

Don't make decisions about your eternity based on false information. You don't get a "do over" with that!

Are there lies you previously have believed but God has shown you the truth?

Satan is the father of lies, while Jesus is the truth. The choice is obvious. Commit to the truth; commit to Jesus.

August 30
Failure

Scripture for Today: Luke 22:60–62

Do you ever feel like success comes easy for others, but difficult for you? It's easy at such moments to play the victim card, and to make excuses. We then use our failures, our race, our age, our intellect, our family, and negative comments from others as an excuse. Once we begin to play the victim card, any excuse will do, and we begin to see a new one around the corner every day.

Have you heard that Thomas Edison's' teacher said he was stupid and could not learn a thing? Did you know that Einstein could not speak until age four nor read till age seven? Or that Walt Disney was once fired for a lack of creativity? Or that Beethoven's music teacher said as a composer Beethoven was hopeless?

Success was not easy for any of them, and it's never easy for anyone. Stop making excuses. Other people see us for who we've been and who we are, but God sees us for who we can become! Believe and then do something to move yourself forward!

One of the great failures recorded in the Bible is Peter denying Jesus during His trial. When Peter realizes what he's done, how does the Bible describe his response (today's scripture)?

Mark 16:7 describes one of the steps Jesus used to restore Peter. How does this make you feel about Jesus' response when you fail?

August 31
New Territory

Scripture for Today: 2 Timothy 1:7

Have you noticed how scary it can be to do something you've never done before or face a challenge you've never faced before? Our brain connects to fear and tells us everything that could possibly go wrong. Walking into new territory can be overwhelming!

We feel it before enrolling for college, getting the results of a medical exam, getting a job, going to a church for the first time, or becoming a parent. As scary as first experiences can be, we must learn to embrace them. It's a challenge we will deal with our entire life. Then we will die, and that's another first experience.

Fear is the opposite of faith. And a solid faith in Jesus Christ overcomes fear. God has not given us the spirit of fear, but of strength, love, and a sound mind. Faith can help you walk forward into new territory with confidence; but walk you must. Don't think you have to run, but don't stand still either. It's time now to take the first step! So embrace Jesus and walk forward!

How often do you deal with fear? Does it ever paralyze you?

One way to increase your faith is to read the biographies of great men and women of the faith. Ask your pastor or someone in your church for recommendations.

September 1
Plans

Scripture for Today: Psalm 39:4; 90:10

Have you paused lately to evaluate what you're learning?

It has been many years since my father's death. It seems like yesterday I sat at his bedside as we talked about life. He was almost 80 years old. His heart was failing, and he was well aware his time in this world was coming to a close.

He talked about his faith in Jesus Christ and that God is always trustworthy. He talked about the brevity of life. Then he made a statement that speaks loudly in my soul every day. He said, "Son, if there is anything you really want to do, make your plans, save up the money, and go do it, because just yesterday I was a teenager!"

Our conversation still reminds me to trust God during the hardest of times. I'm reminded that every day might be my last, or I might live for many more years. So, I've secured my faith in Jesus Christ. And I have set goals and target dates for things I dream of doing. If I die today, I'm ready. And if I live to be an old man, I'm ready for that, too. Thanks, Dad, for the conversation!

Is there anything you'd like to do before you die? Travel somewhere? Work in a certain field? Talk to someone about Christ?

If there is something you'd like to do—or need to do—put it on your calendar, then plan the steps it will take to make it happen.

September 2
Politics

Scripture for Today: Micah 6:8

Do you find yourself whining or boasting after each political election?

I'm thankful to be an American. To live in a country and time period in which we get to help choose our governmental leaders. It's an amazing privilege that is not given everywhere in the world. I pray for our elected leaders. And I pray for the body of Christ-the Church!

I can easily understand why those who are NOT followers of Jesus Christ whine, cry, and march in the streets if their candidate loses. Or if their candidate won to arrogantly boast with an "in-your-face" cynical attitude. But for followers of Jesus Christ, it should not be! We're required to walk humbly, show mercy, trust God, accept one another in love, be kind toward each other, and to love our neighbor as ourselves whether they be a different race, faith, or different political party.

If you spew animosity, don't be surprised if someone spews back. If you light a fire don't be surprised if you get burned by it. A kind word is always a better option!

Do you get tired of people whining? Do people get tired of you whining?

When you focus on helping others you will find less time for you to whine. Ask God to open your eyes in compassion to the people around you.

September 3
Insignificant

Scripture for Today: Judges 6:11–24

Do you ever face the challenge of feeling insignificant? I love the story of Gideon in the Bible. The Hebrew people were being overrun, harassed, and abused by the ruthless Midianites. God called Gideon to conquer them. His calling was a surprise. Gideon was a common farmer from the weakest tribe in Israel. He came from a family of "nobodies," and he was the youngest in his family. He had every logical reason to use his flaws and insignificance as an excuse to do nothing, and he tried. But God insisted Gideon was the man for the job and affirmed, "Go in the strength you have. The Lord is with you, mighty warrior!" Gideon gathered an army of 32,000 men who were ready to fight, but God insisted he take only 300. He did it God's way and conquered their enemy.

God loves to take the insignificant and do the miraculous! In our weakness, He is strong. If you feel like a nobody, remember Gideon. God is looking for nobodies.

Have you ever felt like a nobody God can't use? Has God ever used you in spite of your feeling that way?

God delights to use the lowly, the poor, the ones of no reputation. Thank God for making you a nobody, then thank God for using you anyway for His glory.

September 4
Legacy

Scripture for Today: Proverbs 22:1

Do you ever ponder how your life has been impacted by those who came before you? Or how your life will impact those who come after you? Such questions motivate me to lead, think, and live forward, to do things that will improve the lives of others after I'm gone.

At the beginning of the American Revolution, George Washington spoke to his troops before the first major battle. He said, "The fate of unborn millions now depend, under God, on the courage and conduct of this Army." Many of them died shortly after hearing those words, but they died giving birth to this great nation called America.

Years later Abraham Lincoln challenged Congress to pass the 13th Amendment abolishing slavery. He admonished them, "The abolition of slavery by constitutional provision settles the fate, for all time, not only of the millions who live in bondage, but of unborn millions to come." The amendment passed. Never forget such amazing gifts.

Live your life today in a way that someone's life tomorrow will be better, not worse!

What legacy are you leaving? What legacy would you like to leave?

Leaving a legacy is an intentional choice. Think about the decisions you are making today and how they will affect your legacy years from now, and change the decisions you need to change.

September 5
Death

Scripture for Today: John 5:24

Are you prepared to die? I know it's an intrusive and blunt question, but it needs to be asked. Death is not simply the end of something, but the beginning. The beginning of eternity either with God or separated from Him. And we never know which day will be our last. Some people leave this world slowly through prolonged illness. Others are taken suddenly through tragedy. Either way, we all go! We all have an appointment with death.

I love the promise of Jesus in John 5:24 which reads, "Anyone who hears my word, and believes in him who sent me, has eternal life, and will not come under judgement, but has passed from death to life."

Because of that promise, I live today with peace, and plan to die someday with confidence. Yes, death will find me too. I'm prepared for it. Jesus Christ is my Lord and Savior.

"God so loved the world that He gave His one and only Son, so that whoever believes in Him will not perish, but will have eternal life."

Are you prepared to die? Do you know what's on the other side of death? Do you think it's possible to know what's in the "great unknown"?

Jesus died and rose again. We can have confidence He knows what lies ahead, so trusting Him is a wise thing to do. Believe in Him and you, too, will pass from death to everlasting life.

September 6
Resolving Conflict

Scripture for Today: Proverbs 12:18

Do you ever struggle with resolving conflict? We all do...unless we simply ignore it and hope it will resolve itself. But it never does!

Nobody gets along all the time. I have staff members who've served on my leadership team for 15-20 years. I've been married to my wife since 1982. Our many years together are not because we are all such easy going, nice people all the time. Each of us, at some point, has been completely unbearable, intolerable, and miserable; we likely deserved being kicked to the curb!

What's the answer? Grace and humility. Grace gives people a chance even when they don't deserve one.

Humility seeks to hear and understand the other person more than wanting the other person to hear and understand us.

In some cases, reconciliation will not take place; we won't always agree on the facts. Sometimes people won't be responsible nor respectful. But in every case, we can be honest about our future together knowing we honestly tried.

Why do you think we are so quick to want grace but often slow to show it?

Is there anyone in your life you need to reconcile with? If so, ask for humility to show God's grace to them even if you feel they don't deserve it.

September 7
Destination

Scripture for Today: Luke 9:51

Where have you been this year? The year is almost ¾ over. Do you have anything to show for it?

By this season of each year, I have usually preached many sermons and trained leaders in a variety of places around the world or led a team of people to tour the Holy Land.

But that's not a description of where I'm going. Those are not destinations. They're simply stop-overs on my journey. When I sit down the last week of the year and look back to evaluate, I want to discover that my life stayed on track, my goals were reached, I honored God, I encouraged and invested in others, I led Midway Church with vision and diligence, I loved my family, and I became a better man.

You see, someday I will reach my final destination and stand before God to give an account of my life. I hope to hear Him say, "Well done." Yes, that's where I'm going. Everything else in life is either a stop-over to help me get there, or a distraction to get me off-track. Where are you going?

Have you remained focused on the goals you set back in January?

If not, review them now and get back on track for making progress the rest of the year.

September 8
Courage and Faith

Scripture for Today: 2 Samuel 23:20–21, Hebrews 13:38

How do you face the giants in your life when the overwhelming odds are against you? Facing such times with courage is connected to our faith and trust in God, and there's no guarantee everything will work out to our liking.

I'm inspired by Benaiah, King David's chief bodyguard. He went down into a pit on a snowy day and killed a lion. On another occasion, a massive Egyptian warrior came against him. Benaiah did not have his weapons with him, but instead of running, he fought the Egyptian with a stick, took the Egyptian's own spear and killed him with it! Through courage and faith, he lived to fight again.

But I'm just as inspired by the people who were tortured, imprisoned, and killed as they courageously held tightly to their faith. They did not survive, but their faith gave them courage to face the reality of death with confidence. Hebrews 11:38 honors them by saying, "This world was not worthy of them!" Be courageous and honor God regardless of the outcome.

Do you ever feel like you're facing a lion in a pit on a snowy day?

When is the last time you had to truly exercise courage and faith against an obstacle that looked too big to overcome? How did God come through for you?

September 9
Low Aim

Scripture for Today: Proverbs 29:18

Are you aiming high enough?

I went away for a few days of deer hunting with a friend and when I walked into his cabin to settle in, there it was. Hanging on the wall among mounted deer heads, coyote skins, and old family photos was a framed collection of words with the heading: "Low Aim is a Sin!" The statement drew me in to read every word that followed.

"The tragedy of life doesn't lie in not reaching your goal. Tragedy lies in having no goal to reach!"
"It's not a disgrace to reach for the stars and fail. It's a disgrace to have no stars for which to reach."
"Not failure, but low aim is a sin!" It was a good reminder!

A boy took his pellet rifle one night, aimed carefully into the sky, and pulled the trigger. His dad asked, "Son, what are you aiming at?" "The moon," the boy replied. "You're never gonna hit the moon," the dad said. The boy responded, "Maybe not, but I'm getting closer to it than you are!"

What are you aiming to accomplish this year? Thinking about it, did you aim too low?

Aiming high takes both vision and faith. Ask God to strengthen yours so that you can reach higher and farther than you ever thought possible.

September 10
Do Your Best

Scripture for Today: Deuteronomy 6:4–5

Are you doing your best? I can still hear the voice of teachers from my school days challenging me. "You can do better than that, Todd! You must do your best!"

Whoever you are, and whatever you do, it's likely God gave you a far greater capacity than you are currently living. Success in your marriage, career, or anything else will not come easy. Success won't run you down and jump on your back to make you successful. No, you'll have to give your best.

The Bible clearly teaches the principle of doing your best: "Whatever you do, do it with all of your heart!" "Whatever you do, do it as unto the Lord." "Love the Lord your God with ALL your heart, mind, soul, and strength. And love your neighbor like you love yourself."

Instead, we tend to become half-hearted at some point and do just enough to get by. And in doing so, our success falls far short of what it could and should be. Remember the words of my teachers, "You can do better than that!"

Do you typically do your best toward whatever task is at hand? Why or why not?

God wants us to do the best we can through His strength. Slacking off isn't a gift from God. Ask God right now to help you give your best at whatever He puts before you.

September 11
Priorities

Scripture for Today: Matthew 5:15–16

What is your number one priority each day? You do have one, don't you? Is it to eat a good breakfast? Get out of the house and to work on time with matching clothes? What is it?

Above everything else, God created us to love Him and reflect Him to the world. That's right. Our number one priority should be to reflect an ideal image of God to the people around us through our everyday actions. To love unconditionally. To give people a chance. To empower people to thrive. To rescue a person in trouble. To encourage a hurting soul. To sacrifice to make another person's life better. To be a real friend that sticks even closer than a brother.

It should be easy to do since mankind was originally created in the image of God, but sin, selfishness, and rebellion introduced some competition to these wonderful actions. Living it out every day must begin with a fresh encounter with God Himself. A prayer and a few minutes in His Word is a powerful start.

What image do you reflect to the world around you?

If they don't see Christ in you, surrender every impure reflection to Him and let His light shine through you.

September 12
Growth

Scripture for Today: Luke 2:52

Are you growing?

It's important to grow in wisdom and knowledge about life, in our relationship with God, and in how to deal with the people around us each day. Jesus is the perfect example. The Bible says, "Jesus grew in wisdom and stature and in favor with God and with people."

If Jesus needed to grow in each of these areas, it's likely that you and I do, too. If you don't know which areas in which you need to grow, just ask the people around you. They may not have told you, but they know. They have to tolerate you!

So, what's your plan? Growth is not an automatic process. If we put the right things in, we get the right things out. You will not grow spiritually without regular church attendance. You will not grow in wisdom without reflecting on your actions each day.

And you will not grow with people until you care more about them than your own opinions. Nope; not gonna happen! It's time for you to grow. The next step is yours. What is it?

How are you doing on the foundational items for spiritual growth: Bible reading, prayer, and church attendance?

The more intentional you are about those things, the more regularly you will do them. If needed, rearrange your calendar to make those three things priorities in your daily and weekly decisions.

September 13
Problem Solver

Scripture for Today: 1 Samuel 24:1–7

Do you remember those pesky word problems from school? You know, Sally has 12 apples, Fred has two oranges. If Amanda ate all of them, how much weight would Jim gain? At least, that's the way it sounded in my brain. It was often confusing and did not make sense.

Many times, problems still don't make sense! I did not like solving problems when I was a kid, and I don't like having to solve them now, but it's a necessity of life.

Here's what I have learned: I'm either a problem-solver or an excuse-maker. And so are you. No exceptions. Every problem has a beginning and an end, some last longer than others, and some won't end the way we would like. But almost all problems are temporary.

Rather than make excuses, ask God for wisdom. Brace yourself for the ride and face the problem head on. Develop your plan and begin marching forward! At some point, you'll figure out how much weight Jim gained, or you'll realize it really doesn't matter.

Have you typically been a problem-solver or an excuse-maker? "The dog ate my homework" might get you through first grade, but it isn't a good career option.

Excuse-makers never reach the goals they have in life. Evaluate how you respond to problems and ask God to help you solve them rather than make excuses that you can't.

September 14
Tenacity

Scripture for Today: Philippians 1:6

Do you complete what you start? What's your completion rate? Everybody quits something or changes course from time to time, but we have to make sure it does not become a habit. If it does, then it becomes a character flaw that follows us into every segment of life. At that point, we simply lack tenacity!

Tenacity is the emotional stamina to keep moving forward during difficult times; to finish what we start. If you don't have it, you can get it, but it's never painless. God has a way of using the biggest struggles we face to increase it.

Jesus definitely had tenacity. Learning to complete what we start is a character trait of Jesus we hear little about. But the Bible reminds us that "He who began a good work in you will complete it." Jesus came to die for our sins, and just before breathing His final breath He said, "It is finished!" Do you have a habit of finishing what you start? I'm glad Jesus did and still does. You can too.

Think about how you respond to most challenges? Is there a common factor in challenges along your journey where you lose tenacity?

Ask God for wisdom to press-on further during your next challenge than you normally do. Do the same the next time. This increases your tenacity and helps you finish what you start.

September 15
Decisions

Scripture for Today: 2 Peter 1:3

Do you struggle with making decisions? The very nature of decision-making says that one option is better than another, and we certainly want the best one. But some people approach decision-making like a kid approaches love. They get a daisy, and one by one they pull the petals off, saying, "She loves me, she loves me not." Except this time, they ask, "Should I, or should I not?"

Making good decisions is too important for that. I don't always make the right ones, but here's what I know about decision-making.

Deciding is always accompanied by fear. We feel the pressure of possibly making the wrong one.
Deciding requires cost. Every decision requires resources, energy, and effort to make the decision a reality.
Deciding unleashes problems. Every decision attracts some people to it and repels other people from it. We feel the conflict between the two.
Deciding unleashes passion. Deciding is the hard part, but once a decision is made, we should go all in to make it work.

What is the hardest thing about making decisions?

The most important decision you will ever make is what to do with Jesus? If you have not decided to follow Him, today is the best day and that is the best decision!

September 16
Sacrifice

Scripture for Today: Luke 9:24

When was the last time you sacrificed something to help someone else? Most of us lean more towards "What can I get?" instead of, "What can I give?" In short, we look out for Number 1: me, myself, and I.

But even the animal world is better than that!

As a kid I had a redbone coonhound named Kate. She once gave birth to 12 redbone puppies. They would sell for $100 each. At 15 years of age, I was gonna be rich!

It was winter and a cold front was moving in, so I installed a light in the doghouse to keep them warm. And from that light, the dog house caught fire. There was an opening on either end. Kate could have escaped, but instead she curled around those puppies and sacrificed herself so they might live. And one puppy did live.

Sacrifice is always hard, but it's often necessary to do the right thing. Two thousand years ago, Jesus sacrificed for us. Be thankful for Him.

The way of Jesus is the way of sacrifice. Can you think of when you've looked out for Number 1 rather than sacrificed yourself for another?

Pause and ask God to help you live sacrificially for the good of those around you.

September 17
Wasting Energy

Scripture for Today: Matthew 6:25–34

Are you wasting energy on things you cannot control? Stop it! You need that energy for things you can fix.

I love South Africa and its people. I've been there several times and have many South African friends. One of their great heroes is Nelson Mandela who was imprisoned for twenty-seven years in his fight for racial justice during apartheid. After being released from prison, he went on to become the president of the country. South African whites and blacks today hold him in high esteem as a man who saved their nation and brought the people together.

Many questioned how a man who had felt so abused refused to be bitter or to retaliate. But Mandela lived by the principle of refusing to waste energy on things he could not control. He refused to let the things he could not control control him. He saved his energy to change the things he could control. He let go of the abuses in his past and focused on the possibilities of a better future. You should too.

What is your first response when things get out of your control?

Worry is the result of trying to control what you cannot control. It is wasteful and accomplishes nothing. And, it's a sin. Stop worrying and leave the uncontrollable things in God's hands.

September 18
Eternity

Scripture for Today: Mark 8:36–38

Have you ever worked hard to succeed at something, only to realize it really didn't matter? I'm afraid many people are doing that with harsh eternal consequences. I have watched and listened for years as people prioritize gaining status in their community above gaining character and a transparent relationship with God. They want to be seen as somebody really special and outstanding by their peers. They want to hob-knob with people of whom they are actually jealous. They speak sarcastically about them in private but suck-up to them in public, all in an attempt to move up the societal ladder. They also hope to improve their financial gain in the process. Some even go to church for community status or business reasons!

Jesus asked, "What does it really profit a man to gain the whole world, but lose his own soul?"
Stay focused on the stuff that really matters. Succeeding at the stuff that doesn't matter is much worse than trying and failing at the stuff that does!

What is the biggest challenge you face keeping eternity in view?

Ask God to help weigh every opportunity, challenge, and relationship as if it has eternal consequences, because many times it does.

September 19
Taking Risk

Scripture for Today: 1 Samuel 14:1–23

Are you a high capacity risk taker? Most of us seek safety, not risk. You do know that God designed you to walk with Him and to do the extraordinary, don't you? The Bible is full of people who believed God and attempted the impossible, but often their peers laughed at and mocked them.

They laughed at Noah as he built the ark. Sarah laughed at God when He said she would have a child. They laughed at Paul as he shared his faith. They laughed at Jesus as He hung on the cross. But who's laughing now? These are all facts of history that changed the world!

If God has planted a dream inside your soul, please don't ignore it or write it off as impossible. Yes, it may feel risky. It may require you to walk into new territory. And you may experience some failures along the way. But I have found if you want what you've never had before you'll have to do some things you've never done before! Such actions can change the world.

Is there anything you'd like to accomplish but don't know how to do a significant part of it?

Who can you ask to help you? Sometimes people with expertise will share it for the cost of a lunch.

Taking risks for God's kingdom are the best risks of all. Ask God to make you a risk-taker for His glory.

September 20
Seeking Honest Profits

Scripture for Today: Psalm 119:36

Have you ever been ripped-off in a business deal? Doesn't it make you mad? I was lied to and ripped off in a business deal by someone with whom I went to church. That feels even worse!

In the book of Psalms in the Bible, the writer asks God to "Turn my heart to your decrees and not to dishonest profit." In the book of Proverbs we are warned against using unequal weights and measure in our business dealings. That's a reference to being honest, too.

Seeking profits honestly is a matter of integrity. It speaks to the core of who we are. If you are honest, it's a sign of a healthy core. If you cheat people to get the better end of a deal, your core is unhealthy.

You might remember Bernie Madoff who lived a lavish lifestyle in New York based on a pyramid scheme. He took the money people "invested" and lived off it, leaving them nothing in return. And, he went to jail for it.

So, seek to be faithful and honest in your dealings. Always be fair, and fairness will eventually come back to you!

Have you ever been taken advantage of? Did it make you mad? Confused?

Stop for a few minutes and reflect on the importance of being honest. Write a short prayer below and ask God to help your heart be turned to His Word rather than dishonesty.

September 21
Moral Bearings

Scripture for Today: 1 Corinthians 9:26–27

Are you maintaining good moral bearings? It's possible to have clarity on moral rights and wrongs in one season of life, then be oblivious and self-destructive in another season. We've all been alarmed by the news of someone who lost their moral bearings. And, we've all been astonished by someone with a reputation of immorality who settled down to live a good moral life.

Good moral bearings must be grounded in God's law as found in the Bible. He's the only one with a perfect set of moral bearings. It's something we must strive to develop and maintain until the day we die. They can never be assumed.

In the Bible, Paul tells us he disciplined his body to keep it under control, so that after preaching to others he would not become disqualified. He was speaking about the threat of losing his moral bearings. And it scared him to think of the possibility. It should scare us too.

So, spend time with God each morning. Yesterday's walk with God is never good enough for tomorrow's temptations.

Do you sometimes feel you are living without self-discipline?

Losing one's moral bearings brings all kinds of destruction and damage to that person and the people around them. If you've lost self-discipline, talk to a pastor or other spiritual mentor about getting yourself under God's control.

September 22
Encouragement

Scripture for Today: Isaiah 26:3–4

Are you a good encourager? Encouragement is one of the most powerful gifts you can give someone, and it doesn't cost a single penny.

I'm proud of you. You can do this. I believe in you. I appreciate you. I need you. You've made my life better. Thank you for all you do. You can count on me to be with you. We will do this together.

All of these are simple but powerful words of encouragement. We all need it and we must all learn to give it away! Why? Because, many people have no one who believes in them. Many don't believe in themselves. Many are facing challenges that are absolutely overwhelming. And everyone performs better when they are encouraged!

Your voice is powerful to someone, so use it to breathe life and encouragement.

Jesus understood the power of encouragement. He said to His followers, "I will never leave you nor forsake you." His promise still encourages me as I face challenges of my own. I hope it encourages you, too.

What has encouraged you the most recently? A kind word? A Bible verse? A book or sermon?

Those things that encourage you will tend to encourage others. Plan to be encouraging this week and ask God to help you do it.

September 23
Courage

Scripture for Today: 1 Corinthians 16:13

Do you have enough courage to overcome your enemies? Does the pressure ever get so great you want to walk away and never be seen again? Well courage is what makes you stay!

I love the stories of courage throughout history. They inspire me. I always wonder if I would have found the courage to do the right thing as they did. I'll never know, because their battles belonged to them, and I have battles of my own every day. And you do, too.

You see, courage seeks the truth when we know it might be painful. Courage leads us to change when it would be easier to stay the same. Courage leads us to learn and grow even when doing so will reveal our weaknesses. And courage helps us to lead, when being up front makes us an easy target for criticism, failure, and loneliness.

These are all battles we face every day, and they're battles we must fight to win. Our families and the other people we lead are counting on us.

Do you normally feel courageous?

"Encourage" means to "put courage into." Ask God to encourage you to face the battles or obstacles that you'll face today.

September 24
Real Love

Scripture for Today: 1 Corinthians 13:4–13

Do you wanna know what love is? Regarding love we've been deceived, lied to, tricked, bamboozled, duped, and snookered. In almost every form of modern-day communication we're told that love is a feeling! We sing, "You've lost that lovin' feelin'." and "What's love but a second–hand emotion?" We're told we can find it and lose it. We're told we can fall into it and fall out of it.

But real love is not a feeling; real love is a choice. It's an unconditional sacrificial choice to be devoted to someone until death separates you. It's true in friendship, family, and marriage. It involves devotion, loyalty, faithfulness, and determination to make the other person's life better and brighter. Real love is not about you; it's about them. If you've lost that lovin' feelin', it's because somebody in the relationship has chosen to lose it.

Always remember there are two halves in every friendship or relationship. Make sure your half is the better half. If both halves live this way, endless love can be found.

Who in your life do you have trouble loving? Why?

Love is a decision we make, whether to love God or to love others. Make a conscious decision right now to love everyone you know as God loves you.

September 25
Thunderwood

Scripture for Today: Hebrews 11:24–26

Have you ever been sucked into a devastating personal problem that you never thought would be an issue?

I grew up coon hunting on the Tallapoosa River and its surrounding creeks and swamps. One night our dogs treed a raccoon in a big oak tree and one of my buddies decided to climb the tree to get him. We noticed poisonous vines called thunderwood around the tree. We warned him, but I'll never forget his response: "Thunderwood don't bother me. I'm not allergic!" But the next day, the itching rash on his chest told a different story. To my friend's surprise, the thunderwood had left its mark.

I've seen this kind of surprise many times in people's personal lives, and it can be devastating. It may have begun with a single lie, or trying an addictive drug just once, or a flirtatious comment to someone other than your spouse. You may have thought, "It don't bother me, I'm not allergic!" But all sin is poisonous and leaves a bigger mark than you ever imagined.

Can you remember a time when sin cost you more than you thought? Caused more damage than you anticipated?

When tempted, ask God to help you see the end result of that sin, then trust Him to give you victory over it.

September 26
Patience

Scripture for Today: Proverbs 15:18

How do you rank on the patience scale with those you love?

Another word for patience, is *longsuffering*. It simply means, "to suffer a long time." Many weddings begin with the Bible verse "Love is patient." However, they never look at the other person and say, "I look forward to a long-suffering marriage." No; they expect it to be filled with joy, romance, and bliss every day. To them, there will certainly be no suffering.

But then life happens, and one will say, "I'm no longer happy in my marriage. Don't I deserve to be happy?" To them, that's a perfectly good reason to throw in the towel, quit, and leave. But what time is it really? It's time to be patient; to suffer long. Every 50-year marriage has experienced at least a few thousand unhappy days mixed in.

Someone has said, "Selfishness seeks its own private happiness at the expense of others." That's not love. It never was. Real love will sacrifice its own happiness so the people loved can have a better life. That's what Jesus did for us.

Do you seek your own private happiness at the expense of others? Do you struggle being impatient with others be they family, friends, or co-workers?

The same things that reveal our impatience can make us patient, if we respond to them correctly. Ask God to help you suffer long when trials and unhappiness come your way.

September 27
Shortcuts

Scripture for Today: Proverbs 10:4

When you have to make a choice between the two, do you take the escalator or the stairs? Life is full of such choices. A choice between the easy way or the hard way. The short way or the long way. The way of comfort or the way of hard work and struggle.

I see more and more people taking the escalator these days. Looking for a way to succeed without hard work, sweat, and tears. They're expecting success to come easy, in marriage, in business, in family, and in their spiritual life. They're looking for the shortcuts, handouts, quick fixes, and the path of least resistance.

But you need to know there are no shortcuts that lead to long-term success. Shortcuts give us the illusion of success, all the while setting us up for massive failure. There's something about struggling through the hard times that prepares us for real success over the long haul. The next time you have a choice, avoid the escalator and take the stairs. Trust me. You need the stairs!

When have you noticed people taking shortcuts that resulted in inferior work or craftsmanship?

Commit to doing the full work, whether in your family or job, rather than taking shortcuts that result in relationships or work not done well.

September 28th
Reflection

Scripture for Today: Philippians 1:6

It's that time of year again! Time for the nights to get colder, the days to get shorter, and the leaves to change colors. Migratory birds journey southward. Squirrels finish storing their nuts. Salmon begin their amazing swim back to their spawning grounds. And bears make their final preparations to take a long winter nap. Autumn is an amazing and important season of the year for all of nature.

God designed it that way. It's important for you and me too. The year still has a couple of months left, and autumn is a great time to reflect on where we've been and where we're going. Reflection is essential for a successful life. Life's experience does not automatically make a person better; it's an evaluated experience that's required. Reflection about your past helps build deep roots, roots that will help keep you strong in the future. God has begun a good work in you, and HE promises to continue that good work. But if you don't pause to reflect, you'll be completely unaware of HIS amazing work.

List some major events, memories, decisions or experiences from this year thus far.

How have these events impacted your life?

September 29
True Happiness

Scripture for Today: Ecclesiastes 12:13

What are you working for? Most would say they are working for money, of course! And it's a necessary thing in this world, but money without meaning and purpose leaves us empty. Others are working to collect stuff, some to acquire knowledge, success, and fame, while others are working to have a life of fun, pleasure, and security. But to be honest, these things motivate all of us to some degree. They are the cravings of our human nature.

However, acquiring all of these things in abundance will not deliver the happiness for which we had hoped. King Solomon was wiser, richer, and more famous than anyone in the world. He had several vacation homes. And with 700 wives and 300 concubines to satisfy his lustful desires, he would certainly be labeled a "ladies' man." All of it left him disappointed, yet he challenged us to "Fear God, and keep His commandments." This is the path to true happiness. Many of us don't take advice very well, but that's great advice from a man who learned it the hard way!

Have you ever chased something you thought would bring real happiness only to have the happiness fade away?

Fearing God requires us to love His Word; they are hand-in-glove. Seek to spend as much time in scripture as you can. It will point you directly to the One who is the source of true happiness.

September 30
Family

Scripture for Today: Colossians 3:19–21

How are you investing in your family? The family was the first and most important institution God created. And our family has a greater impact on our lives than anything or anyone else. When we were kids, our parents, grandparents, and siblings formed our approach to life. Our experiences during childhood, whether good or bad, infuse every thought, attitude, and decision we will ever face.

Except through adoption and marriage, we don't get to choose our family, but we do get to choose how to invest in them. Regardless of our childhood experiences, as we become adults, we must decide how to lead our family now that we're the decision makers. Some will want a family exactly like the one in which they grew up. Others will want the opposite.

But keep in mind that God created the family. The Bible teaches that love, honor, and respect are essential, and worshipping God should be at the center. Yes, there's a price to be paid. But your kids and grandkids are worth the investment.

Are you making good family investments right now?

If not, what changes do you need to make in your family investment strategy?

October 1
Betrayal

Scripture for Today: Psalm 49:1, Matthew 26:47–54

Have you ever felt betrayed? It happens in business, family, and friendship. Few things are more painful and humiliating. Betrayal always leaves us confused, because it happens with someone we love—and we thought loved us. We knew the person well—or at least we thought we did! We've all felt betrayed and we remember it well.

But have you ever been the betrayer? Sure, you have, but it's likely you don't remember quite as clearly. We have long memories about those who've hurt us, but easily forget when we've hurt others.

If you've been betrayed, you'll need to work to find forgiveness to protect your own soul from bitterness and resentment. If you've been the betrayer, you'll need to work hard to help restore the trust and relationships you've destroyed.

Neither is easy, but forgiveness and restoration are essential, or you'll walk through life with the heaviness of a wounded, flawed, and destructive soul. And such a soul will strike again, and it usually strikes at the people you love the most.

Write a few words below that describe how it feels to be betrayed.

Jesus has experienced this hurt Himself and can heal you from the hurt you feel. Talk to Him about it in prayer and trust His power to make you whole.

October 2
Hustle

Scripture for Today: 1 Kings 19:1–5

Have you lost your hustle? I can still hear my boyhood baseball coach yelling, "Hustle, Todd! Hustle!"

It's easy to lose our hustle when we're losing. When things aren't going so well. Or when we aren't having fun anymore. Sometimes difficulties and hardships become the norm in life. And such difficulties simply suck the energy and excitement we have about the future right out of us.

But when it happens, you can get it back, and you'll likely need a mental re-start with a plan to do so. Here's how:

Re-establish your dream for the future.
Re-commit to excellence in all your actions.
Re-create a timeline to reach your goal.
And *re-determine* yourself to complete what you start and to finish well. Your life has massive potential, but you won't reach that potential without maintaining your hustle.

Hustle, Todd! Hustle! It was a great challenge from a boyhood coach, but I need to hear it today as much as ever. But today I usually have to say it to myself. And you will too!

Are you at a place in life where you've lost your hustle? Can you find a specific reason? Is it something in your control or out of your control?

If it's something in your control, pause and ask God to help you eliminate the obstacles so you can follow the steps above to hustle to your goals.

October 3
If

Scripture for Today: Mark 9:14–24

Do you ever catch yourself using the word "if" to make excuses?

"If" I'd been born rich, I could live a good life. Well, you weren't, and all the ifs in the world won't change it. "If only" I'd won the lottery I wouldn't have lost my home. Well, you didn't, and nothing is going to change that either. It's easy to use "if" as an emotional crutch, but it's a trap. Such thinking locks you in a make-believe world and locks you out of the real world where you can excel to become all God intends for you to become.

If you're determined to use "if" to control your life, make sure you use it in the right way. Instead of "If only," how about asking "What if"? What if I go back to school, what difference can it make in my financial future? What if I go all in with my marriage, what difference can it make with my family in the future? "If" is a powerful word if it's used in the right way! What if you try that for a while?

Do you have a lot of "if only" regrets in your life?

Take some time to think about the "what ifs" that are possible in your life, then write two or three of them below.

October 4
Humility

Scripture for Today: Proverbs 3:34, Proverbs 11:2

Do you understand the power of humility? I know, it's not really our favorite attitude to embrace. Too often we'd rather feel the power of domineering confidence, arrogance, and pride. But such desires are misguided.

Real humility flows from the greatest confidence possible. It's about giving someone else a chance. Even if you know the answer you don't have to be the first to blurt it out. I remember those kids in school, don't you?

Humility is the awareness that you don't know everything, and you're not right about everything. There's no need to be quickly critical of other people's thoughts and ideas as if you're brilliant and they're idiots. Humility invests in people who often have nothing to give back. And it gives public credit to the people who work privately behind the scenes to help you succeed and look like a genius.

Jesus is the perfect example of humility; through humility He changed the world. Don't you think a little humility can change your world, too?

What's the difference between being humble and being a doormat?

Ask God to teach you to be humble so you can gain His favor in return.

October 5
Playing it Safe

Scripture for Today: Matthew 10:16

Are you living by the philosophy of playing it safe? I meet people often who're afraid to live an adventurous life. It's ironic that many of them profess to be Christians, with the promise of God's constant presence in this world and eternity with God in the next.

Yet, they're afraid of what they know and what they don't know. They're afraid to make a decision. They're afraid to fly or to go out of the country. They're afraid to leave home in the morning and afraid to go home in the evening.

Jesus did not die so we could live safely. He died so we could live dangerously. He said, "I'm sending you out like sheep among wolves." Now that doesn't sound very safe to me!

As believers, we're to be salt and light to people who need Jesus, but we can't do so while cowering safely and cowardly in our homes and church gatherings. Go find some wolves to walk among today. Our Shepherd promises to never leave us nor forsake us.

Do you tend to play it safe in life decisions or do you tend to go for broke?

Are there any areas in your life where you are playing it safe when you should be walking by faith? Reading God's word, the Bible, will strengthen your faith and help you have the confidence in God not to play it safe.

October 6
Fight

Scripture for Today: 2 Timothy 4:7

Are you ready for a fight? I hope so, because life will bring you one fight after another.

Regardless of your views about Andrew Jackson and his complex legacy, one thing is for sure: He was a fighter! The hardened General's leadership in the War of 1812 and the Indian wars that followed earned him the nickname "Old Hickory." Before becoming President of the United States, he fought 13 face-to-face duels. Of himself he said, "I was born for the storm. The calm does not suit me." Jackson did not run from a hard fight. He pressed in to it!

At some point, you'll have to fight for your marriage, your friends, your health, your career, your family, and your honor. And you'll definitely have to fight for your moral life, because you have an enemy who is relentless at taking you down, destroying the very fabric of your soul and everything you treasure. And he does not fight fairly. The Apostle Paul said, "I have fought the good fight!" I'm committed to do the same. Are you?

Have you given up on your goals, maybe the ones you set this year, or are you still fighting to reach them?

Paul's counsel to "fight the good fight" is a great reminder to press on until the end. If you've become weary in the fight, ask God for strength to continue on to your goals.

October 7
Strength

Scripture for Today: Psalm 23; Romans 8:28

Where do you get strength when life gets tough? I love history. One of my favorite characters is Jedidiah Smith, explorer of the American West.

His personal journal describes the beauty of God's creation in its rawest forms. For inner strength, he spent hours reading his Bible as he explored the wilderness. Then in the Black Hills territory of today's South Dakota, he faced his greatest battle ever. He was savagely attacked by a grizzly bear. His ribs were crushed as the bear slammed him into the ground. The bear sunk his teeth into Jedidiah's head, attempted to crush his skull, and ripped his scalp from his head. It was left hanging by one ear! But somehow, the bear then left and Jedidiah lived. Fellow explorer Jim Clyman sewed his scalp and ear back on, and after just ten days of rest, he was leading his exploration team again. From where did Jedidiah get his strength to survive? He said he got it from the 23rd Psalm. You can too!

What's the worst trial you've ever had to persevere through? What things did you learn from it? Did you feel strong or weak when you were in the middle of it?

God has promised to work all things out for good for those who belong to Him. If you don't know Him yet, stop right now and ask God to bring you into His family.

October 8
Grace, Greenbacks, Grit

Scripture for Today: James 4:1–6

Have you found that magical formula for a great life? You know, like ice cream on a brownie? Once you've had it together, you just know it's magic.

Many years ago, just after beginning as a pastor, I received a magical formula from my dad's friend and Tallapoosa legend Herschel Kirkland. He said, "Todd, three things are needed to build a great church. Lots of grace, lots of greenbacks, and lots of grit!" Herschel was right on all three points. But it's not just true about church; it's also true about life.

We and the people around us are flawed, so grace is required. God shows it toward us. Be prepared to show it toward others.

It takes lots of greenbacks to raise a family and live each day. Get a good education, work hard, spend wisely, and save. Greenbacks are needed until you die.

Life is hard and we must find the grit to plow through the hard stuff. You'll want to quit, but you must find the grit. Thank you, Hershel, for the magical formula.

Of grace, greenbacks, and grit which seems the biggest challenge for you to reach or manage?

God promises both wisdom and strength to us to help us show grace, manage greenbacks, and find grit. If you are lacking in one, ask God to provide it to you.

October 9
Don't Worry Be Happy

Scripture for Today: Matthew 6:25–34

What are you worried about? I'm sure you could easily provide me with a list. And maybe if I read it, I might begin to worry a little myself. That's the problem with worry—it's contagious! And it does absolutely nothing except increase your blood pressure. So, stop it.

I remember the song like it was yesterday. "In every life we have some trouble, but when you worry you make it double. So, don't worry, be happy!"

Jesus said, "Don't worry about your life. About your body. What you will eat or drink or what you will wear. Today has too many challenges of its own, so don't worry about tomorrow either!"

If you're a believer, your heavenly Father promises to provide what you need, and He knows what you need before you need it. Above everything else, seek first the kingdom of God and His righteousness, and all of these other things will be provided for you.

"In every life we have some trouble, but when you worry you make it double. So, don't worry, be happy!"

Are you in a state of worry? What is causing you to worry?

Someone once said worry is taking on responsibility God never intended us to have. Give back to God that which only He can carry. You'll find you won't worry, but will be happy.

October 10
Autumn

Scripture for Today: Proverbs 16:3

Autumn is my favorite time of year. It's the third quarter season.
It's a reminder to get ready for winter, which is just around the
corner. The changing of the leaves. The coolness in the air. The
warmth of a fire. How can you not love it?

My wife and I went to Bar Harbor, Maine with some friends to
enjoy autumn in a different region. I'd heard about the brightness
and beauty of the colors, but I found it to be even more than I
expected. The fresh lobster was a real treat also.

But I'm reminded that once I moved over the age of 50, I began to
firmly rest in my third quarter season of life. The changing color of
the hair I have left is clear evidence. It's a good time to be
intentional as I reflect upon my first half-century of life, enjoy each
day, and plan for my future ahead. I don't know what my winter
season will be like, but wisdom tells me, "Don't wait till it arrives to
prepare for it!"

Are you prepared for the next season of life?

*If not, take some time soon to make a plan for your next season and ask God
for His wisdom as you move into it.*

October 11
Echoes

Scripture for Today: Matthew 7:12, Galatians 5:14

What is echoing back your way? Some years ago my wife and I took a dream trip with some friends to the Swiss Alps. As we climbed higher and higher, we saw beautiful lush green hillsides, surrounded by massive snow-capped mountains in the distance. All we could say was, "Wow!"

Then it hit me. And with all of the force I could muster, I took a deep breath, cupped my hands around my mouth and yelled, "Ricola!" And yes, I heard that same word echo back to me several times. I even tried yodeling a time or two. I mean, how could I not?

I'm reminded that life is much like an echo. Jesus taught us that we get what we give. Treat people the way you want to be treated. If you want your wife, husband, or friends to be kind, supportive and forgiving, then let those actions begin with you. If you expect to have good things echo back your way, remember, they must begin with you. Life is like an echo!

Do you normally treat people like you want to be treated? You can tell by the echoes coming back to you.

Ask God to help you in every situation to treat people like you want to be treated.

October 12
Stabilizing Force

Scripture for Today: Joshua 2:12, Proverbs 19:22

Are you a stabilizing force in our shaky world? My mom certainly was. She was a smiler and encourager, who gave each away freely. She believed in people who often didn't believe in themselves. She made people feel stable when they were in her presence. In short, Mom loved like Jesus.

Some time ago a man dropped by our family home to visit Mom. We knew each other well as kids, but he had made some decisions early in life that led him down a difficult road. But Mom had always shown him love and kindness. She prayed for him and with him. He'd been away for several years and didn't know Mom had died years earlier. When he asked my brother, "Is Mrs. Dean here?" He was informed she'd passed away. The news was difficult for him to absorb as grief overtook him. He wept uncontrollably. Why? Because a stabilizing force in his life was gone.

This world gets shaky at times for all of us. Stabilize it for somebody today while you can. All it takes is a little love and kindness.

Who has been a stabilizing force for you through your life? Write their names here.

Do you think you've been a stabilizing force for anyone? Your kids or spouse? An ailing parent? A hurting friend?

If you have, thank God that He used you to help someone else. If you've been helped, thank God for using someone in your life. Then, thank God for being the source of all stability.

October 13
Clothes for the Soul

Scripture for Today: Colossians 3:12–14

Have you ever left your house in the morning without first putting on the necessities? You know, your clothes, glasses, deodorant, or shoes? Putting these things on is an intentional choice because we know that doing so will make our day go so much better. Not doing so will likely make us feel naked and create some embarrassing moments.

Well, there are a few other things we'd better put on every day. They're just as important, but for some people they're not as obvious. The Bible tells us to put on love, put on compassion, kindness, humility, gentleness, and patience. These too require an intentional choice. Without question, they will make our day go so much better. They're what I call "clothes for the soul!" You wouldn't go to work without first putting clothes on your body. Make sure you put the right stuff on your soul, too.

There are too many people walking around today with a naked soul. They think no one notices, but we do. Make sure you're not one of them.

What article of soul clothing is the hardest for you to put on?

Develop a practice of putting on your soul clothes each day as you get dressed. You will find yourself more prepared for life when your soul is as dressed as your body.

October 14
Breath of God

Scripture for Today: Genesis 2:4–7

Are you using your breath for which it was given?

We learn from the Bible that God made Adam from the dust of the ground, but Adam was not yet alive. He was without function and purpose. Then God breathed into the nostrils of Adam, and Adam became a living soul. It was the breath of God that became the breath of Adam. God loaned His breath to Adam for a purpose: to worship God, to speak of His goodness, and to give Him gratitude for His many blessings.

Sure, you can use the breath God loaned you for many things. You can curse, complain, and criticize, and even deny God's existence. You can use it to blow out your birthday candles each year. But keep in mind that someday you'll blow them out for the last time and God will take His breath back. And you will give an account for what you did with it while you had it. So, use it to confess your faith in Him and worship Him today while you still can.

Are you using your breath to honor God or to dishonor Him, to praise Him or ignore Him?

If you've been using your breath to sin, stop now and confess your sins to God, then live in forgiveness, using each breath to honor Him.

October 15
Why?

Scripture for Today: Psalm 67:7

But why? Why this? Why me? Why now? These are the most tormenting questions we ask. They follow every tragedy or shred of disappointing news for which we're not prepared. We yearn to make sense of it all, but sometimes we can find no answers.

Your business is destroyed, your belongings are stolen, and employees murdered. All ten of your children are killed in a storm. Yes, all of this happened in the Old Testament to Job's family within a short period of time. But why? Why this? Why me? Why now?

As Job and his wife stood beside the fresh graves of their children, the heavens were silent and without answers. With bitterness, Job's wife said, "Curse God and die!" But in the midst of brokenness and confusion, Job asked a different question, "Shall we accept good from God and not adversity?" So perhaps the next time something good happens, your business prospers, a deal goes through, you get a promotion, or give birth to a healthy child, you should ask, "But why? Why this? Why me? Why now?"

Do you find yourself asking why regarding bad things and taking blessings for granted?

Take some time to list some good things you've been taking for granted, then thank God for them.

October 16
Complaining

Scripture for Today: Philippians 2:14

Are you making it personal? I hope you are, because it's the only way you can improve. When you think of problems in the human race today, do you remember that you are a part of the human race today? You might be the problem! When you complain about problems in your church, your community, and your nation, do you remind yourself that you ARE the church? You ARE the community. You ARE the nation. And more often than not, you ARE a part of the problem you complain about.

When we talk about problems, we love to speak in generalities. We love to imagine that everyone else is the problem. But the fact is, we are all flawed by sin, and at some point we must face the person in the mirror and make it personal—me, myself, and I. That's the biggest problem I must deal with every day. It's true for you, too. So, before you complain today about somebody else, make it personal. Do a little complaining about yourself, then go to work on the problem.

Do you do all things without grumbling or complaining as the scripture tells us?

What is there in your life you would complain about in other people did it? Ask for God's help in correcting it, then remain focused on your own "complaint areas" than those of others.

October 17
New Life

Scripture for Today: Romans 7:6

Did you know you really can have a new life in Jesus?

Born in Haralson County in 1892, Taylor was an arrogant and troubled kid. According to his brother, Taylor woke up every day thinking about who he was going to fight. He carried a sharp knife for the special occasion. One such fight happened outside of church while services were being held inside. He cut a boy so badly he almost died. As a teenager, Taylor was in and out of jail, quickly becoming a community criminal. He was shot in a fight and couldn't walk for several months as a result. He had to learn how to walk again.

Then in his early 30's, Taylor heard the gospel and called out to Jesus for forgiveness and a new life. He became one of the most humble, loving, and respectable men imaginable. He became a pastor, telling others how to find hope and forgiveness. Taylor was my grandfather. He found new life in Jesus. I'm glad he did. You can find new life in Christ, too!

Do you have new life in Jesus Christ, been forgiven of sins, and made part of God's family?

God can change your life just like He changed my grandfather's life, my father's life, my life, and billions of others throughout history. Simply ask Him today.

October 18
Lost

Scripture for Today: Psalm 28:6, John 14:6

Have you ever lost your way? I've been lost in a foreign country, in a large city, in the Rocky Mountains at night in the cold winter, and I've been lost in a good ole Georgia swamp. It felt the same every time. It's a frightening and unnerving experience to wander aimlessly with no sense of direction and no guide or device to help you get back on track. To make things worse, when we're lost, our mind plays tricks on us. We hear, think, and see things that are simply not true. Those tricks will often make us think we're going in the right direction when we're not.

Well the Bible describes the spiritual condition of mankind as lost. You might think you have it all figured out. You may think you're a genius. Others might even affirm that you are. You may think you're going in the right direction. But unless your faith is firmly fixed in Jesus Christ, you're lost. There's only one way to heaven. Jesus said, "No one comes to the Father except through me."

Many people believe we make our own way to God, but Jesus claims to be the only way. Does that challenge your current way of thinking?

Without Christ we are lost because He is "the way." Ask Him today to show you the way to Himself so you will no longer be lost.

October 19
Potential

Scripture for Today: Ecclesiastes 9:10, 1 Corinthians 9:24–25

What are you doing with your God given potential? You have skills, training, influence, time, and opportunity. What are you doing with all of that? God created you to do great things. To do wonderful works as the Bible calls them. So, are you? You have the potential.

Too often we sit on the sidelines of life and make excuses. We have a poverty mindset: "I don't have the time." "I'm too young." "I'm too old." "I don't have the ability." You say, "I would…if I could." You simply stop short of your potential.

But the opposite is true. You say, "I would…if I could," but in reality "you could…if you would." God designed you on purpose, for purpose, and with great potential. Un-attempted potential leads to massive regret. Yes, sometimes we try and fail. And falling short while trying is painful. But the pain of falling short is nothing compared to the pain of stopping short. Don't be half-hearted in what you do. You're better than that. Reach your God-given potential!

Are you currently living with a poverty mindset, poor-mouthing your abilities and efforts?

When you live according to God's purpose for your life, it is easier to realize your potential, so start by seeking His purpose, then let Him fully use you.

October 20
Harmony

Scripture for Today: John 17:9–11

Have you ever wondered what was on the mind of Jesus as He prepared to go to the cross? The Gospel of John chapters 12-18 explain many of His thoughts in great detail. But the fact that He prayed for me and every other believer throughout history is inspiring. His specific prayer for us is that we would be one. It was the concept of unity, harmony, and togetherness that He desired for us to display so the world might believe.

Divisiveness among believers and in churches is a great hindrance to people believing the Gospel.

I heard about a town that had a church named Harmony Church. Down the road was Old Harmony Church. Farther down the road was New Harmony Church. And a little farther was 2nd New Harmony Church. I have a pretty good feeling that "harmony" was not one of their real character traits.

Togetherness must be centered around a clear mission. The mission Jesus gave us to go make disciples. Let's do that and leave the fussing and fighting to someone else.

Can you think of a time when a team or organization you were involved with was in harmony? What about a time it wasn't in harmony?

Harmony depends on all of us. Why not ask God to make you an instrument of harmony in your family, church, and workplace. Everyone will benefit as a result.

October 21
Listening to God

Scripture for Today: Revelation 2:7, 11, 17, 29; 3:6, 13, 22

Are you hard of hearing…especially when it comes to God?

"If you have ears to hear, please listen!" That challenge is given at least fourteen times in the Bible. Listening and paying attention to what's being said is an age-old problem. It's a problem when we don't listen to the people around us, but it's an even bigger problem when we don't listen to God! Many question whether or not God still speaks. But I believe the bigger problem is we don't listen. Often, we aren't really interested in what God has to say.

Or perhaps we're mistaken in thinking God's voice is a deep baritone or loud bass sound. I've often thought it would be funny if God has a high-pitched tenor voice, and when I get to heaven He says, "Hey, Todd, come on in!"

The fact is, God speaks to us in a variety of ways, including the Bible, events, circumstances, and other people. But more often than not, God speaks with a whisper in our spirit. And when you hear that whisper, pay close attention.

Do you regularly pay attention to what God says to you while reading scripture, listening to a sermon, or sharing with a Christian friend?

God is not silent. Start by listening to Him speak to you through His word, the Bible; be reading it as often as you can.

October 22
God's Ability

Scripture for Today: Philippians 4:13

Are you aware of God's ability to do great things in your life?

"Let there be light!" These are God's very first words recorded in history. He spoke them in the midst of darkness and chaos. As a result, the sun, moon, and stars came into existence. They were the foundation for everything else God would create, including us. Without light, we would have no vision. There would be no life. There would be no universe. Just four words set it all in motion!

As Pastor Mark Batterson observed in his book, *Whisper,* the universe is God's way of saying, "Look what I can do with just four words!"

You also are a part of God's creation. He gave you the ability to learn, grow, and become wise. He gave you the ability to choose between right and wrong, to be wise or foolish, to live for Him, or live for yourself. God has the ability to do great things in your life, but He also gave you the ability to mess it all up if you choose to.

Are you currently living according to your ability or God's ability?

Limiting yourself to your own ability separates you from God's power. Leave behind your own strength and ask God for His.

October 23
Bible

Scripture for Today: Luke 4:1–4

Did you realize you can read through the Bible in one year by reading just four chapters per day, or in two years with two chapters per day? You can read through Proverbs every month reading one of its 31 chapters each day. Five chapters a day will get you through the entire book of Psalms in just a month (save 119 for day 31).

It's a big book, but its value to your life is even bigger. Our modern culture of tolerance says there is no absolute truth: no one is right, no one is wrong, that everyone who tries wins.

But the Bible teaches a different principle. There is absolute truth. You should know that truth, and that truth will set you free. Yes, sometimes truth is painful and frustrating, especially if it condemns something we're doing and requires us to change. But if we align our life with truth every day, it sets us up to win this thing called life. I hope that's at least one of your goals.

Has regular Bible reading been part of your life? Was it in the past but now is not?

If you need to, sit down with your calendar or planning app and make Bible reading a priority. A few verses a day read slowly and thought-over are far better than not reading at all.

October 24
Pain

Scripture for Today: 2 Corinthians 11:24–30

Have you ever heard the statement, "No pain, no gain?" Man, I hate that statement! I started going to the gym and working out again after being out for a while, and I must have been doing something right, because I was in pain constantly!

The fact is, we all hate pain of every kind, but pain is one of God's great gifts. One of the ways God speaks to us and guides us to get better is through pain.

Pain can be a parent, college professor, marriage counselor, or friend who challenges us to excel and do better!

Pain can be an illness, death, disappointment, or tragedy that makes us rethink our life, redirects our journey, and drives us closer in our relationship with God. Aging is a pain that can do the same.

Since the beginning of time, we see pain as our enemy, but if you'll lean in and listen to the pains you face, it just might be that you hear the voice of God speaking clearer than ever about your next adventure.

Is something in life causing you pain?

Ask God to show you what He's trying to show you in it, then embrace the gift He gives you in the pain.

October 25
Priorities

Scripture for Today: Joshua 24:14–15

What God are you leading your family to worship and serve? Our culture has a variety of gods to choose: sports, politics, education, entertainment, wealth, and so many more. Each of these play a role in all of our lives, but where does your devotion rate for these when compared to your faith? Wherever it rates sends a clear message to your kids and grandkids where their devotion, passion, and worship should be aimed.

The historic leader Joshua gave a clear challenge to his fellow countrymen. "You can worship whatever god you choose," he said, "but as for me and my family, we will serve the Lord!"
It was a powerful declaration coming from the much-revered leader of his family.

No voice will ever speak louder to your kids and grandkids than yours. You're the most influential person in their life, good or bad. You help shape their thinking, priorities, and choices. Make a clear statement that you and your family will serve the Lord. Such a decision will help them long after you're gone.

It's been said that Sunday morning church is a Saturday night decision. When does your family prepare for Sunday morning?

Worshipping God personally and with other people of faith should be a top priority. Take a personal inventory and see where it ranks. If not near the very top, refocus yourself toward God.

October 26
Future

Scripture for Today: James 4:13–17

Are you consumed with wondering about the future? When I was a kid, I wondered what it would be like to be married, to have kids, to get old like my parents. And now I am a grandparent, and by many standards I fit into the OLD category! Yes, I still think and dream about the future and I plan for it, too. But, the longer I live, I realize some of the future I dream about will never happen. So, more and more, I appreciate the here and now.

A good cup of coffee on a cold morning. A dinner and conversation with friends. A smile and sparkle in the eye of a grandson or granddaughter. Yeah, I have always been a dreamer and planner for the future, but the peace of contentment can be found in the small stuff every day. So, I choose to stop and look for it.

The Bible warns us about saying, "I'm going to do this or that in the future" because "nobody knows what a day might bring." That changes everything. Pause today and enjoy the small stuff.

Think about a few small things in life you can be thankful for today: maybe light traffic on the way to work, a cool breeze when walking, or an unexpected financial blessing.

Think about a small thing you can do for someone else: an anonymous gift, an encouraging card, or a cheerful text message. Make a few notes below or on your calendar to help you remember to do it.

October 27
A Person's Value

Scripture for Today: Romans 5:8

Have you ever seen or heard of the actions of someone and thought, *"Well that person is just worthless!"* Such statements demonstrate a lack of understanding of ourselves and most importantly, a lack of understanding God's love. It's so easy for us to judge a person's value based on that person's actions. You know: bad actions = worthless person, and good actions = valued person?

But we forget, we are all bad actors at some point.

The Bible reminds us that Jesus died for the ungodly. "God showed His love toward us in that, Christ died for us while we were still sinners!" That means that while we were at our worst, God gave His best and most for us! Our value was massive, even at our worst. And it's at our worst that God has chosen to meet us with His love, grace, and forgiveness.

Never confuse the behaviors of a person with the value of a person. Choose to meet people where they are; that's what God does, and we should do the same.

Do you remember a time you misjudged a person based on a single act?

Jesus was known for meeting people where they were: tax collectors, prostitutes, religious sinners, etc. Love people where they are and see if God doesn't open a door for the gospel.

October 28
Stuck

Scripture for Today: Acts 1:4–8

Okay, what's next? That's the primary and essential question to help you get the most out of life. It's a question to ask, not only at the beginning of a new year, but it should be asked every day.

It's easy to get stuck in the disappointments of yesterday or the frustrations of today. And yes, once we're stuck, it can last for days, weeks, and even years. And it's often hard to get moving again.

I know what it's like to get stuck. I know how hard it is to start moving forward again, but it sure feels good when it happens, especially when other people depend on your leadership. And it doesn't happen automatically.

Asking, "What's next?" will help you focus on where you're going tomorrow. That's a great thing to focus on to help your life and the lives of those around you get better. So, "What's next?"

Where in life are you stuck? What's the next thing you need to do to get unstuck?

Asking "What's next" requires us to listen in faith to what God says and where He leads. Be attentive as He responds then do what's next.

October 29
Billy Graham

Scripture for Today: Daniel 12:3

How much can one life really matter? How much can your life matter?

It was an inspiring couple of weeks when the nation and the world honored the life of the late evangelist, Billy Graham. With clips of him preaching the message of forgiveness through Jesus Christ playing again and again, His death provided another chance for his bold, clear, and unmistakable voice to speak of God's love to hurting hearts around the world.

From an obscure dairy farm in the hills of North Carolina to the world stage, no human in history has preached to more people. He led millions to embrace Jesus by faith; they will spend eternity in heaven. He was honored well for his good life and devotion to Jesus, the gospel, and humanity. His life now matters for eternity.

But your life can matter, too. Encourage someone to embrace Jesus today. Then tomorrow, do it again. People need to hear the good news. God promises those who turn many people toward a righteous life will shine like the stars forever and ever.

Who in your family, school, or workplace needs to hear the gospel?

Ask God right now to use you in sharing the good news of Jesus with them.

October 30
Finishing the Race

Scripture for Today: 1 Corinthians 9:24–27, 2 Timothy 4:7

Are you committed to finishing well in the important races of life? You know, things like school, marriage, parenthood, career, and your faith? Quitting is the easy way out, especially when we get tired, weary, and wounded. But quitting always leaves an empty spot inside.

It was the 1968 Summer Olympics in Mexico City. The Gold, Silver, and Bronze medals for the marathon had already been awarded and most of the stadium cleared. However, the race was not over.

John Stephen Akwari from Tanzania was still dragging himself through the course. He had fallen, was badly injured and in excruciating pain with a dislocated knee, but he refused to quit. Over an hour after the winner had crossed the finish line, Akwari finally dragged himself across the finish line.

When asked why he continued in pain with no chance of winning, he gave a response that can inspire us all: "My country did not send me 5000 miles to start a race. They sent me 5000 miles to finish a race!" Finish well. You'll be glad you did!

Are you on pace to finish the race of life well? What is hindering you?

If you are discouraged in the race, ask God to renew your strength, then refocus on the race set before you.

October 31
Rumors

Scripture for Today: 2 Corinthians 12:20

Have you ever wondered how rumors get started? Shakespeare said a "rumor is a pipe blown by jealousies and conjectures."

Yes, a rumor kept poor old Abraham Lincoln from resting in peace even twenty-two years after his death. A rumor developed that his tomb was empty. So, in 1887, they opened his casket and there he was. After being seen by several witnesses, they sealed his casket with lead. But not for long: fourteen years later they opened it up again. Why? For the same reason: another rumor began to circulate that his tomb was empty. But, when they looked the second time, He was still there.

All rumors are cruel, unfair, and destructive attacks perpetrated by needy, suspicious, busybodies. "Have you heard…" "They say…" "Did you hear…" "Somebody told me…" "Well, I heard…" All of their info is based on rumor and innuendo.

Here's a fact: if it's about someone else, it's none of your business. None! Read a book or eat a hamburger instead. At least you can't talk with your mouth full!

Have you ever been made aware of rumors being told about you? How did it make you feel? How did you respond?

Rumors, slander, and false innuendo are tools of Satan. Commit to neither listen to nor spread unfounded information about others.

November 1
Voting

Scripture for Today: Proverbs 29:2

Are you ready to vote? Voting is one of our most sacred freedoms in America, and every citizen should do so. Soldiers have fought and died so we could have the privilege. It's irresponsible to not participate.

I recently visited an extremely poor country where they had the same leader in office for over 30 years. Corruption and abuse of power was rampant. Their unemployment rate was extremely high, their currency was almost worthless, and their people felt hopeless about the future. Leadership does matter!

The United States of America is in no way a perfect nation, and neither are our leaders, but we do get the privilege to choose our leaders. We can decide to keep the leaders we have, or we can vote them out and replace them with new leaders we can believe in. The choice is ours. So if you're an American citizen, be responsible and vote. If you don't vote, you should never complain about your leaders. When you don't vote, you are actually one of the biggest problems the nation has. And if you don't live in the United States, but are in a country that allows you to choose your leaders, make sure you participate!

What are some reasons people don't bother to vote?

How can Christians encourage faithful, godly people to step into careers of governmental service?

November 2
Fun

Scripture for Today: Proverbs 17:22

Are you taking the time to have some fun in life? I heard about a dad who told his family he could not go on the annual family vacation because of work. But he helped them plan every detail of the vacation, including the route they would drive, and then sent them on their way. But the dad had planned to go all along. He had a friend drive him over a hundred miles and drop him off ahead of his family so he could pretend to be a hitch-hiker on the side of the road.

The man stood there and watched car after car pass, and when he saw his family's car coming the dad stepped to the edge of the road and put his thumb out. The kids said, "That man looks like Dad!" Then another said, "That is Dad!" Mom said, "It can't be Dad because Dad had to work!" But it was Dad. They had the best vacation ever. And they laughed about the experience for years.

Parents, be remembered for more than rules, work, money, and a bad attitude. Go have some fun today!

When is the last time you did something fun with your family? What was it? What made it fun?

Are you ever concerned God doesn't want us to have fun? Well, He does. In fact, laughter does us good. Look for opportunities for fun and enjoy it to the glory of God.

November 3
Nitpicker

Scripture for Today: 1 Corinthians 10:10

Are you one of those troublesome nitpickers?

To some people, everything is a big deal. Their opinion is all that matters. And according to them, everyone with basic intelligence should think, act, dress, and look like them. And yes, it's those people who make mountains out of mole hills.

Such an attitude will destroy relationships in a family, at work, and at church. They bring division and animosity wherever they go, instead of unity and love.

I know of a church that decided to put a soda machine in their fellowship hall. The decision passed the church vote unanimously. But whether it would be a Coca-Cola or a Pepsi machine, well that didn't go so well. One person made such a big deal of it that an entire group left the church. Coca-Cola won! Yay! But the message of Jesus lost!

I've watched people do this over music, carpet, stained glass, and lots of other stuff that doesn't matter. There are a few things worth fussing about, but very few. Make sure you're not a nitpicker.

Do you enjoy being around nitpickers, people who criticize nearly everything? Who does, right?

You can avoid being a nitpicker by looking at the big picture and leave the details to others. Ask God to help you avoid needless criticism and commit to encouraging those around you.

November 4
Anger

Scripture for Today: Ephesians 4:26, 1 John 1:9

Have you ever had somebody say something bad about you? It's frustrating and painful, but could it be what they said is actually true? She gossips. He's rude and hateful. She's untrustworthy.

If it's true, that's even more frustrating and painful!

I went through a season when wisecracks were made about my anger and temper. They initially said these things behind my back, but after a while I began to pick up on it. I denied their accusation and often got angrier as a result. I had always been an easy-going kind of guy, but I began to realize my personality and temperament were changing for the worse.

I traced it back to when my parents died, and realized my grief had turned to anger, resentment, and bitterness toward God for the loss. My critics were right, I was wrong, and so was my behavior.

If the bad stuff people say about you is true, you will never fix it until you agree that it's wrong. Could it be you're as bad as they say?

Do you have a pattern of anger in your life? Can you trace it to a single root?

Most anger does not please God and should be repented of. Ask God to deliver you from any patterns of anger you have in your life.

November 5
Faulty View of God

Scripture for Today: Psalm 16:4, Galatians 4:8

Although you may be a follower of Jesus, do you still have a faulty view of God?

Some people view God as an aggravating uncle to a 5-year-old nephew. In their view, the uncle gives his nephew a new toy, and the kid is so excited. Then all of a sudden, the uncle grabs the toy from the kid and says, "Nope, you can't have it! I was just kidding!" The uncle smiles and laughs as the little boy screams and cries. No, God is not constantly looking for ways to make us miserable.

The Bible says, "Every good and perfect gift comes from our Father above." And, "If an earthly father knows how to give good gifts to his children, how much more does your heavenly Father."

Sure, life is often painful and disappointing. And yes, there are times when we don't understand things that happen or don't happen. But one thing is for sure: God is a good, good heavenly Father. He loves you more than you can imagine, and you can trust Him.

Have you ever become aware of faulty views of God that you've held in the past? What were some of them?

Faulty views of God come very close to causing us to worship a god created in our own mind. That's idolatry. Ask God to identify any idols in your heart, then repent of them and seek the true God in His Word, the Bible.

November 6
Peacemaker

Scripture for Today: Matthew 5:9

Are you a peacemaker or a troublemaker? Jesus said happy are the peacemakers. And my experience says miserable are the troublemakers!

We have many choices to make every day, but one of the most important is to be a peacemaker not a troublemaker. This is even more important in today's toxic political climate. A single positive or negative comment about a president can easily make you a target of demonization, and scores of people are eager to jump in and participate, and bring the emotions of hate, anger, and insults to the discussion.

Being a peacemaker doesn't mean you don't have thoughts and opinions of your own. And it doesn't mean you shouldn't share them. It simply means you work to remove as much negative emotion from a discussion as possible. It means you treat everyone with respect and dignity, including the people who differ from you. We are blessed to live in a free society and I'm thankful we do. But respect and civil discourse are necessary to keep it free. Be a peacemaker and be happy.

Do you enjoy the company of peacemakers or troublemakers? Which would most people around say you are?

Peacemakers will be called the children of God. Pause and ask God to make you be a peacemaker.

November 7
Admiration

Scripture for Today: Philippians 4:8

Who is it that you admire and honor these days? Admiration and honor are disappearing concepts. Taking their place is a commitment to highlight the flaws and faults of the people in our lives. But be careful; you are not flawless yourself.

As a kid, I admired my parents, grandparents, teachers, pastors, coaches, and several others who invested in me. But they were not perfect people. I knew it, and it was okay.

Not long before writing this I heard about the criticism of a man I admired at a distance for many years. I still do. But he is being attacked for a statement he made many years ago in a sermon, and for his handling of a situation over thirty years ago. Some were calling for his resignation.

I hope no one goes back thirty years and listens to some of my sermons. I've listened to some of them, and I don't even agree with me anymore!

If you highlight the flaws and faults of other people, you'll have no one left to admire and honor. You're not so perfect yourself.

Why do you think it's easy to highlight flaws in other people? Who do you admire in spite of their flaws?

Make it a practice to think on the good characteristics in other people and withhold criticism unless it is truly needed. Ask God to guide your thinking in this way.

November 8
Refreshing

Scripture for Today: Proverbs 25:13, 2 Timothy 1:16

Does your soul need a little refreshing?

One winter, I noticed severe damage to my lawn due to the harshness of the season. But after some fertilizer, rain, and sunshine to refresh it, it got more beautiful every day.

Our soul is much like our lawn. Life is often tough. After prolonged seasons of difficulty, we feel trapped in hardship with no end in sight. It seems like the harshness and brutality will last forever. I know that story. I've been there on many occasions, and you have too! But it can change.

You'll need to give your soul a little refreshing. A day at the lake or a night camping with family or a friend. Or it could be that you've ignored your spiritual life and it needs some personal attention. God created you and knows you better than you know yourself. Ask Him to refresh your soul and give you wisdom to live life His way. A few steps in the right direction and your life can begin to be more beautiful every day!

How does the lawn of your life look?

Rest, relaxation, the Word of God, and prayer are all ways God refreshes us. Make time for one or more of them this week so God can refresh you.

November 9
Not Alone

Scripture for Today: Psalm 139:7–10

"Alone" is a powerful concept. Sometimes we crave some "alone time." Yet too much time alone can leave us feeling lonely, as if no one cares about us. In frustration someone will say, "I wish everybody would just leave me alone!" But be careful, you might get what you wish.

The Bible teaches that as a follower of Jesus, I am never alone. Jesus promised to be with me, even to the end. And the 23rd Psalm reminds me that "even when I walk through the valley of the shadow of death, I will fear no evil, because I'm not alone. He is with me." The Christian life is a relationship with Jesus Christ. And yes, He is a friend that never forsakes us.

But the Christian life is also a relationship with other followers of Jesus. That's what church is all about. Believe me, I know church people are flawed and sometimes a little messed up in the head. You might think it's better to stay home and alone. But it's not. Find a church where you can be a part and serve God and others there.

In a normal week, how much time do you spend alone? Is it too much, too little, or about the right amount?

Ask God to help you find balance in your alone time, but whatever you do, find a church family that can be with you if you feel alone.

November 10
Starving to Death

Scripture for Today: Deuteronomy 8:3, Matthew 4:4

Are you starving to death? Sometimes we make such a claim just before pulling into a fast food drive thru for a biggie sized combo. We quickly scarf down enough food to feed three people, and in doing so we add to our already bulging waistline. We might be eating ourselves to death, but we are certainly not starving to death; not physically anyway.

But we might be starving ourselves spiritually. Jesus warned us about feeding our physical being without feeding our spiritual being. He said we must not live on bread alone, but feast on every word that comes from God. The essence of a healthy and successful life is so much more than feeding our physical bodies. Are you spiritually starving to death? Possibly so.

I've seen physical starvation in the Sahara Desert. I saw a boy and a vulture eating from the same garbage pile. Are you eating from a spiritual garbage pile, or worse, not feeding your spiritual being at all? Don't starve to death: read your Bible today and go to church this weekend.

What if your physical appearance looked like your spiritual reality? Would people see you and think you are healthy or starving?

Ask God to give you an appetite for His word, then eat it until you are filled.

November 11
Christian

Scripture for Today: Mark 1:16–20

Are you a follower of Jesus Christ? Over two billion people worldwide identify themselves as Christians. But being a Christian is more than getting baptized, joining a church, burning a candle, or taking communion.

Jesus invited His first potential followers this way. They were fishermen, and He said, "Come follow me, and I will make you fishers of men." In His own words, He defined what it means to be a Christian. It's someone who's following Jesus. Following Jesus is the most adventurous life possible. Are you following Him?

Then He said, "I will make you." He refers to a shift from who they've been to who He will help them become. So, a Christian is someone willing to be changed by Jesus. I'm thankful He doesn't leave us the way we've always been—He changes us.

Then He said, "I will make you fish for people." To reach others with His message of hope and forgiveness is His mission for all of His followers. If we do this, the world will be a much better place.

Do you share Jesus' view of what it means to be a Christian? If not, stop now and ask Him to make you His follower. Eternity depends on it.

November 12
Blessing Others

Scripture for Today: Acts 20:35, 2 Corinthians 9:7

When was the last time you blessed someone for no particular reason? You know, you saw a need and met it, expecting nothing in return: a tank of gas or a meal or whatever comes to mind. I've been on the receiving end of someone's generosity on several occasions and it's always a little overwhelming. It feels even better to be on the giving side.

A while back I was pumping gas in my truck and I saw a lady sitting in her car on the other side of the pump, and she was counting out a few one-dollar bills to see how much gas she could afford. Immediately there was that voice inside me that said, "Be a blessing! Make her day! Fill hers up too!" I tried to ignore it, but I'm glad I didn't. The tears in her eyes and the look on her face said it all.

The Bible tells us it feels even better to give than to receive. Try it today. When we do so, it's a win-win every single time!

Can you remember a time when you were blessed for no particular reason?

Blessing others is one of the greatest things we can do. Look for opportunities every day.

November 13
Erosion

Scripture for Today: Hebrews 2:1

Do you have an erosion problem? I was mowing my lawn and I noticed a new root showing above ground. It was large, and had been under the surface for many years, providing life to the towering oak tree that hovered above it. Now it was bare, and open to the destructive elements of the sun, rain, and lawnmower blades. Over time, erosion had removed it from the safety and coolness of the soil; now it was facing new dangers that were never intended.

Erosion can also impact our physical and spiritual health. Erosion doesn't happen suddenly. It happens slowly over time, as the seasons of life often bring one challenge after another. Age will certainly erode our physical health at some point.

However, our spiritual life can actually get stronger and deeper as we get older, but it's not a guarantee. We fight against spiritual erosion as we walk with God through daily prayer, Bible reading, and worship. And regardless of what life brings on the outside, we can be strong and stable on the inside.

Can you see erosion happening in your soul right now? Are you sliding in your relationship with God?

The deepest soil for every human is to be in the Word of God and in regular prayer. If those things have eroded away from your life, stop right now and renew your commitment to them.

November 14
Generous Words

Scripture for Today: Proverbs 18:21

How generous are you with kind words? How quickly do you jump in and compliment or encourage someone when you have the chance, highlighting a good quality or a good action? Or to actually affirm to someone how much they mean to you and how you appreciate them?

Regarding generosity, we often feel we have nothing to give. But all of us can give kind words, and that action costs us nothing. And it might be the most generous and life-changing gift a person has ever been given!

We live in a world of constant critique, judgment, and comparison. Most people don't feel like they measure up. And even if someone appears to have it all together on the outside, they're likely not so confident on the inside.

You and I have the power to speak life or death into other people's hopes and dreams, and even their self-esteem. That's a powerful gift to give. Choose kind and affirming words and be generous with them. Don't speak death to other people. Speak life!

When is the last time you turned someone's day around by speaking life to them?

The power of one's words can build or destroy. Be intentional about speaking words of life to those in your family, church, school, or work. God will honor you for it.

November 15
Border Walls

Scripture for Today: Revelation 21:9–14, 22–27

Should we or should we not build a wall at our nation's borders? Some time ago, this was the big question with which the United States was grappling. I was asked my opinion on several occasions. But it's a trap! My answer could lead to an explosive discussion.

Besides, our elected officials who've been placed into office are the ones who must answer that question. I have no authority to affect government policy except at the voting booth. Once leaders are voted into office, the Bible demands that I honor them and pray for them!

But here's something I can do, and so can you! As followers of Jesus, we can and should make sure we don't build any walls around ourselves. We must keep our hearts, minds and souls open to God, and HIS plan for OUR life. And we must also keep our hearts open to people who are culturally different than us, whether they're from another country or across the street. Jesus is their only hope, and it's OUR job to take HIS message of salvation to them. The Government will do what it's going to do. But we have an important job of our own!

What are some ways you can avoid building walls around your life?

What are some ways you can actively reach out with Jesus' love to people around you who don't share your religion, race, or life experiences?

November 16
Self-Talk

Scripture for Today: Psalm 103:1–5

What are you saying to yourself these days? You know, that inner voice and conversation you have with yourself every moment of every day? It's your self-talk. And it's powerful!

If someone else spoke to you the way you speak to yourself, would you consider them an enemy or a friend? Would you be drawn to those people or hide from them? Would you be offended or encouraged?

Your own voice is the most prominent voice you listen to, so you'd better make sure it's a voice of wisdom and encouragement. It's a part of leading yourself to do the right things, to lay a good foundation for your future.

In Psalm 103 David spoke to his own soul. He demanded that his soul praise the Lord. He demanded that his soul never forget all of the benefits of a God-centered life.

Don't be your own worst enemy! Be a good friend to yourself and to your future. Tell yourself to put God first in everything, and to praise Him. Then listen to your own advice.

Does your self-talk condemn or encourage you?

Don't let your heart condemn you. God loves you. Train yourself to have the mind of Christ so your self-talk will be as He speaks.

November 17
Waffler

Scripture for Today: Matthew 5:37

Have you become a waffler? That is not a good thing, but I see it and hear it a lot these days.

I ask someone for a commitment to do something or participate in something. All I need is a simple yes or no. If it's yes, then I can move forward with my plans. If it's no, then I can move forward and ask someone else. It doesn't seem that difficult. But more often than not, I don't get a yes or no. I get a "maybe." Or "I'll try." Or "I hope to." Or "Let me wait and see." Or "I might."

If such responses have become a pattern for you, then you've become a waffler. Wafflers are not dependable. They lack the character to make a simple decision, put it on the calendar, and then follow through with that commitment.

The Bible reminds us, "Let your yes be yes, and your no be no."

Stop trying to avoid commitments and stop leaving the door open for something better. Stop being a waffler!

Are you finding it harder to make and keep commitments?

Being a waffler makes it impossible for people to depend on you. Ask God to make you a faithful person whose word can be counted on.

November 18
Being Thankful

Scripture for Today: 1 Chronicles 16:34

What are you doing for Thanksgiving this year? I have been asked that many times before. It's a reminder that Thanksgiving is a really special American holiday that should be approached with intentionality. Intentionally spending time with certain people, doing certain things, eating certain foods, and telling God you're thankful for certain blessings.

Most Thanksgiving Days follow a pattern and are very similar in nature. But it was November 1987 I broke with tradition. I was 23 years old. On Thanksgiving Day that year I was in a remote village in West Africa telling people about Jesus Christ, the one and only savior of the world. It was my first time not sitting with my family for the meal on Riverside Road. I ate rice instead of turkey and dressing! There was no electricity, running water, or modern conveniences. That's the year I became more thankful than ever for lots of things. We often don't know how thankful we should be for something until we don't have it anymore. And the same applies to the people in our lives.

What are you the most thankful for right now?

What's gone now that you're more thankful for than when you had it?

During this Thanksgiving season, take some time to make a "Thanksgiving" list and be intentional about your thankfulness to God.

November 19
Caught

Scripture for Today: Romans 10:9–10, 13

Are you fully aware that today could be your last? No, I don't mean to sound morbid, negative, or put a dark cloud over your day. But, I'm a realist.

One morning, as my wife and I sat on our back porch eating breakfast, we noticed a beautiful red fox coming across our pasture. But he was not alone. He carried a massive white rabbit in his mouth. A rabbit that at one point was likely a safe and cuddly pet of a kid. The night before, it had an amazing life, but something went horribly wrong. Just like that, it was over.

I've experienced the same thing with several family members and friends. Someday it will be me. I'm fully aware that today could be my last, or yours. We are not promised tomorrow. But we are promised eternal life if we've trusted Jesus as our Lord and Savior. That requires a decision on our part. I've made that decision. I know where I'm going when I leave this world. Do you?

If today was your last day on earth and you left tonight, do you have confidence God would welcome you into heaven?

If not, Jesus wants a relationship with you. He died for you and was raised from the dead so you could have eternal life. Ask Him today to bring you into His family.

November 20
Responsibilities

Scripture for Today: Luke 10:38-42

Are you busy? It's a question we often hear from the other side of the office door or the other end of the phone. And while we usually are busy, we usually answer that we're not.

The fact is, we're under the constant frustration of feeling busy, but it's a feeling we learn to live with. It's the weight of having responsibilities. That weight feels even heavier at certain times and for certain tasks. How can we survive the pressure?

First, plan some "alone time" to nourish your soul; a moment to stop the fast pace. You may get two weeks or just two hours. But plan some alone time. Just peace and quiet to reflect, to pray, and to renew your inner strength.

Remember that God is trustworthy to meet every need you have. That's what He promises, and that's what He will deliver.

And remember that someday, your responsibilities will stop. And then what? Don't live your life wishing they were all gone. Just carry them out with diligence while you still can.

Do you struggle with being too busy? Do your responsibilities sometimes overwhelm you?

How do you deal with it when that happens?

Strive to reach a life-balance so your normal patterns enable you to cover your responsibilities. Ask God for wisdom in doing so.

November 21
Pride and Humility

Scripture for Today: James 4:10

Are you aware of the power of humility?

The people we most admire in life possess a sense of confident humility that is stabilizing and magnetic. Their persona and presence add strength to themselves and the people around them. When they speak, people are eager to listen. Some see humility as a weakness, but these people are actually bigger than life.

One of God's laws in the Bible is "Humble yourself before the Lord, and He will exalt you." When we humble ourselves, we get God's help to become strong.

Humility means to be honest about yourself, with yourself, and with God. Pride on the other hand is to think more of yourself than you really ought to think. These are difficult concepts to work through in our culture of self-promotion and fakeness. We're tempted to become professional pretenders. But Jesus gives us a sobering warning. "Everyone who exalts himself will be humbled, and everyone who humbles himself will be lifted up!"

Who do you know that is truly humble?

Do you struggle with humility personally?

Ask God to keep you humble so when you are lifted up, He gets the glory for it.

November 22
God's Greatness

Scripture for Today: Psalm 145:1–13

Do you know people who have too high an opinion of themselves? Sometimes we might say of them, "They need a good dose of humble pie!" Well, all of us likely fall into that category occasionally.

Aspirations toward greatness are clearly evident throughout history:

Alexander the Great
Alfred the Great
Catherine the Great
Constantine the Great
Fredrick the Great
Peter the Great

There are many more, but you get the picture.

King David seemed to have a better perspective on greatness. He wrote, "The Lord is great and should be greatly praised. His greatness is unsearchable." He made it personal by saying, "I will praise you every day, and I will honor your name forever and ever."

I'm not sure who you are or what you've accomplished, but God is greater. Lead your own heart to tell Him so every day.

Who do you consider the greatest person you've ever known personally?

How much greater is God than that person? Stop for a minute and tell God you recognize His greatness and praise Him for it.

November 23
Thanksgiving

Scripture for Today: Psalm 7:17

Have you really paused this week to give thanks to God for His many blessings? Thanksgiving is so much more than a day or two of vacation, eating turkey, or going on a shopping spree. It's a time to hit the pause button of our busy lives. To stop complaining, wishing, wanting, and worrying. To take inventory of every good thing in life, and to give God thanks. A simple thank you is not much to ask!

For some people, this week is a sad one. It's a reminder of someone special who was with you last year but has since passed away or moved away. Or it's your first Thanksgiving after a divorce. May I remind you that Thanksgiving is not a time to focus on what you don't have, but what you do have, and to give thanks. Stop! Sit down for ten minutes and list the things for which you are thankful.

And if you're an agnostic or atheist, you should be even more thankful! God has blessed you even though you don't believe in Him.

Most of the time we are too busy around Thanksgiving to give thanks. Purpose in your mind to take those ten minutes to list things.

Make thankfulness a practice. Use a notebook or note app to regularly list things to thank God for.

November 24
Thanksgiving

Scripture for Today: Psalm 136

"What are you doing for Thanksgiving?" I've heard that question many times through the years. Some go out of town to be with family, while others have family come visit with them. Some look forward to a parade, a ballgame, or a hunting trip, while others enjoy some time to relax.

I've now watched more than 55 Thanksgiving seasons come and go. I have some wonderful memories. It's become my favorite holiday of the year. Family gatherings, great food, and, of course, giving thanks for God's many blessings in my life.

Times have changed. Many who used to sit at our Thanksgiving table are no longer alive. One by one it was the absence of grandparents, then my brother, and then my parents. Their loss reminds me of my greatest blessing of all. Through Jesus Christ I have eternal life, so I'm certain we will be together again someday.

Until then, I will continue to give thanks to the Lord, because He is good!

What blessing are you most thankful for?

If you haven't thanked God lately for His many blessings, make a list and thank Him for each one.

November 25
More Like Jesus

Scripture for Today: John 3:27–30

If you're a follower of Jesus, do you really think that everyone else in the world must think and look exactly like you to be a Christian? Are you the one person that has it all perfectly figured out? Are you really the standard to which everyone else in the world should conform? I seriously doubt it.

Stop avoiding, judging, fearing, and alienating people different than you. Jesus died to bring people together around Himself! He is the unifying factor for believers—not race, politics, social class, language, denomination, music, nor any other cultural identifier. Stop hiding from the very people Jesus died for and wants you to reach with His message.

Jesus did not sing in a southern gospel quartet, a band, nor a choir. He was neither white nor black. Nor did He wear a suit and tie when He preached. Stop imagining that Jesus was exactly like you; instead, become more like Him.

What's the danger in everyone wanting a Jesus who looks and acts like them?

Read the Bible to know Jesus as He really is, rather than seeking a Jesus defined by our culture. It will be worth the effort to know Him as He is.

November 26
Peter Reflecting Doubt

Scripture for Today: 2 Peter 1:13–18

Do you ever struggle with doubt in your spiritual journey? It's a common challenge for all of us.

The Apostle Peter faced the same challenge, but he learned the value and discipline of "reflecting, remembering and reminding" himself of certain things to help overcome his doubts.

In his older years, in the book of Second Peter, he reflected and reminded himself of the amazing journey God had taken him on. The great things God had done throughout his life. The challenges he'd faced and overcome. The character that God had built into him. The truth he had learned and embraced and that had changed his life. He even mentioned a mountaintop experience he had with Jesus, James, and John, when they were all young men. But, he's not on the mountain anymore; he's now in the valley.

When life gets hard it's easy to forget God's faithfulness. We wonder if God was ever there in the first place. And, we doubt.

Never doubt in the valley what you experienced on the mountain. Reflect. Remember. And remind yourself of all God has done.

Is there something God once showed you on a mountain you later forgot while in the valley?

Mountaintop experiences don't last, but the memory of them can serve as encouragement for a long time. Reflect on it, remember that it happened, and remind yourself He hasn't forgotten it either.

November 27
Letting Go

Scripture for Today: Exodus 5:1–3

Do you ever hold on when you ought to let go?

I'll never forget my first water skiing experience. My brother was amazing on a set of skis. He was skinny and looked like a mosquito skimming across the water. He made it look so easy.

When it was my turn, he told me to hold on. "Don't turn loose," he said. So, when the boat launched forward, I held on. Then I fell forward, and the skis came off, but I still held on for dear life! I looked like a torpedo plowing head-first under the water. Now, my brother was yelling, "Let go! Let go! Let go!" But I found it difficult to do, until it felt like my arms would be pulled out of their sockets.

In the Old Testament, Pharaoh refused to let go and it cost him his kingdom. Too often we do this in life, too. We hold on to certain things even though they bring us pain and destruction. We hold on when we should let go. We hold on to hurts, wounds, betrayals, and disappointments from the past. Let it go! You'll be better for it.

Have you ever seen someone suffer because they refused to let go of something?

Are you holding on to anything you should let go? Drop it now and trust God to replace it with something better.

November 28
Difficult Tasks

Scripture for Today: 2 Thessalonians 3:13

What do you do when you face difficult tasks? They come often, so you'd better have a plan.

Crying is not a plan. Wishing things were different is not a plan. Postponing the inevitable is not a plan. And staring at it is not a plan. We are often overwhelmed and paralyzed by not knowing what to do. So, pray for wisdom. God promises to give a generous amount of wisdom to those who ask Him for it.

Then embrace reality. Don't start dreading the task before you even start. And don't get hung up on "what ifs" and "I wish." It is what it is; deal with it!

Then, make a decision. No, we don't always get it right. We don't ever have all the information we need but make a decision anyway.

And finally, jump in there and start. Regardless of the size of the task, it will not disappear by crying, wishing, postponing, or staring. If you'll start, after a while, you can look back with gratitude at a task well done.

What's the hardest thing about persevering through difficult tasks?

What are some excuses you've used for not persevering?

Face reality about it and ask God for strength to go through the difficult tasks you face.

November 29
Endurance

Scripture for Today: Proverbs 18:10

Do you suffer from the "I want it now" syndrome? It's always been a problem for humanity, but it's gotten much worse with the invention of modern-day conveniences. Microwaves, cars, airplanes, and such are awesome, but they greatly complicate the matter of patience and our expectations.

Once my wife and I made a trip from Atlanta to Anchorage, Alaska in around 7 hours. Just 150 years ago the same trip would have taken over a year. Most of us in our generation struggle to take journeys. We'd much rather take short trips. Even then we constantly ask, "Are we there yet?"

And this mindset greatly influences how we live spiritually. We pray today and get disappointed with God if He doesn't answer by tomorrow at noon.

The fact is that God knows the destinations of each struggle we face, but He does His greatest work in us during the journey. We are consumed by the destinations. We should be consumed by the journey. The journey is where the great stuff happens.

Why do we tend to focus on the destination rather than the journey?

The journey is where God does His greatest work in our lives. Ask God to meet you along the way and show you what there is to learn as you journey with Him.

November 30
Aging

Scripture for Today: Ecclesiastes 11:8–10

How old are you? Growing old is certainly not for sissies! And it happens so quickly! I remember thinking the age of sixteen would never get here so I could drive. Now in my 50s, I wonder where all the time has gone! A white beard, bald head, slowing metabolism, diminishing muscle tone, and some aches and pains are now like flashing billboards advertising my current season of life.

Getting old is one thing, but getting old, bitter, and sour is another. Dark days, tragedies, and heartaches in life can take a negative toll, but instead of bitterness they can also create depth of character through which others can be strengthened.

On the one hand, Solomon reminds us that, "If a man lives many years, he should rejoice in them all, and always remember the dark days since they will be many."

On the other hand, he said, "Remove sorrow from your heart because youthfulness is fleeting."

Instead of being bitter because something bad happened, celebrate and rejoice as you remember what God has brought you through!

Have you reached the point where you really feel the reality of aging?

Don't take your youth for granted and don't give up in your older years. God can use you in all your years if you yield yourself to Him.

December 1
Purpose

Scripture for Today: Acts 13:36

Just why exactly are you still hanging around in this world? It's a question about purpose. Why are you still here? Everything and everyone is uniquely designed with purpose and for purpose. God created you for a reason—likely many reasons. You are not here by accident.

Purpose is your reason for getting up each morning with passion and enthusiasm. Purpose defines the mission for your life. It's about investing your life each day in the things that matter most, so you can live a life of meaning. And it will define the memory people have of you when you're gone.

So, what's yours this week?

What matters to you, frustrates you, or inspires you? What problem could you do something about if you went all in? Once you answer these questions, you'll be much closer to understanding your purpose. And when you do, life will make more sense than ever before.

If you don't know where to start, ask God. He's the one who knows exactly why He created each of us!

Have you determined your purpose for being in this world? Are you living in that purpose?

If not, pray and seek the wisdom of your pastor, mentors, or parents to help you determine it. Then pursue it with all of your might for God's glory.

December 2
What If…

Scripture for Today: Ephesians 5:16

Have you experienced the pain of wondering "what if…?" As an Atlanta Falcons fan, I recall how frustrating it was to host the Super Bowl in Atlanta a few years ago without the Atlanta Falcons playing in the Super Bowl. It had been a difficult year for players and fans alike. At the BIG game, their players were reduced to spectators in the stands in their own stadium. They now sat in the stands wishing they were on the field. They looked back through the year at small failures that made the difference between losing and winning and wondered, What if…! What if I had not fumbled that ball? What if I had given my absolute best to my team? What if…? And the list goes on.

Well, I have plenty of what ifs of my own. Times when I quit when I should have reached deeper. I should have said yes, but I said no, or vice versa. I should have spoken up, but I remained silent. Or times I should have remained silent and I opened my big fat mouth!

Try to remember the pain of what if BEFORE you make a decision.

Can you think of some what ifs in your own life? Have you recognized them in the lives of others?

Can what ifs be changed? Maybe you can finish college, change careers, reconcile a relationship, make a move to the mountains or the beach. Take a personal inventory and determine if you can resolve some what ifs this month.

December 3
Disappearing Dreams

Scripture for Today: Galatians 6:9

Do you ever have those moments when you almost reach your dream, and then poof! Just like that it moves farther away or disappears altogether?

One day I was turkey hunting and a gobbler sounded like he was just over the next ridge. I called occasionally and he answered every time. He was moving in my direction with excitement. It was going to be a successful hunt. He would appear at any moment. In my mind, he was already on my table for supper. And then...I waited. And then...nothing! He went silent and I never heard from him again. And just like that, my dream of killing a big gobbler was over. It had seemed so close to reality just a few minutes earlier.

So, what's next? Well, I get up and go try again!

If at first you don't succeed, try, try again! Or as the Bible puts it,

"We shall reap in due season if we do not quit!" And so it goes with every dream!

Did you once have a dream that has now disappeared, that you've given up on completely?

It's almost never too late to start pursuing a dying dream or to dream a new one. Spend some time in prayer and dream for God's will again.

December 4
Joseph

Scripture for Today: Genesis 50:15–21

The events of our life can be confusing. Are you sure you have the right perspective?

He was sold into slavery by his own brothers. Sent to a foreign country and sold again. Served his master with honesty and integrity, but was falsely accused of sexual assault and rape. He was sent to prison and forgotten. And then many years later was elevated to the position of prime minister and hero of the country. Yeah, this really happened to Joseph in the book of Genesis.

Then during a great famine, who came before him for food? His brothers who had sold him into slavery so many years earlier. At such a moment, we might be prone to take revenge on those who'd harmed us; but not Joseph.

He said to his brothers, "Yes, you planned evil against me, but God planned it for good for the survival of many people." And Joseph comforted his brothers and spoke kindly to them.

Joseph recognized that he was not the master of the Universe. God is, and God is always trustworthy!

Have you ever had the opportunity to show mercy on someone who didn't deserve it? Did you?

It's a biblical practice to show mercy, so look for opportunities around you to bless people who haven't earned it, especially those who don't deserve it.

December 5
Endurance

Scripture for Today: Hebrews 10:35-39

Are you running out of steam? Some journeys, challenges, and seasons in life seem like they'll never end. One disappointment and heartache after another pile onto our already fragile emotions. We're tempted to walk away and quit. But if we do, we're settling for less than the best for our lives and the lives of those around us.

So many people are settling for less these days in life, love, relationships, and in their walk with God!

But somehow, we must find the strength to endure. Yes, endurance requires discipline and strong character. But it's also where strong character is built. Endurance means striving to take one more step, to see one more sunset, and one more sunrise. It's always worth the effort to finish the challenge before us, because that's where great reward is found.

We are reminded in the Bible that as followers of Jesus, we are not those people who draw back and run out of steam. We are those who have faith and endurance and a great reward.

Do you want to hear God say "Well done, good and faithful servant" when you stand before Him?

Don't give up! Keep your eyes on the prize and ask God for strength to reach it.

December 6
Spiritually Dry

Scripture for Today: John 7:37–38

Have you ever been really thirsty with no water in sight? Nothing makes us more aware of our need for water than going through dry barren places. I have spent days in the Sahara Desert region serving the people there. I slept on a hard dirt floor. I stayed in a village where the nearest water pump was over a mile away. The people there have known what it's like to be truly dry and thirsty. For me, it was a short and exciting adventure. For them, it was life!

Jesus promised "If anyone is thirsty, let him come to me and drink. Whoever believes in Me will have rivers of living water flowing out of his heart."

You may be going through a dry, barren, and difficult time in your life. You don't have to remain thirsty. Jesus can turn you into a mighty river, bringing life to others!

Are you feeling spiritually dry right now? How long has it been this way?

Remind yourself that Jesus is the fountain of living water. Return to Him as often as you need to be refreshed.

December 7
Joy

Scripture for Today: John 15:11

Is your joy overflowing and abundant?

Do you remember your school days at the science fair? There was always somebody who made a clay volcano around a Coca-Cola bottle using baking soda and vinegar. They demonstrated lava overflowing and abundant. In the real world a volcano overflowing with lava is a powerful force to be reckoned with.

In John 15, Jesus challenged believers to obey Him. And if we would, our joy would be full, abundant, and overflowing. Yes, and just like the lava, overflowing joy is a powerful force to be reckoned with, a good force that impacts the lives of others daily. A force that leaves every person we come in contact with a little better, happier, and more hopeful than we found them.

There is a deep level of joy in living a God-centered life through Jesus Christ. Whether things go your way or not, that joy can and should remain strong.

People in this world need some bright spots in their journey each day. Be one!

Do you typically have joy in your life or not? What tends to rob you of joy?

Joy truly is found in Jesus. If you don't know Him yet, stop, pray and surrender to Him as Lord. If you know Him but have lost joy, ask Him to restore the joy of salvation to you.

December 8
Christmas

Scripture for Today: Luke 2:8–14

Have you felt that everything that could go wrong actually does? During a two-week stint, I got the full-blown flu, had five flat tires, the clutch went out on my tractor, septic tank clogged up, and I needed a surprise home repair costing several thousand dollars. Yes, all of that happened to me during a two-week period just in time to celebrate Christmas!

Such challenges can dampen our spirits and suck the joy right out of us. That is, if we forget that these are all just temporary challenges in a temporary world.

Jesus came to bring good news of great joy to all people. That good news is that eternal life in Heaven is offered to all who put their faith in Jesus. Forgiveness and eternal life are offered as a free gift to all who'll believe in Him.

My tires have been fixed or replaced, repairs were made, and the flu finally passed. Most importantly, I'm ready to celebrate the greatest gift of Christmas; forgiveness and eternal life through Jesus our Savior.

What do you do every year to get ready for Christmas?

Do you ever feel something is trying to steal your joy during this season?

Remember your main focus: our Savior has come. Ask God to help you remember Jesus is the reason for the season.

December 9
Tim Lee

Scripture for Today: Philippians 3:7–11

Do you need some inspiration, perspective, and encouragement? I'll never forget the first time I heard Vietnam veteran United States Marine Tim Lee tell his story. He rolled onto the stage in his wheelchair. His dress Marine uniform was captivating. His chest was full of colorful awards and medals. But his legs were missing! Yet the man without legs I saw on stage appeared to be so much bigger, stronger, and taller than I.

Then he opened his mouth and began to tell his story with a typical thundering Marine voice, and I was immediately challenged to overcome obstacles, and stirred to aspire toward greatness!

He lost his legs in combat, but his story of battling through the physical, emotional, mental, and spiritual battles that followed is a story that every person needs to hear. Life is hard for everyone and harder for some. Expose your heart and mind to stories of overcoming obstacles. Doing so will help you whine a little less and become an overcomer yourself!

Have you ever been tempted to quit with less of an excuse than losing part of your body?

If you have lost part of your body due to injury or disease, have you been able to regain your sense of self? How long did it take?

In today's scripture, Paul counts everything as a loss for the glory of Jesus. Whether you have physical impairments or not, everything pales before Jesus. Ask Him today for that perspective on life.

December 10
Investing in Young People

Scripture for Today: 1 Timothy 4:12

Have you invested in a young person lately? I recall many people who invested in me when I was younger. They chose to spend time with me. They spoke truth in an encouraging way. They believed in me. They gave me opportunity, and even did so again after I failed! They spoke words of affirmation. Every success I experience today is built on the shoulders of someone from yesterday who invested in me! I am better and wiser because of them.

I hear lots of criticism of today's younger generation. But I'm pretty sure they're no more frustrating than we were to our parents' and grandparents' generation!

"Wise counsel to the younger is the duty of the aged!" We don't know who said it, but we do know they were wise!

In the Bible, Moses invested in Joshua, Elijah in Elisha, and Paul in Timothy.

I would at least be a little kinder to those who are young. You might need them to help you operate your phone, computer, or remote control!

Are you investing in any young people today? If not, how long has it been?

Whether church, business, or just life, young people do better when older people help them out, so be aware of younger folks you can mentor or disciple along the way.

December 11
Influence

Scripture for Today: 2 Timothy 1:5

Do you know how powerful your presence is? There are at least three men who have been present in my life for the last 25 years. As I reflected about our meeting, I realized how powerful their presence in my life has been. No, we do not spend time together every day. At times we've gone years without much interaction; but they've always been there, just a phone call away.

When we have gotten together, the value of their friendship, the power of their influence, and the wisdom of their advice was planted deeply in my soul. Their willingness to be present in my life has helped shape me into the man I am today!

As a result, I realize the power of my own presence in the lives of others and know the outcome will be the same. I don't have to be a genius or have the answers for every problem, but if I can find a few minutes to simply be present, I can help shape the future for somebody! How awesome is that?

Write down the names of a few people who you have that kind of relationship with. Pause for a minute and ask God to bless them today.

Now write down the names of two people you can reach out to and start that kind of relationship. Ask God to give you wisdom to influence them well.

December 12
Baptism

Scripture for Today: Matthew 3:13–17

From where do you get your inner strength?

I get mine from the resurrection of Jesus from the dead, the most powerful event in history. Jesus' resurrection is God's way of giving eternal life to those who'll believe. It's God's way of moving us from death to life spiritually, just like He did for Jesus physically. When I got baptized, I was put under the water to identify with His death. Then I was raised to identify with His resurrection. Baptism has been a symbol of Christian faith for over 2,000 years.

Many people think baptism is what makes a person right with God, but that's wrong. Baptism shows outwardly what God has already done inwardly! Going under the water represents death and burial. Coming up again represents our resurrection to a brand-new life in Jesus Christ. Anyone can get in water, but only God can make a person truly clean.

Have you settled the issue of faith in the resurrected Jesus? Do you believe? Have you followed through with baptism as a symbol of your faith? It's time to get a new start!

If you have never died to yourself and been resurrected in Christ, ask God to make that a reality in your life today, then find a church to be baptized in and join.

December 13
Love at Christmas

Scripture for Today: Mark 12:28–31

How are you doing with God and people? As we near the end of one year and get ready to start another, it's a great thought to ponder. We know it's an important topic because God built the 10 Commandments around it. When Jesus was asked which is the greatest commandment, He responded with just two thoughts: Love God with all your heart, mind, soul, and strength, and love your neighbor like you love yourself.

That's a good summary of what a successful life is all about. Most of the trinkets, toys, and stuff we purchase and accumulate during the Christmas season will soon be worthless. But the relationships we have with God and people will continue to be of great value.

So, as you prepare to wrap up one year and launch your most successful year ever, make sure you consider these two relationships. You'll find that the end result is a better you, a better year, and a better life!

What's your plan for a better relationship with God?

How can you improve in your relationship with people?

December 14
Winter
Scripture for Today: Daniel 2:21

What are you doing this winter? I know. We usually ask that question about summer, but you should know that winter is just as important. You should have a plan for it as well.

By the way, Winter officially begins today, so if you haven't developed a plan for it, you're already behind, and you'd better get started.

The Prophet Daniel wisely referred to God as, the God of the times and seasons. Winter is likely not your favorite season of the year, but God designed it on purpose. Among other things, winter is a time when the leaves die and return to the ground. They become fertile top-soil for the blooming flowers of springtime.

For us, it's a time to reflect upon the past and to dream about our future. It's a time to let go of bitterness, disappointment, and resentment. It's a time to make sure our heart is fertile so our dreams about the future can flourish. Winter is an awesome gift from God, so don't waste it!

What is your favorite season? Most of us experience winter as a "season of life" periodically. Are you in a winter season now?

Remember to thank God during the winter times and look forward with expectation for the new life of spring.

December 15
Christmas

Scripture for Today: Luke 2:8–14

Well it's Christmas time again. It seems to come around more quickly as I get older. When I was a kid it took a lifetime before it rolled around each year. I have some great Christmas memories: family gatherings at MawMaw and PawPaw's house, seeing my cousins I hadn't seen in a while, acting as a shepherd or a wise man in the church play, and getting a much needed break from school.

I have sad memories around the Christmas season, too. My Grandpa died on Christmas Eve. My brother died the week before Christmas several years ago. My mom died two weeks before Christmas. She knew death was coming and she gave us our presents early.

But these sad events make the Christmas season even more special. Jesus was born into this world to give us hope, joy, and eternal life. Because of Jesus, I will see them again. Now that's a gift only God can give.

What is the best Christmas gift you've ever received? What is the gift you had the most joy giving?

The best gift ever given was Jesus Christ, the One who brought joy to the world. He's the best gift ever given and eternal life is the best gift you'll ever get. Have you accepted His gift? Why not today?

December 16
Irritation

Scripture for Today: Isaiah 40:31

How do you deal with those nagging irritations that drive you crazy? You know, weeds that keep coming back, long lines that seem to go nowhere, whiny kids and the parents who ignore them, phone calls at all the wrong times and from the wrong people, cold food that was supposed to be served hot…and the list goes on!

Such irritations can build up inside of us to the point that an explosion is inevitable. I love the sign that reads, "I'm planning to have a nervous breakdown! I've earned it…I deserve it…I've worked for it…and nobody's going to keep me from it!"

Why are we so sensitive to such irritations? It's because we struggle with being impatient. One of my closest friends recently looked at me and said, "I think you are the most impatient person I know!" I laughed and said, "I've never been accused of that before!" Both of us knew I was being sarcastic!

Patience is a virtue I'm still struggling to acquire. I wish it would hurry up and arrive!

Have you ever thought about how all of our impatience is really impatience with God?

The Bible says, "Those who wait on the Lord will renew their strength." Waiting on God means trusting His heart and His plan. If you struggle with impatience, confess it to God, and learn to trust Him moment by moment.

December 17
The Person of Christmas is Here

Scripture for Today: Matthew 1:18–21

I don't have to ask what you are doing this week. You're either making your final plans and purchases for Christmas, or you're cleaning up after Christmas, including returning gifts, making exchanges, and taking advantage of "After Christmas Sales." But somewhere in the midst of it all, you should have a moment to reflect upon your own relationship with Jesus Christ.

While it's true that Jesus came to be the Savior of the world, at some point that reality must be personalized for your own life. Jesus is not a rude and obnoxious intruder who forces His presence into a life that doesn't want Him. He offers His gift of eternal life to all who will receive it. Like every gift, someone pays the price and offers it to someone they dearly love. But the other person must not reject the gift but instead, with gratitude and humility, receive it as their own. Jesus offers to you something no one else can offer— eternal life. Do you reject it, or will you receive it today?

God offers a priceless gift to every person. Have you received His Son as the satisfaction for your sins?

If you know someone who needs to receive God's gift of eternal life, pray for them right now.

December 18
Breaking Down Barriers

Scripture for Today: Ephesians 2:13–18

Are you ready for Christmas? I hope so, because it's here. When I was a kid it seemed like a lifetime between Christmas seasons. But as an adult, they come and go faster than cars at a NASCAR race!

I especially love how Christmas helps break down barriers: a gift to a friend, a kind word to a stranger, a donation to someone in need, a meal with someone we haven't seen for a while, or a party with people we usually only work with. It's a great time to pause and focus on the valued relationships we have or new ones we'd like to invest in.

Breaking down barriers is the very nature of Christmas. That's why Jesus was born. God became flesh and was born in Bethlehem to break down the barrier between God and mankind. The struggle between ourselves and God is real, and everybody feels it. But Jesus came to break down that barrier. To bring forgiveness of your sin, peace to your soul, and as a result, joy to the world!

Are there any personal barriers you'd like to see broken down this Christmas?

Look for opportunities to intentionally break down barriers through acts of generosity large or small. Ask God to open doors for the gospel through them.

December 19
Controlling Your Emotions

Scripture for Today: Proverbs 16:32; Galatians 5:22–23

Do you control your emotions, or do your emotions control you? Usually when we think about someone who can't control their emotions, we think of anger. That boss who flies into a rage and cusses out everyone around, or a parent who is constantly yelling at their kid. We often recognize it as wrong in other people's lives, but make excuses for it ourselves: "I was tired" or "She was getting on my nerves."

We don't need to be ruled by our emotions; we need to rule our emotions.

The Bible says we should be patient and have self-control. We can't be flying off the handle all time and expect people to have confidence in our leadership. We need to be self-controlled when people make mistakes. The Bible also says that being able to control one's emotions is better than being able to capture a city! Living an emotionally out of control life leaves you open to attack. It's like letting down the gate to a city so the enemy can easily enter!

Emotions are good; God made them. But we are supposed to control our emotions. They aren't supposed to control us.

Are you prone to emotional outbursts of any kind: anger, frustration, hurt?

How do you think it affects those around you?

Stop and pray about your emotional life. Ask God to help you control your emotions so patience and self-control cause your life to be a strong city.

December 20
Disoriented

Scripture for Today: Proverbs 3:5–6

Have you ever been disoriented? You know, when something happens and you just can't figure out what's going on, and nothing makes sense? Life gets that way sometimes.

President Harry Truman loved to tell the story of a man who got hit in the head at work. His co-workers and his family thought he was dead, so they called the undertaker to prepare him for his funeral. However, in the early hours of the morning the man awoke, sat straight up in his casket, but was disoriented.

Confused, he thought, "If I'm alive, what am I doing in this soft, satin filled box? Yet, if I am dead, why do I feel like I have to go to the bathroom?"

Being disoriented is the pits, but in today's busy world—and especially at certain times of the year—it's sometimes hard to avoid. A good reality check is often required. There is an awesome God who created and cares deeply about us. And He will give us perspective and wisdom to understand if we'll only ask.

Have you ever been physically disoriented from vertigo or losing your sense of direction? What about emotionally or spiritually disoriented?

Setting Jesus as your True North each day will help keep you oriented on His plan for your life. Take some time to acknowledge Him so you will remain oriented in the right direction.

December 21
Peace with God

Scripture for Today: Romans 5:1, 8; 12:18

Do you have true peace in your soul? There are three relationships of peace that must be maintained every day.

First is peace with ourselves. Like every person in the human race, we were each born with a sinful nature. As a result of our own moral failures our conscience becomes conflicted and develops within us a restless spirit. Confessing our sins to God and accepting His forgiveness is essential for maintaining peace with ourselves.

Second, is peace with others. Wrong actions can destroy the relationships we treasure most. Sometimes it's our wrong action and at other times it's the actions of the other person. Usually it's both! Either way, someone must take the initiative to salvage, restore, and heal the relationship. A true heartfelt apology is a great start.

Third, is peace with God. Too often, we argue with God, debate God, or ignore God. But God is the perfect peacemaker. He showed His love toward us while we were still sinners. Accept His offer of peace through Jesus and let your soul experience true peace.

Is there something you've done for which God has forgiven you, but you haven't forgiven yourself?

Is there an apology you need to make that might help restore a fractured relationship?

December 22
Jesus' Birthday

Scripture for Today: Matthew 2:1–12

Are you giving anything to Jesus this Christmas? I'm assuming you do know that you should give Him something. Christmas is the celebration of His birthday. Why is it that we typically get everyone else a gift for Jesus' birthday but give Him nothing? I mean, how would you feel if, on your birthday, everyone got a gift except you? I don't think you would feel very special. You can give Jesus a gift by giving to someone in need, giving a special gift to your church, or supporting a charity that helps hurting people or furthers the gospel message.

It's certainly okay to give the special people in your life a gift at Christmas, just to let them know how special they are. But you should really give Jesus your most expensive gift, because Christmas would not exist without Him. Neither would forgiveness or eternal life. You could make a statement by giving Him your most treasured possession this Christmas. If you haven't done so already, why not give Him your life?

What will you give to Jesus?

Have you given Jesus Christ your life?

You can no matter where you are as you read these words. If you will turn from controlling your own life and give Him control, you will receive the gift of eternal life. Why not do that now?

December 23
New Year

Scripture for Today: Proverbs 16:9

Well it's that season again, and I love it! It's the ending of one year and beginning of another. It's time to start over, but with much more experience and wisdom this time. Which areas of your life need the most improvement? If this is your last year to live, what should you do differently? These are questions I address every December as one year comes to a close and another one is ready to begin.

A New Year is one of God's great gifts to help us leave our failures behind and prepare for a much better life. Start back to school. Lose weight. Exercise. Go to church every week. Start a savings account. Read the Bible all the way through. Just be nice! The list goes on and on, and all of those things are good.

But many people won't do anything differently. They think their lives will improve and get better just because they continue to breathe, but another year of disappointment awaits them.

But that's not you. What are you going to do differently next year?

Why do you think New Year's resolutions so often fail? Can you think of any of yours that have?

Rather than going overboard, write down three goals below you think you can realistically reach this year and focus your time and energy on those three. Ask God for wisdom to reach them by next December.

December 24
Christmas

Scripture for Today: 1 Timothy 3:16

Are you ready for Christmas? Ready or not, it has arrived! When I was a kid, my entire year revolved around it. Within a week after one Christmas, I was already dreaming about the next one. Every trip to a store, or even a look at the Sears Catalog led to one more item on my wish list for the next year.

Now past 50 years old, Christmas has changed. I now approach December with mixed emotions. It's the month of my dad's birthday, and he's no longer here for us to celebrate. It's when death took my granddad, step-granddad, brother, and mother.

I can identify with the many people who have to work through some sadness first in order to find a joyful spirit. I can no longer say my year revolves around Christmas; it's a little bigger than that. Today, my entire future revolves around it! For it's on Christmas Day that I celebrate the birth of my Savior, Jesus Christ. Because of Him, I'll be reunited with my family again someday.

Do you look forward to Christmas with anticipation or sadness?

Do you have hope in Christ of seeing your loved ones again? If not, you can ask Jesus to give you eternal life right now, and I pray you will.

December 25
The Best Christmas Gift

Scripture for Today: Isaiah 9:6

Well it's Christmas time again, and it seems to come around more quickly as I get older. When I was a kid it felt like a lifetime. I have some great Christmas memories of the past: family gatherings with grandparents, seeing my cousins I hadn't seen in a while. The excitement of Christmas morning. Acting as a shepherd or wise man in the church play. And getting a much-needed break from school.

Oh, like many of you, yes I have some sad memories around the Christmas season too. One Grandpa died on Christmas Eve and another died the week after Christmas. My brother died one week before Christmas, and My Mom died two weeks before Christmas.

But these sad events make the Christmas season even more special. I don't focus on the bad. I'm thankful for the good. Jesus was born into this world to give us hope, joy, and eternal life. Because of Jesus, heaven is my home. Now that's a gift only God can give. Have you accepted His gift? Why not today?

The focus of Christmas is Jesus as the Savior of the world. Is He yours?

Why not make the Christ of Christmas your Lord and Savior today and have the best Christmas you've ever had.

December 26
Roadmap

Scripture for Today: Psalm 119:105

Where's your roadmap leading you? You do have one, don't you? A map, that is? Or maybe it's an app these days.

Too often people approach life like one of those carefree vacations. You know, when you just get in the car and head out with no plans and no goals and go from place to place until you get tired and want to head back home. That may be fine for an occasional vacation, but it's not a good way to approach life. There's too much at stake. Your family, your future, your health, your wealth, and your eternity will all pay a heavy price.

You will pay the most obvious and immediate price in your heart and your spine, for if you have no map, you will certainly have no heart and no spine. If you have no heart, you will lack compassion and passion, and if you have no spine, you'll have no courage, no conviction, and no confidence. So, pause today and look at your map. If you don't have one, get one. It will help your heart and your spine.

What does your map look like? Is it worn from much use, or in pristine condition from being forgotten?

Take some time over the next few days to create a map so you can bring focus and direction to the rest of your life.

December 27
Happy New Year

Scripture for Today: Psalm 37:37

Happy New Year! You're going to hear that a lot this week, but a great year, like a great life, will require much more than a wish. And good intentions alone won't make much of a difference either. Some people are even holding out for that elusive friend called *luck*, so they are sure to eat some turnip greens and black-eyed peas on New Year's Day!

Each year is filled with events we describe as blessings and tragedies, good times and bad. The good doesn't have much meaning without the bad, but a good attitude and perspective are required or we'll miss the most valuable things of life.

I remember just recovering from my dad's death when I found out mom had brain cancer. Ten weeks later she was gone. Sure, it was tragic, but watching her live out those final weeks was perhaps the most inspiring and amazing thing I've ever witnessed. I don't know what the New Year will hold, but I've already decided it's going to be a good one.

Has this year been relatively good or bad for you?

What are some practical steps you can take to get next year off to its very best start? Think about it and write some ideas below.

December 28
Look Around

Scripture for Today: Psalm 16:11

Have you paused this week to take a look around? It's Christmas week and it has the potential to be the most joyous week of the entire year.

I know. You may not have as much money as you'd like to have. You may not get all the stuff you'd like to get. You might have to take a few things back that don't fit or that you don't like. And there might be a few friends or family members who aren't present around the tree this year. But all of that is a focus on what you don't have and what you don't like.

Intentionally take a look around this week to see what you do have and what you do like. Count your many blessings and name them one by one. Turn the chaos and stress into a time of joy, celebration, and thanksgiving. Jesus came to bring good tidings of great joy to all people everywhere. And at least once this week, let your family hear you say, "This is my best Christmas ever!"

Did you feel like you had the joy of Christmas this year?

Our tendency is to focus on the negatives which robs us of joy. Commit to focus on God's blessings next year so that joy may follow.

December 29th
Hezekiah's Tunnel

Scripture for Today: Psalm 103:14

Are you a responsible leader to the roles God has given you? Regardless of our role in life, a parent, a supervisor, a pastor, or political leader, God has entrusted something very important into our hands. We feel the pressure to do the right thing to protect, serve, and lead the people for which we're responsible and sometimes we are required to make great sacrifices to do so.

Recently on a visit to the Holy Land in Israel, I walked through Hezekiah's Tunnel with a steady flow of cold water flowing over my feet and legs. It was built over 700 years before Christ, during the days of the Prophet Isaiah. King Hezekiah in Jerusalem had heard the King of Assyria was planning an attack. And to protect his people, Hezekiah's men dug the tunnel to channel the water from outside the city walls to the inside. It remains today as one of the great manmade wonders of the world. It also reminds us to be exceptional in our own roles in life.

All of us occasionally feel pressured because of various roles and responsibilities. Have you ever felt under too much pressure from them? Do you now?

God knows how much we can carry and that we are frail. Whatever your current burden, ask Him for the strength He has already promised to give you.

December 30
Relationship that Impact Us

Scripture for Today: 2 Timothy 4:9–11

Have you ever wondered why certain people come into your life? It's an important question as we seek to learn from the people around us. Sometimes for a short season, yet others remain for a lifetime. But all of them help define who we are and how we think. Sometimes they even become closer than family.

But it also important to ask, why are you in their life? You see, every relationship is a two-way street, and our impact in their life is bigger than we might think. Each relationship must be lived with honesty, commitment, respect, and attempts to make their lives better. As life moves on, we will look back and cherish some amazing memories together.

As I celebrate and get started into a New Year, I am more thankful than ever for the people God has placed in my life. Many of them have died or moved away. Some were only there for a brief season. And still others allow me to spend time with them every week. I'm thankful for them all!

Below or in the margins, list the names of people you think you have impacted for good this year.

Then, write the names of people you think you can impact for good next year. Pray that God will give you influence in their lives for His glory.

December 31st
What Time is It?

Scripture for Today: 1 Peter 1:24-25

I began writing my very first "Keeping Life in Focus" devotional with that question. There was a total of eight years in between my first and last inspirational writing for my radio audience and for this book. My focus each time was to write a simple thought-provoking challenge, with my life and yours in mind. My life is better for it and I hope yours is too!

Time passes each day whether we do something to help ourselves and others become better or not. As I reflected on those eight years, it dawned on me how much has happened during that time frame. Both of my parents have passed away. People who were best of friends have vanished from my daily life. New friends have taken their place. I now have 4 grandchildren and another on the way. Eight years ago, I had none. My world has changed. Perhaps yours has too.

Time is like that: It brings good and bad, blessing and heartache. But it never leaves things the same. Make the most of every day. Thank you for allowing my time to intersect with yours!

SCRIPTURE INDEX

JOB
1:6-9 – January 31st
1:13-22 – May 26th
7:6-10 – March 10th
7:7 – January 14th
24:12 – May 8th

PSALMS
7:17 – November 23rd
16 – June 27th
16:4 – November 5th
16:11 – December 28th
18:2 – July 11th
18:30-33 – January 23rd
23 – October 7th
24:1-2 – August 28th
27:1-3 – February 5th
27:14 – August 23rd
28:6 – October 18th
31:19-20 – May 5th
32:8 – August 11th
32:9 – August 15th
37 – August 18th
37:8 – November 4th
37:37 – December 27th
39:4 – September 1st
40:3 – March 28th
42:1 – August 4th
46:10 – May 9th
49:1 – October 1st
55:2 – September 17th
55:22 – April 12th
62:5 – May 28th
62:8 – July 15th
67:7 – October 15th
73:1-3 – January 26th

74 – June 26th
78:1-4 – January 28th
90:10 – September 1st
90:12 – February 22nd
95:2 – January 4th
103:1-5 – February 14th
103:1-5 – November 16th
103:14 – December 29th
112:1 – June 10th
115:1-3 – March 27th
118:22-24 – March 29th
119:1-6 – May 20th
119:33-40 – May 7th
119:36 – September 20th
119:105 – June 6th
119:105 – December 17th
127:3-5 – April 21st
131:2 – May 8th
133:1-3 – June 22nd
136 – November 24th
139:7-10 – November 9th
139:13-18 – March 18th
145:1-13 – November 22nd

PROVERBS
3:5-6 – December 20th
3:5-6 – April 9th
3:21-26 – January 8th
3:34 – October 4th
4:18 – May 17th
6:6-8 – July 18th
8:33 – July 7th
9:9 – August 1st
10:4 – September 27th
11:2 – October 4
11:3 – May 14th

12:18 – September 6th
13:4 – July 2nd
13:22 – May 21st
14:12 – February 9th
15:38 – September 26th
16:3 – October 10th
16:9 – January 10th
16:19 – July 26th
16:20 – July 9th
16:25 – January 16th
16:32 – December 19th
17:22 – November 2nd
18:10 – November 29th
18:10 – July 25th
18:21 – March 11th
18:24 – April 14th
19:22 – October 12th
20:4 – December 23rd
20:6 – January 27th
21:5 – May 18th
22:1 – September 4th
22:1 – February 12th
23:7 – January 18th
23:24 – September 29th
25:13 – November 8th
27:1 – April 8th
27:23-24 – June 2nd, June 6th
29:2 – November 1st
29:18 – February 6th

ECCLESIASTES
2:13-14 – June 3rd
3:1 – January 1st
3:1-8 – April 27th
7:11-10 – November 30th
8:6 – May 3rd

9:10 – October 19th
12:13 – September 29th

ISAIAH
2:12 – July 8th
6:1-5 – August 7th
9:6 – December 25th
26:3 – February 27th
26:3-4 – September 22nd
40:8 – April 7th
40:31 – July 7th
41:8 – August 8th
41:10 – February 21st
40:31 – December 16th
43:2 – July 17th
43:18-19 – March 22nd
50:7 – July 27th

JEREMIAH
10:23 – July 23rd
22:21 – February 1st
29:11 – February 2nd
32:27 – July 14th

EZEKIEL
12:2 – May 13th

DANIEL
2:21 –December 14th
12:3 – October 29th

HOSEA
4:6 – September 9th

JOEL
2:23 – August 19th

MICAH
6:8 – September 2nd

HABAKKUK
2:4 – April 26th
2:20 – March 20th

ZECHARIAH
13:9 – October 7th

MATTHEW
1:18-21 – December 26th
2:1-12 – December 22
3:13-17 – December 12th
4:4 – November 10th
5:3-7 – November 17th
5:3-10 – May 11th
5:9 – November 6th
5:16 – May 30th
5:15-16 – September 11th
5:37 – February 3rd
5:43-47 – April 15th
6:25-34 – February 23rd
6:25-34 – October 9th
6:33 – March 14th
6:34 – January 14th
7:1-5 – January 3rd
7:12 – July 30th
7:12 – October 11th
7:7-12 – March 19th
10:16 – October 5th
10:38 – August 26th
11:7-10 – March 13th
11:28 – March 15th
13:31-32 – February 7th
15:10-11 – January 18th

16:24-26 – May 22nd
18:11 – August 14th
18:15-16 – January 29th
19:19 – June 28th
19:24 – May 27th
23:13-17 – May 12th
23:11 – April 13th
28:1-7 – April 3rd
27:45-47 – March 12th
28:18-20 – March 12th
28:19-20 – August 24th

MARK
1:14-15 – December 8th
1:16-20 – November 11th
4:35-41 – March 30th
8:34-37 – January 2nd
8:36-38 – September 18th
9:14-24 – October 3rd
9:18-27 – March 26th
10:13-16 – April 22nd
10:45 – August 5th
12:28-31 – December 13th
12:35-37 – June 16th

LUKE
2:8-14 – December 15th
2:52 – September 12th
4:1-4 – October 23rd
4:16 – February 1st
9:24 – September 16th
9:51 – September 7th
10:20 – July 20
10:28-42 – November 20th
12:7 – April 18th
12:29-30 – February 28th

14:28 – June 18th
16:10 – April 11th
22:31 – June 29th
22:60-62 – August 30th

JOHN
1:1 – February 3rd
3:16 – June 1st
3:27-30 – November 18th
4:31-32 – July 21st
5:24 – September 5th
7:37-38 – June 11th
7:37-38 – December 6th
8:44 – August 29th
14:6 – May 6th
14:6 – October 18th
14:16 – June 9th
14:26 – January 7th
14:26 – July 16th
15:11 – December 7th
17:9-11 – October 20th
20:19-22 – February 15th

ACTS
1:4-8 – October 28th
3:19-20 – August 2nd
9:1-9 – April 4th
10:1-2 – June 20th
11:22-26 – May 2nd
11:24 – March 3rd
13:36 – December 1st
20:35 – November 12th

ROMANS
2:7 – August 10th
3:10, 23 – May 1st

6:23 – February 10th
5:8 – April 19th
5:8 – October 27th
7:6 – October 17th
8:18 – July 1st
8:28 – April 28th
8:31 – August 24th
10:9-10 – July 3rd
10:9-10,13 – November 19th
12:10 – July 5th
12:18 – December 21st
16:21-24 – March 6th

1 CORINTHIANS
1:26-29 – July 3rd
9:24-27 – October 30th
9:26-27 – September 21st
10:10 – November 3rd
10:13 – April 24th
10:31 – February 24th
13 – March 16th
13:4-13 – September 24th
13:11 – February 4th
15:33 – April 25th
16:13 – September 23rd

2 CORINTHIANS
2:20 – October 31st
4:17-18 – April 9th
5:7 – April 1st
5:14 – June 1st
5:17 – March 5th
5:17 – March 28th
8:1-6 – January 15th
9:7 – November 12th
11:24-30 – October 24th

GALATIANS
4:8 – November 5th
5:14 – October 11th
5:22-23 – January 20th
5:22-23 – June 13th
6:7 – February 9th
6:9 – June 28th
6:9 – December 3rd

EPHESIANS
2:11-22 – May 30th
2:13-18 – December 18th
4:2 – May 29th
4:26-27 – August 27th
4:29 – March 11th
4:31-32 – April 5th
5:4 – July 28th
5:15-33 – March 2nd
5:16 – December 2nd
5:19 – January 5th
5:25 – May 19th
6:4 – August 25th
6:9 – May 15th
6:10-18 – June 12th

PHILLIPPIANS
1:6 – September 14th
1:21-26 – January 17th
2:14 – October 16th
2:19-23 – July 13th
2:25-30 – February 25th
3:7-11 – December 9th
3:12-14 – July 29th
3:12-16 – January 21st
3:13 – August 3rd
4:1-2 – March 7th

4:1-7 – January 13th
4:2-4 – January 29th
4:4-7 – January 24th
4:7-10 – April 7th
4:8 – February 13th
4:8 – November 7th
4:13 – October 22nd

COLOSSIANS
2:6-7 – August 22nd
3:9 – March 1st
3:12 – July 6th
3:12-14 – October 13th
3:13 – June 24th
3:15 – May 31st
3:17 – March 24th
3:18-21 – February 8th
3:19-21 – September 30th
3:23 – May 24th
4:1 – May 15th

1 THESSALONIANS
2:12 – July 19th
5:11 – January 5th
5:18 – January 4th

2 THESSALONIANS
3:13 – November 1st

1 TIMOTHY
3:16 – December 24th
4:12 – December 10th
6:10 – April 30th
6:12 – April 10th

2 TIMOTHY
1:5 – December 11th
1:7 – February 5th
1:7 – August 31st
1:16 – November 8th
1:16-18 – February 8th
2:2 – January 12th
2:2 – July 12th
2:15 – March 23rd
4:2 – March 17th
4:7 – October 6th
4:7 – October 30th
4:9-11 – December 30th
4:13 – July 24
4:19 – February 8th

HEBREWS
1:1-2 – February 3rd
2:1 – July 4th
2:1 – November 13th
2:1 – August 12th
2:1 – November 13th
3:13 – August 21st
4:9-11 – June 4th
5:6-9 – March 21st
12:1-2 – January 6th
9:27 – April 23rd
10:12-14 – July 10th
10:35-39 – December 5th
10:38 – August 20th
11 – January 25th
11:1-2 – April 29th
12:1-2 – August 13th
13:8 – March 8th
13:38 – September 25th

JAMES
1:56 – June 23rd
3:3-12 – January 9th
3:3-12 – June 14th
4:1-6 – October 8th
4:8 – January 11th
4:10 – November 21st
4:13-17 – June 8th
4:13-17 – October 26th
4:14 – June 5th
5:12 – March 9th

1 PETER
1:3-5 – May 25th
1:23-25 – June 30th
1:24-25 – December 31st
2:2 – June 21
5:8-9 – June 25th
5:10 – June 17th
5:12 – January 19th

2 PETER
1:3 – September 15th
1:5-9 – November 14th
1:13-18 – November 26th
1:24-25 – December 31st

1 JOHN
1:9 – August 17th
1:9 – November 4th
2:15 – April 30th
4:7-8 – April 19th

REVELATION
2:7,11,17,29 – October 21st
3:6, 13, 22 – October 21st

21:9-14 – November 15th

TOPIC INDEX

WRITE YOUR OWN
OBITUARY NOW
July 20th

LIFE

ADVENTURE
April 1st
BETTER
June 2nd
COMMITMENT
May 22nd
DEFINING MOMENTS
April 4th
LIFE VERSE
June 10th
PSALM 119
May 20th
RHYTHMS OF LIFE
May 3rd
SHELTER
May 5th
THREE WAYS TO LIVE
YOUR LIFE
April 9th
WHERE'S YOUR MARGIN
May 4th
WILLPOWER
May 18th

LOVE

March 16th
April 19th
LOVE SOMEONE
June 1st

LOVING YOUR
NEIGHBOR
June 28th
REAL LOVE
September 24th

MARRIAGE AND FAMILY

CHILDREN
April 21st
FAMILY
February 18th
September 30th
FAMILY REUNION
April 22nd
MEMORIES OF FAMILY
June 20th
MARRIAGE
March 2nd
TRAINING KIDS
August 25th

MENTORING

INVEST AND MENTOR
January 12th
INVESTMENTS AND
DIVIDENDS
March 25th
INVESTING IN YOUNG
PEOPLE
December 10th
LISTEN AND LEARN
July 7th
MOTIVATED
April 28th

TENACITY
February 16th
September 14th
THE SIFTING OF PETER
June 29th
WEIGHTS
August 13th
WHAT TO DO WHEN YOU
DON'T KNOW WHAT TO
DO
April 10th

PERSONAL VALUE

A PERSON'S VALUE
October 27th
INSIGNIFICANCE
September 3rd
KNOWING YOUR VALUE
March 18th
RICH PEOPLE
May 27th
WORTH OF YOUR SOUL
January 2nd

PLANNING

BIG GOALS
January 22nd
DIE CLIMBING
January 21st
CLIMB MOUNTAINS
January 23rd
DAYS
February 22nd

DECISIONS
April 10th
September 15th
DIRECTION
January 16th
DESTINATION
September 7th
LIFE DIRECTION
July 23rd
LOOK AROUND
December 28th
PLANS
September 1st
ROADMAP
December 17th
THREE WAYS TO LIVE
YOUR LIFE
April 9th
VISION
February 6th

PRAISE/WORSHIP

FAITH OF JOB
June 9th
GOOD NOISE
January 5th
WORSHIP
July 31st

PRIORITIES

June 8th
September 11th
ETERNITY
September 18th

FIGHT
October 6th
October 25th
MATH
February 28th

PROMISES

GRACE, GREENBACKS,
AND GRIT
October 8th
MISSING OUT
May 25th

PURPOSE

ENGAGED
January 11th
INTENTIONS
February 2nd
HARMONY
October 20th
HUNGRY
July 21st
MISSION
August 14th
THE BREATH OF GOD
October 14th

RELATIONSHIPS

February 25th
April 14th
August 21st
December 30th

FATHERS
September 29th
NOT ALONE
November 9th

RESOLVING CONFLICT

September 6th
CLEAN UP
July 5th
CONFLICT
January 29th
PROBLEM SOLVER
September 13th
PROBLEMS AND
SOLUTIONS
March 24th
PEACEMAKER
November 6th

RESPECT

ADMIRATION
November 7th
APPRECIATION
March 6th
BORDER WALLS
November 15th
ECHOES
October 11th
INFLUENCE
December 11th
KINDNESS
June 13th
PEOPLE ADDING VALUE
August 16th

POLITICS
September 2nd
RESPECT
April 17th
STANDING OVATION
February 26th
TOLERANCE
January 3rd
VALUING YOUR
EMPLOYEES
May 15th

REST

February 19th
March 15th
FUN
November 2nd
HAPPY TIMES
July 9th
HAVING A HOBBY
February 20th
QUIET
March 20th
REFRESHING
November 8th
RESPONSIBILITIES
November 20th
SIMPLICITY
June 4th
STILLNESS
May 9th

SALVATION

BAPTISM
December 12th
CAUGHT
November 19th
CHANGE
March 5th
CHRISTIAN
November 11th
DEATH
September 5th
FLIP-FLOP FAITH
June 9th
GRACE
January 24th
JESUS CHRIST
June 27th
JESUS IS ALIVE
February 15th
JOY
December 7th
LOST
October 18th
MORE LIKE JESUS
November 18th
NEW LIFE
October 17th
PEACE WITH GOD
December 21st
SIN
May 1st

SEASONS OF LIFE

AGING
November 30th
AUTUMN
October 10th
CHANGE
March 8th
EVALUATING OUR
AGING
April 20th
GROWING OLD
February 4th
SEASONS
April 27th
TIMES/SEASONS
January 1st
WINTER
December 14th

SELF-EVALUATION

CLOTHES FOR THE SOUL
October 13th
HALFTIME
June 18th
HUSTLE
October 2nd
IF
October 3rd
LIFE APPRAISAL
March 14th
LOOKING BACK
July 16th
NOBODY
July 3rd

OUR BOOK
July 19th
PURPOSE
April 23rd
December 1st

RAIN
August 19th
REGRETS
January 8th
RESET BUTTON
August 17th
SELF TALK
January 18th
November 16th
THINKING
February 13th
WHAT IF…
December 2nd

RUMORS AND GOSSIP
January 9th
October 31st

THANKFULNESS

January 4th
February 14th
BLESSINGS IN BURKINA
FASO
July 28th
SACRIFICE
July 10th
THANKFUL FOR
TEACHERS
August 1st

CPSIA information can be obtained
at www.ICGtesting.com
Printed in the USA
LVHW050556140621
690137LV00002B/2